VOODOO DIVORCE®

Put a Hex on Your Ex
Through Preparation and Knowledge

All Rights Reserved
Stephen R. Rue, Esq.
MBA, J.D.
New Orleans, Louisiana
(504) 443-2400
Facsimile: (504) 443-5533

www.voodoodivorce.com
www.stephenrue.com
stephenrue@aol.com

Forbes/FCP

New York • Chicago • Washington D.C. • Los Angeles • Toronto

Copyright © 1998 by Stephen R. Rue. All rights reserved.

Voodoo Divorce® and Voodoo Divorce Doll® are registered trademarks of Dream Boy L.L.C.

No portion of this work may be reproduced or transmitted in any form or by any means, electronic or mechanical, including photocopying and recording, or by any information storage or retrieval system without written permission from the copyright and trademark holders.

CIP Data is available.
Printed in Canada

10 9 8 7 6 5 4 3 2 1

ISBN 0–8281–1290–8

DEDICATION

This book is dedicated to my mother, Jeannie Rue Pearson, a divorcée and widow, who has not only survived, but is living a beautiful, giving life with her new husband. She is my inspiration and my catalyst, providing me with the will and desire to help others experiencing similar situations. May this book help you to survive and flourish, as well.

We shall conjure a voodoo spell, "a hex on your ex," made of powerful ingredients derived from this recipe for success and from your own active participation in your divorce process. This book is not for the squeamish or for the faint of heart. The spell requires your desire to win and to take advantage of the many secret tools disclosed in this manual—things your own lawyer may never tell you. If you are willing to unleash the powers of these insights, turn the page...

Table of Contents

PREFACE:
Conjure a Voodoo Spell through Preparation and Knowledge xi

    Voodoo Ingredient Number 1
    DIVORCE YOURSELF FROM YOUR EMOTIONS. 1

    Voodoo Ingredient Number 2
    HIRE THE RIGHT LAWYER 9

    Voodoo Ingredient Number 3
    CONTROL YOUR LEGAL FEES, COURT COSTS,
    AND OTHER LEGAL EXPENSES 19

    Voodoo Ingredient Number 4
    GET POSSESSED! GET POSSESSION
    OF EVERYONE AND EVERYTHING 33

    Voodoo Ingredient Number 5
    INJUNCTIONS AND *EX PARTE* RELIEF 45

    Voodoo Ingredient Number 6
    GROUNDS FOR DIVORCE 51

    Voodoo Ingredient Number 7
    ALIMONY 65

    Voodoo Ingredient Number 8
    PATERNITY/MATERNITY 75

    Voodoo Ingredient Number 9
    CUSTODY AND VISITATION 79

Table of Contents

Voodoo Ingredient Number 10
CHILD SUPPORT 109

Voodoo Ingredient Number 11
PROPERTY DIVISION 153

Voodoo Ingredient Number 12
PRENUPTIAL AND POSTNUPTIAL AGREEMENTS 165

Voodoo Ingredient Number 13
**DON'T STAND FOR ABUSE OR
BEING FALSELY ACCUSED OF ABUSE** 171

Voodoo Ingredient Number 14
**PREVENT PARENTAL KIDNAPPING AND PROHIBIT
YOUR SPOUSE FROM TAKING YOUR CHILDREN
OUT OF THE STATE AND COUNTRY** 185

Voodoo Ingredient Number 15
TAXES 193

Voodoo Ingredient Number 16
CREDIT CONCERNS AND BANKRUPTCY 207

Voodoo Ingredient Number 17
DISCOVERY PLEADINGS 219

Voodoo Ingredient Number 18
MEDIATION AND ARBITRATION 223

Voodoo Ingredient Number 19
BE PREPARED FOR TRIAL 227

Voodoo Ingredient Number 20
CONCLUSION 235

APPENDICES 237

    Voodoo Spice Number 1
    Voodoo Divorce Checklist 238

    Voodoo Spice Number 2
    Financial Information 243

    Voodoo Spice Number 3
    Your Expenses 245

    Voodoo Spice Number 4
    Summary of Your Income and Expenses 250

Table of Contents

Voodoo Spice Number 5
Your Ownership Interest in a Business 252

Voodoo Spice Number 6
Real Estate 253

Voodoo Spice Number 7
State Bar Associations 254

Voodoo Spice Number 8
Divorce Statistics 257

Voodoo Spice Number 9
State by State Divorce Statistics 258

Voodoo Spice Number 10
Divorce Statistics. 260

Voodoo Spice Number 11
Divorce Statistics 261

Voodoo Spice Number 12
My Novel to My Attorney 262

Voodoo Spice Number 13
Custody/Visitation Resource Worksheet 263

Voodoo Spice Number 14
Your Child's Identification Record 264

Voodoo Spice Number 15
Voodoo Divorce Telephone Log 265

Voodoo Spice Number 16
Letter to Attorney. 266

Voodoo Spice Number 17
States that Exclude/Examine Fault 267

Voodoo Spice Number 18
Your State's Time Limit to Establish Paternity 268

Voodoo Spice Number 19
Thresholds for Genetic Test Results 270

Voodoo Spice Number 20
Support Groups. 271

Voodoo Spice Number 21
Regional Offices of Child Support Enforcement 273

Voodoo Spice Number 22
**State Child Support Enforcement Agencies
and Enforcement Support Groups** 274

Voodoo Spice Number 23
Collecting Child Support from the Military 287

Voodoo Spice Number 24
**Child Support Contacts for Countries
with Reciprocal Agreements** 288

Voodoo Spice Number 25
Child Abuse Statistics 291

Voodoo Spice Number 26
Domestic Abuse and Violence Hotlines 292

Voodoo Spice Number 27
Missing Children Hotlines 300

Voodoo Spice Number 28
Alcohol and Substance Abuse Support Groups 301

Voodoo Spice Number 29
**IRS Form 8332: Release of Claim to Exemption
for Child of Divorced or Separated Parents** 302

Voodoo Spice Number 30
Bankruptcy Statistics 303

Voodoo Spice Number 31
Sample Discovery Pleadings: Interrogatories 304

Voodoo Spice Number 32
Sample Discovery Pleadings 308

Voodoo Spice Number 33
Directory of Mediation Resources 312

Voodoo Spice Number 34
Actual Voodoo Ingredients 313

Voodoo Spice Number 35
Subscribe to the "Voodoo Divorce Newsletter" 317

Voodoo Spice Number 36
Disclaimer 318

Voodoo Spice Number 37
About the Author; to Consult with the Author 319

INDEX 321

PREFACE:
Conjure a Voodoo Spell through Preparation and Knowledge

This book is different.

This book is quite different from any other book on the market. It goes far beyond the mundane goals of setting forth the law. This book provides you with aggressive tips that you either may use or be aware of so that these powerful principals aren't used against you. Hence, you shall have significant, competitive advantages over your spouse in your divorce proceedings. It will empower you. The concepts provided here are to be used within the constraints of your own morals, the laws of your state, and the advice of your attorney. This book will provide you with valuable knowledge that many lawyers don't possess, or are afraid to tell you. Many of the topics are considered taboo for lawyers to talk about. Quite frankly, most lawyers don't know much of the information contained in this book. Furthermore, even if a lawyer possesses this information, he would rarely take the time and effort to fully discuss these working concepts with you.

This book is empowering.

The filing of a divorce pleading may be the first step to your declaration of war on emotions, finances, security, and hope. A symbolic voodoo spell, made from ingredients of your preparation, shall ward off the evil spirits of ignorance and lack of preparation. Each chapter is a sequential ingredient to your voodoo spell. The chapters are full of "Real Life Experiences" throughout the country. You will readily see that many people are experiencing similar problems. You will quickly see that you are not alone.

Reviewing and successfully acting upon each ingredient will create a potion to eliminate your emotion of loss and will create the reality of your control.

Each chapter is an ingredient to your recipe for success, based on your increasing knowledge and preparation that will lead you toward your goals of personal (and family) happiness, security, and justice.

This book can make or save you money.

The application of just a few of the concepts set forth here will significantly enhance the results of your divorce experience, as well as earn or save you money.

This book provides you with valuable and extensive worksheets and resources.

You are provided with an extensive Appendix ("Voodoo Spices"), complete with vital forms and resources. These forms will guide you to find virtually any information and/or documents that your lawyer might need for your case, saving you money while eliminating emotional and financial stress.

The resources cited here will lead you to further sources of assistance in your neighborhood and around the country.

This book is for you.

We begin with the notion that you have already decided that you want a divorce or that your spouse wants a divorce. It is not our intent or desire to promote or discourage divorces. This book is not for those seeking legitimate reconciliation or resumption of the marriage. We recommend marriage counseling, mediation, therapy, religious counseling, consumer credit counseling, and the use of self-help books and tapes for attempts to salvage a marriage. It may be to your advantage to read this book if your spouse does not have a legitimate desire to continue the marriage. You need to protect yourself from being exploited by your spouse, and knowledge is always power.

For the rest of us, we must deal with the unpleasant reality of divorce and become empowered by the concepts revealed in this book. The vast majority of civil lawsuits brought in American courtrooms are regarding divorces and their aftermath.

This book is written to be gender neutral. The author does not favor wives, mothers, husbands, or fathers. And he disdains any gender, racial, or sexual orientation biases that still permeate the judicial system. The author does, however, favor the best interest of any children involved.

This book is dynamic.

Each of the fifty states has peculiarities in their laws, and each case can only be properly analyzed after considering your particular circumstances and needs. We have worked diligently to provide the most recent facts as they pertain to the nation and each state; however, the law is dynamic and laws do change. Your lawyer should be able to advise you as to your state's current laws and how they relate to you. Each topic discussed does not contain recommendations, but rather ideas for you to consider in the light of your current situation.

We strongly recommend that you seek professional advice and not handle the divorce without a lawyer. You may wish to consider consulting an attorney, accountant, certified financial planner, tax advisor, and other such professionals. This book is not to be used in place of a competent lawyer in your state. Discuss the concepts disclosed in this book with your lawyer and consider his advice on each of the issues presented.

As an extra benefit, you have become part of the "Voodoo Divorce Family." Through the web site and toll free telephone numbers, you have links to the author for further assistance.

This is *your* Voodoo Divorce Book.

Finally, this book uses "VOODOO" merely as a metaphor for the apparent magical and miraculous results that you can achieve with your use or knowledge of the facts and concepts disclosed in this book. The "VOODOO" metaphor is not intended to be sacrilegious; but, rather, should be taken in the spirit in which it was intended—that being to empower you with information, insight, and humor. Recipes for voodoo spells and hexes are provided as means of comic relief and are provided for entertainment purposes only. So without further a due, let's begin!

VOODOO INGREDIENT NUMBER 1

Divorce Yourself from Your Emotions

There is no question that getting divorced is a very stressful event in one's life. The commencement of a divorce proceeding brings concerns about children, money, property, and being single again.

We must cope with our emotions, however. We should not allow our emotions to guide us into acts and decisions that are irrational and/or not in the best interests of our children and ourselves. Divorce yourself from the emotions of the divorce process. Separate your emotions from the decisions that affect your finances and your family. The more that emotions become involved in your divorce proceeding, the more your divorce will likely last and cost. Take control of your divorce proceeding. Become at peace with yourself and enjoy your new life. One step towards peacefulness is knowing what you may encounter in your litigation. The knowledge in this book should put you at further ease. This book will save you time and money by assisting you in preparing all of the information and documentation that your attorney should request from you.

You may experience anxiety, doubt, denial, depression, loneliness, guilt, anger, sadness, feelings that overwhelm, forgetfulness, and frustration. You also may feel a sense of relief. We often must go outside of our comfort zone in order to grow. Moving past the familiar into the realm of unknown is never easy.

Real Life Experience Susan A.

   Age 34, Married, Two Children
Teacher; Los Angeles, California

"My husband left me for another woman. Now, the kids seem to be my sole responsibility. I am overweight and feel totally abandoned. I don't know what to do. I don't know where to turn. Please help me!"

Voodoo Tip 1.1

REMEMBER THAT YOU ARE NOT ALONE

Quick Fact: Over two million people get divorced each year. Nearly half of all marriages will ultimately end in divorce.

The world is changing. The once hallowed halls of the institution of marriage are now less sacred and secure. Being divorced no longer carries with it the scarlet letter of shame. We all know many people who are divorced. Many divorces are needed transformations into a new phase of life, full of new adventures and chances for happiness.

You will survive. You will be happy again. You are not alone.

Real Life Experience   *Barbara K.*

Age 42, Divorced Twice, One Child
Housewife; Boston, Massachusetts

"I can't believe I am getting divorced again!"

Voodoo Tip 1.2

BE HAPPY—LIGHTEN UP

One of the reasons that humor is used sporadically in this book is because we must learn to laugh at ourselves and not take ourselves too seriously. We might as well smile, laugh, and celebrate a new beginning. After all, what other choice do we have. Certainly not to return to unhappiness.

Smile!

A woman went into her divorce lawyer's office. She showed him a beautiful three carat diamond wedding ring that was placed on the pinkie finger of her left hand. The client said, "I want to make sure that I get to keep this ring." The attorney replied, "I'm sure that will be possible, but did you know that you are wearing your ring on the wrong finger?"

With a smile, she said, "I know, I married the wrong man!"

* * *

> **Real Life Experience**   *Patrick S.*
> Age 44, Received Divorce Papers
> Two Months Ago, Married, Two Children
> Insurance Agent; Atlanta, Georgia
>
> *"Ever since she filed for divorce, I just come home from work and sit on the couch, drink beer and order pizza. I feel so sluggish and depressed."*

Voodoo Tip 1.3

EAT HEALTHY AND EXCERCISE

Take good care of yourself. Eating healthy and exercising regularly will allow you to be physically and mentally prepared for this time of inherent stress and uncertainty.

If you haven't eaten well or exercised regularly in the past, now is a great time to start; after all, you are now starting a new phase of your life.

Be cautious of any susceptibility to drugs or alcohol abuse and addiction. If you need assistance for a substance abuse problem, contact the good people listed in the Appendix (see Voodoo Spice Number 28: Alcohol and Substance Abuse Organizations).

Voodoo Tip 1.4

FORGIVE AND LIVE

Anger and bitterness will eat you up. The person most hurt by the rage is yourself. Don't forget, don't regress, but do forgive your spouse for your own sake, and for the sake of your children. This is not to say that you should forgive and reconcile, but rather, forgive for the sake of being happy. Forgive for the sake of being healthy. Forgive for the sake of moving on. Get what is just and fair to you and the children. But forgive.

Although you may reach a point of forgiveness, be suspicious of attempts to reconcile. A temporary reconciliation may have legal ramifications on your divorce proceeding and/or may allow your spouse additional opportunity to protect his assets and/or solidify his position in other matters of custody and the like. Consult your attorney about your options and how to best protect the rights of yourself and your children.

Guilt is another emotion that robs you of happiness. Do not wallow in your guilt and certainly do not let guilt motivate your decisions. If you feel guilty about events that led to your breakup, forgive yourself. Forgive and live.

Real Life Experience	*Debra F.*
	Age 53, Married, No Children Waitress; St. Louis, Missouri

"I cry all the time. I am so depressed, all I want to do is sleep."

Voodoo Tip 1.5

IF YOUR STRESS IS SEVERE, CONSULT A COUNSELOR

Expect stress! It will come. It will hide. It surely will return. You are helping cope with your stress by discovering the many tips in this book. You will know what to expect and how to deal with things that may come your way.

If you feel overwhelmed, please consider seeking advice from a mental health professional and/or religious and spiritual advisor.

Although it is true that your spouse may try to use the fact that you sought counseling against you in the divorce proceeding, the chances are that the benefits obtained by counseling shall far exceed the misplaced stigma that your spouse may attempt to place on your constructive acts to help yourself and your loved ones. Many people who criticize counseling are often the very people that need counseling the most.

Be careful of using friends or family members as your confidants. They are not covered by the same privileges against testifying as are many mental health care professionals and clergy. Other alternatives are local self-help and support groups. Along with your local newspaper, the extensive listings provided in the Appendices of this book will assist you in your pursuit for emotional support.

Do what you need to do to manage and control your stress and emotions. Remember that stress will always be there in some shape or form. Feel it. Recognize its existence, and don't let it control you.

Real Life Experience:	*Bernadette F.*
	Age 27, Married, One Child Advertising Executive; Dallas, Texas

"I want to make sure that my husband and my attorney won't take advantage of me. I want to get out of this divorce as cheaply as possible, and I want to make sure that he pays as much child support as possible."

Voodoo Tip 1.6

READ BOOKS ABOUT DIVORCE AND RELATED ISSUES

After reading the chapters in this book that apply to you, consider reading other books on the subject. You shall discover a wide variety of publications, with different slants on various issues. As with this book, take the ideas that work for you and discard the rest.

Voodoo Tip 1.7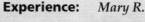

GET BUSY—GET ON WITH GETTING ON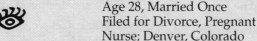

Don't have an idle mind that dwells on pity and despair. Get up and fight for yourself and your children.

Procrastination and feeling overwhelmed are typical responses to the potential emotional aspects of a divorce proceeding. You have already taken the first step to climb out of this funk by reading this book. You are already getting on with your life.

> **Real Life Experience:** *Mary R.*
>
> Age 28, Married Once
> Filed for Divorce, Pregnant
> Nurse; Denver, Colorado
>
> *"How will I survive? I am expecting to deliver my baby in September. My husband refuses to pay any of the bills. I cannot afford to pay the mortgage, the utilities, the car, and the credit card bills by myself. What about the baby's expenses? How can I pay for day care? He has always handled the money matters. Obviously, he still wants to control me. Now that he can't have me, he wants to ruin my life."*

Voodoo Tip 1.8

PREPARE FOR FINANCIAL CHANGES

Divorce always has financial ramifications. New and/or additional expenses and less sources of funds are usual ramifications of divorce. Read on and you will be much better equipped to deal with these financial pressures. After you have read this book, you will have direction on how to solve many of your financial concerns.

> **Real Life Experience:** *Brian H.*
> Age 36, Divorced Once, One Child
> Hotel Assist. Manager
> San Francisco, California
>
> "My ex is such a *****. I cannot stand her. Every time I call my attorney to complain, he tells me that he is doing everything that he can do. I want her to pay."

Voodoo Tip 1.9

YOUR LAWYER IS NOT TRAINED TO BE A PSYCHIATRIST

Remember that your lawyer is not a therapist. Other professionals are better equipped to handle your emotional needs. Plus, most counselors and therapists are less expensive than your attorney.

If you do not have or want a counselor or therapist, vent your feelings by writing in a diary/journal that will go to your attorney. By addressing the diary/journal to your attorney, you may be able to keep your writings out of evidence as an attorney-client privilege. Nonetheless, do keep your writings out of the hands of your spouse.

> **Real Life Experience:** *Karen S.*
> Age 27, Married Once
> Filing for Divorce, Three Children
> Restaurant Hostess; New Orleans, Louisiana
>
> "The kids are so quiet. They haven't said a word about there father's absence. I want John and me to talk to the kids. I'm just so mad and hurt right now that I don't know whether I can go through with it."

Voodoo Tip 1.10

TALK TO YOUR CHILDREN

Take time to talk with your children and explain that you are getting a divorce. Tailor your statements to the age of the children. Emphasize that the break up is not their fault and that your decision to divorce is made and that they cannot change it. Do not speak badly of the other parent. Frequently reassure the children that both of you are still their parents and that they are loved and will not be abandoned. Tell them that you will take care of them and keep them safe.

It's O.K.!

Summary of Voodoo Tips from Number 1

DIVORCE YOURSELF FROM YOUR EMOTIONS

Voodoo Tip 1.1   Remember that you are not alone.

Voodoo Tip 1.2   Be happy—Lighten up.

Voodoo Tip 1.3   Eat healthy and exercise.

Voodoo Tip 1.4   Forgive and live.

Voodoo Tip 1.5   If your stress is severe, consult a counselor.

Voodoo Tip 1.6   Read books about divorce and related issues.

Voodoo Tip 1.7   Get busy—Get on with getting on.

Voodoo Tip 1.8   Prepare for financial changes.

Voodoo Tip 1.9   Your lawyer is not trained to be a psychiatrist.

Voodoo Tip 1.10 Talk to your children.

**A Quick Note That Applies to
All Voodoo Divorce Spells Found in this Book**

As with all voodoo spells found in this book, the spell recipes are derived from historic Haitian and New Orleans voodoo origins. The spells refer to actual voodoo ingredients, including candles, incense, herbs, oils, roots, voodoo dolls, gris-gris bags, and other items. Although actual voodoo ingredients are used, literary license also is added for comic relief. Use of the following voodoo spells are for amusement and entertainment purposes only (Please refer to the Disclaimer.) To get voodoo dolls, gris-gris bags, and other items used in these voodoo spells, contact our web site at:

WWW.VOODOODIVORCE.COM

or telephone toll free 1-877-4VOODOO.

**VOODOO SPELL
FOR YOUR EMOTIONAL HARMONY**

Place a picture of your spouse in a preserve jar. Write his name on a piece of paper. With a red marker, scratch through his name. Place the paper in the preserve jar. Light one white and one blue candle. Place the following ingredients in the preserve jar: Broom Tops, Huckleberry, Linseed Oil, Myrrh, and Mississippi River Water. Tightly close the lid of the preserve jar. Shake the jar three times. Bury the jar in a public place.

Put the following ingredients in a red flannel bag (known as a gris-gris bag): Argue Root, Basil, Catnip, Corn Flower, Dog Grass, Frankincense, Gardenia, Garlic, Goat's Leaves, Horseradish, Magnolia, Peony, Rose Buds, St. John's Wort, and Yarrow. Keep the gris-gris bag with you at all times.

Go home and relax. By then you should be feeling much better. A smile will come easier.

VOODOO INGREDIENT NUMBER 2

Hire the Right Lawyer

Choosing the right lawyer is one of the most important factors in winning your case. Most people haphazardly use the telephone book or merely ask a friend for a recommendation. Their search and investigation in choosing a lawyer ends there. If you're lucky, your spouse will choose this random method.

If you have a simple uncontested divorce, then most divorce lawyers can handle your case. Simply shop for the best price.

> **Real Life Experience:** *Elizabeth V.*
> Age 58, No Minor Children
> Physician; Seattle, Washington
>
> *"I want to hire the very best attorney in the city. Of course, I have heard about certain divorce lawyers, but I am not sure whom to use. Throughout the past twenty six years, my husband and I have accumulated substantial assets. It seems that everyone wants to give me advice as to whom to hire."*

Voodoo Tip 2.1

INQUIRE BEFORE YOU HIRE

Voodoo Divorce
Top Ten List for Finding the Best Attorney

In a hotly contested divorce, your lawyer can make all the difference in the world. The following are suggestions in finding the best lawyer that you can afford:

1. Ask friends and family.

Warning: Do not base your decision merely on the advice of your friends or family. They may not have done their homework in finding the best attorney. However, word of mouth is usually one of the best indicators of the quality of an attorney. Also remember that no two divorce cases are identical and the results a lawyer got for your relative may not be the same results that lawyer could get for you. Each case has its own characteristics.

2. Ask lawyers.

    If you know any lawyers, ask them who they would recommend and why. Remember that a personal injury attorney may not be the best individual to represent you in a divorce proceeding.

3. Ask your accountant and/or certified financial planner.

4. Ask therapists and members of divorce support groups (see Appendix: Voodoo Spice Number 20).

5. Call the clerks in charge of the domestic docket at your local courthouse and ask for three recommendations.

    These individuals see the divorce lawyers in court on a regular basis and if you get the right person on the telephone, they can tell you the good, the bad, and the ugly about the superior domestic lawyers.

6. Ask mediators that do domestic mediation.

7. Ask marriage counselors that advise divorcing couples.

8. Ask personnel of battered women's shelters (if abuse is an issue in your current situation.)

9. Ask your local or state bar association for a list of their local domestic lawyers (see Appendix: Voodoo Spice Number 7 for a listing of all state bar associations).

10. Call the VOODOO DIVORCE NATIONAL LAWYER REFERRAL HOTLINE at 1-877-4VOODOO (See Appendix for more details).

After you have done your research by speaking with your personal and professional contacts, it's now time to interview several potential divorce lawyers. But first, be sure to neutralize your competition.

Real Life Experience: Michelle H.
Age 34, Married, No Children
Pharmacist; Santa Fe, New Mexico

"I am afraid that my husband is going to hire the very best lawyer in town. I would attempt to hire that lawyer myself, but I'm not sure who he will get. I think that he has two or three attorneys in mind that are well-known here in Santa Fe."

Voodoo Tip 2.2

NEUTRALIZE YOUR BEST OPPOSITION

If you anticipate a major domestic battle and you live in a community that has a limited amount of good domestic attorneys, you can prevent your spouse from hiring a select group of these attorneys. Find out who the very best attorneys are not necessary in your spouse's anticipated price range and set up appointments with all of them. The lawyers may charge a consultation fee. This gives you an opportunity to compare the lawyers before you make your choice. And here's the kicker . . . your spouse cannot hire any attorney that you have consulted because you previously have a professional relationship with that lawyer. This is especially effective in a small community with a mere handful of good domestic attorneys.

When you have your face to face meeting, be certain that you pay for the consultation, but don't pay cash; use a check so you can later prove that you consulted with that lawyer on a certain date. If the lawyer originally refuses to take a consultation fee, drop a check written in his or her name or in the law firm's name for a nominal amount (i.e., $25.00). The chances are high that the check will be deposited in the lawyer's bank account and your canceled check will be evidence that prevents your spouse from using that attorney or anyone in that attorney's law firm.

Don't worry about what you disclose to the lawyer during the consultation. What you say is confidential and the lawyer cannot tell the information to anyone even if you do not hire him or her.

> **Real Life Experience:** *Clifton L.*
>
> Age 40, Second Marriage, Three Children
> Car Salesman; Charleston, South Carolina
>
> *"I have used a divorce attorney for my first divorce, and I was very unhappy with the results. My wife took me to the cleaners. When I first met the lawyer, I had some doubts about his abilities, but I thought he would do a satisfactory job. I mistakenly thought that all divorce lawyers were alike. I don't plan on making that mistake again."*

Voodoo Tip 2.3

INTERVIEW SEVERAL ATTORNEYS

Most prospective clients merely go into the lawyer's office and the lawyer takes complete control over the discussion. In essence, the lawyer interviews you as if he is already your selected attorney. Turn the meeting around. First listen to what the lawyer has to say, without prompting. This will give you a general idea of his competency level. Then take control by asking your potential lawyer the following questions: (Remember, you are the client and customer.)

1. Ask how long he has been a lawyer.
2. Ask how long he has practiced divorce law.

    Lawyers who do not normally handle divorce cases are more likely to make mistakes. They are also more likely to procrastinate on your case because the work is unfamiliar to them.

3. Ask the lawyer how often he goes to trial in contested cases.
4. Ask how much of the lawyer's practice is devoted to domestic law. If the lawyer says that he devotes less than half of his time to divorce cases, then thank the attorney for his time and leave.
5. Ask the lawyer to rate himself as to his ability as a litigate on a scale from 1 to 10 (10 being best). If the lawyer scores himself less than an 8, the honest lawyer probably does not have the confidence or arrogance necessary to be the type of litigator that you need. After all, if he does not have confidence in his own ability, how can he possibly have greater confidence in his ability to win for you? A confident attorney not only knows the law, he challenges any attack on his client's position. The judge will sense the level of confidence and competency. In a tight decision, the extra aura of righteousness very well may be the intangible factor that allows you to have custody or have a child support award in your favor.
6. Ask the lawyer whether he will personally handle the case or will an associate be assigned the case. Make sure that you are speaking to the lawyer that you want to handle your case. It's a waste of time to interview an attorney that will not actually be representing you. If you are in a true battle over custody, property rights, or other vital issues, don't ever settle for second best. It's usually worth the extra money to hire the lead attorney.
7. Ask for the attorney's home, car or beeper telephone numbers. Be able to contact him when you need him. Many lawyers are extremely hesitant to give their private telephone numbers; however, you should insist on a means to contact the attorney on an emergency basis. Clients often need to immediately contact their attorney when visitation disputes arise when one spouse refuses to return the children, etc.
8. Ask to review the retainer agreement. Don't be afraid to ask to take the retainer agreement home and study it prior to signing it.
9. Ask the attorney how he charges for his legal services and expenses. If he charges by the hour, ask at what intervals of an hour

does he charge. For example, some lawyers bill for legal services on a quarter hour basis (.25 of an hour) while others may charge by a tenth of an hour (.10 of an hour). Also, ask if he charges for any questions that you may have regarding your bill.

10. Ask the lawyer what he charges for a photocopy, a facsimile, travel, etc.
11. Ask the lawyer what other charges he expects to be incurred during the litigation such as investigators, mediators, experts, evaluators, etc.

    By your numerous inquiries of your prospective attorney, you should get a good idea of the range of hourly rates that lawyers charge for services in your community.
12. Ask how many months the lawyer would estimate the case to last.
13. Ask the attorney to give you references of at least three recent clients that are happy with his services. He should be able to contact these clients and ask them if it is all right to disclose their identity and give the prospective client their telephone number. You should contact the former clients and get the scoop on the attorney.
14. Ask your prospective lawyer if he will send you copies of each letter and pleading that he sends out on your behalf. It is important that you stay informed.
15. Ask yourself if you can get along with your attorney. Is the attorney someone that you can have faith in? Are your personalities compatible? Trust your instincts; they are rarely wrong.
16. Ask yourself if the lawyer appears to be genuinely sensitive to your needs.
17. Did the lawyer promptly see you at the time of your scheduled appointment?
18. Ask yourself whether the lawyer gave you his undivided complete attention.
19. Ask the lawyer if any of the legal fee is non-refundable.
20. Ask the lawyer if he knows all of the federal and state tax implications that may result from your divorce case. (Refer to Number 15 on "Taxes").
21. Ask the lawyer for the names of other good domestic lawyers that he would recommend. This gives you a good idea of who the other good lawyers are in your area.

22. Be totally honest with your attorney. He cannot help you to his fullest abilities if you do not disclose the skeletons in your closet. Whatever you tell him is confidential, so go for it and tell all!
23. Ask the lawyer if he has payment plans and what are the methods of payment. Can you use credit cards?
24. Ask the lawyer if he or she charges interest on unpaid balances.
25. Provide your chosen lawyer with a copy of your completed VOODOO DIVORCE FORMS (See Appendix).

Real Life Experience: *Peggy P.*
Age 29, Divorced, One Child
Accountant; Ft. Lauderdale, Florida

"I like to keep track of my time and money. I called my attorney on many occasions and seldom got a returned phone call. When I got my monthly statement for the lawyer, I was astonished to see charges for my telephone calls that went unanswered. I also received expensive charges for telephone calls that only lasted a few minutes. I am deeply offended by these business practices. If I do not get proper resolution of these billing issues, then I shall change attorneys."

Voodoo Tip 2.4

KEEP A RECORD OF YOUR CALLS TO YOUR ATTORNEY

Keep a telephone log of when you call your attorney and when he returns your telephone calls. You will also be creating a document that can be used to confirm the telephone conferences charged on your billing statement. Use the VOODOO DIVORCE TELEPHONE LOG found in the Appendix (Voodoo Spice Number 15).

Voodoo Tip 2.5

MAKE YOUR LAWYER PROMPTLY RETURN TELEPHONE CALLS

Quick Fact: One of the greatest complaints about lawyers is their failure to promptly return client telephone calls.

Ask the attorney how promptly he returns client telephone calls.

If your lawyer does not promptly return your telephone calls, send him a certified letter indicating so. Note the times and dates of each call. Also, the letter should include all inquiries that need to be addressed or facts that you need to relate to your attorney. To save time, simply use Voodoo Spice Number 16 found in the Appendix. You can expedite the process by faxing your letter to your attorney. Tell your prospective attorney that you intend to send him these letters should he not promptly return your telephone calls. Remember, the squeaky wheel gets the grease!

Good divorce attorneys are busy. Keep in mind that they are often in court, at depositions, in conferences with other clients, and may not be available to immediately receive or return your telephone call. Indicate to the attorney that you expect to be able to talk to his secretary, paralegal or other lawyer on your case, in order to convey any message that is vital to you. A lawyer should return telephone calls within twenty-four hours. Have the lawyer pledge to you that he will return your calls within the twenty-four hour period.

> **Real Life Experience:** *Jean F.*
> Age 24, Married, One Child
> Receptionist; Akron, Ohio
>
> *"Every time I call my attorney, she makes me so nervous that I don't seem to be able to collect my thoughts. After I get off the phone with her, I remember something that I forgot to ask her."*

Voodoo Tip 2.6

COLLECT YOUR THOUGHTS BEFORE YOU CALL YOUR ATTORNEY

If your attorney charges you for every telephone call that you make to him, write down and collect all of the topics that you want to discuss, then make one call.

If a lawyer charges $175.00 per hour and charges on each quarter of an hour (every fifteen minute intervals), a 12 minute telephone call that addresses three issues would cost you $43.75. However, if you do not collect your thoughts and make three separate calls for each issue over the next day or two, your same total twelve minutes of conversation with your lawyer would cost you $131.25 (3 times 43.75).

> **Real Life Experience:** *Anne G.*
> Age 32, Married, Two Children
> Retail Store Manager;
> Charlotte, North Carolina
>
> *"My divorce has been going on for five months. I've been to one hearing. Besides that hearing, I have no idea what's going on."*

Voodoo Tip 2.7

STAY INFORMED

Tell your lawyer to send you copies of each correspondence and pleading that he files on your behalf. Keep a file of your case for your own review.

Once you hire the attorney, give him all of the documents that you have collected and the information that you compiled with your VOODOO FORMS. (See the forms in the Appendix).

> **Real Life Experience:** *Steve S.*
> Age 32, Married, Two Children
> Mechanic; Birmingham, Alabama
>
> *"I went to one of those advertised clinics that promote cheap divorces in the yellow pages. Once I got into their office, they said it would cost me more money to fight the child support and visitation problems."*

Voodoo Tip 2.8

WATCH OUT FOR ADVERTISED LOW PRICES

Be cautious about hiring a legal clinic or law firm that advertises a very low flat fee for your divorce. Often there is an advertised fee for a very limited legal service such as merely the divorce. The firm may be advertising the low fee to get you in their door, then they may inform you that there are additional fees for litigation of child support, custody, visitation, property rights and other issues. If all you need is a simple uncontested divorce, these legal clinics are quite affordable and serve your limited purpose.

Once you have an idea of what the lawyer charges, then you should ask him to give you an estimate of the expected cost of the litigation. Many attorneys will not be able to answer this question with much accuracy because many factors that affect the cost of the litigation are beyond his control, such as the extent that your spouse's attorney to fight each issue, as well as how much discovery he tenders to your answer.

> **Real Life Experience:** *Helen D.*
> Age 23, Married, No Children
> Student; Chicago, Illinois
>
> *"My husband said that we can use just one attorney and split the cost."*

Voodoo Tip 2.9

ONE LAWYER CANNOT REPRESENT BOTH OF YOU

A lawyer can only represent one spouse. If he would represent both spouses, then a conflict of interest would exist. A lawyer likely would not be able to serve the best interests of both parties. If your spouse insists on using one lawyer to handle your domestic case, be sure that you are the client, not your spouse. This creates a fiduciary responsibility of the lawyer to you. Ask your lawyer to inform your spouse that you are the client, not him or her.

> **Real Life Experience:** *Evette Y.*
>
> Age 47, Married, One Child
> Small Business Owner; San Antonio, Texas
>
> *"Last week, we went to court for a hearing and lost miserably. My lawyer was totally out gunned by my husband's attorney. I have lost faith in my lawyer's abilities. I truly believe that he was intimidated by the other lawyer. Now, I have to battle over the property. I fear that I will lose again. What advice can you give me?"*

Voodoo Tip 2.10

YOU ARE NOT WED TO YOUR DIVORCE ATTORNEY

When you hire your attorney, you have accomplished one of the most important acts towards the success of your case. If you are later dissatisfied with your attorney, don't hesitate to fire him and get a new one. Your prior research on attorneys will have come in handy. Hopefully, if you have done your homework properly, you will be very happy with your selection of an attorney.

Remember, you may terminate your attorney at any time. It is not usually wise to do so just before a scheduled hearing. On occasion, after terminating your attorney, the attorney might refuse to release your file until his bill is paid in full.

Because if you have followed the tips found in this book, you will have on copies of all pleadings... as the case progresses, thus you will not be put under any major duress because of the actions of your terminated attorney.

Ask your new attorney to request your file from your last one. Having to personally fight with your old lawyer over your file merely puts unecessary stress upon you during this naturally stressful time in your life. Let the new lawyer get the file for you.

Summary of Voodoo Tips from Number 2

HIRE THE RIGHT LAWYER

Voodoo Tip 2.1 Inquire before your hire.

Voodoo Tip 2.2 Neutralize your best opposition.

Voodoo Tip 2.3 Interview several attorneys.

Voodoo Tip 2.4 Keep a record of your calls to your attorney.

Voodoo Tip 2.5 Make your lawyer promptly return telephone calls.

Voodoo Tip 2.6 Collect your thoughts before you call your attorney.

Voodoo Tip 2.7 Stay informed.

Voodoo Tip 2.8 Watch out for advertised low prices.

Voodoo Tip 2.9 One lawyer cannot represent both of you.

Voodoo Tip 2.10 You are not wed to your divorce attorney.

VOODOO SPELL
FOR CHOOSING THE RIGHT LAWYER

Place a compass in a brown paper bag. Write the names of each lawyer that you are considering on separate sheets of paper. Place each piece of paper in the brown bag. Add the following ingredients to the bag: Acacia, Adam and Eve Root, Althea, Black Pepper, Calendula, Cascara Sagrada, Celery, Galangal Root, Lemongrass, Marigold, Nutmeg, Rose Petals, Sandalwood, and Shark Cartilage. Throw the bag over your right shoulder.

Light one black and one brown candle.

Take your voodoo doll and pin a one dollar bill to it's right hand.

Follow your instincts, and make your decision following the recommendations found in this chapter.

VOODOO INGREDIENT NUMBER 3

Control Your Legal Fees, Court Costs, and Other Legal Expenses

Money is the life's blood of your domestic case. No one wants to spend money on lawyers and related court costs and expenses. And very few consider legal costs as regular bills that must be paid on a monthly basis. Most people want to spend as little money as possible. In contested domestic disputes, the spouse that harshly restricts paying money for a good lawyer is often penny wise and pound foolish.

> **Real Life Experience:** *Jan S.*
> Age 52, Married, Three Adult Children
> Computer Consultant
> Concord, New Hampshire
>
> *"These lawyers want so much money, it's ridiculous. I have to pay my attorney and still find a way to live. I want to get through this without a huge financial burden."*

Voodoo Tip 3.1

CONTRARY TO POPULAR OPINION, PAYMENT OF LEGAL FEES CAN BE A SOUND FINANCIAL INVESTMENT

The quality of your lawyer often is revealed by the hourly rate that he charges or the initial retainer fee that is required for representation. There very well may be excellent lawyers who charge minimal fees for their services. Although they may be excellent lawyers, they are clearly poor businessmen. Get a quality lawyer that believes that the services that he provides are worth it.

It's remarkable the return on your investment that you may receive by biting the bullet and hiring a quality lawyer. Just imagine the cash flow of a mere two hundred and fifty dollars ($250) per month in child support during the eighteen years of a minor child's life. That's $54,000! In our illustration, if you hire a superb lawyer that is able to get you five hundred dollars ($500) per month, your recovery totals $108,000 (Not to mention other future increases in child support due to changes in parent's income or the child's expenses). A child support award of seven hundred and fifty dollars per month totals $162,000 over the first eighteen years of your child's life. Are you willing to pay a few thousand dollars in legal fees for a return of your investment of one hundred percent (100%) or more than the results that might be accomplished with an inferior attorney?

On the other hand, can you afford not to hire a quality domestic attorney? As a payer of child support, can you afford $250, 500, or 1,000 dollars a month more in child support over the remaining minor years of your child's life?

What is the value of the real estate, retirement, and other valuables that you will fight about in your divorce case? A house and retirement are usually the greatest financial investments that most people make during their lives. Do you want to put these investments in the hands of an attorney that is inferior to the attorney of your spouse? And, of course, there is no value that can be placed on your children.

WELCOME TO PLASTIC PARADISE!

> **Real Life Experience:**   *Brooke O.*
> Age 35, Married, No Children
> Unemployed Housewife; Detroit, Michigan
>
> *"We have an American Express, a Gold Visa, two Mastercards, and a Discover card. Each of us can sign on these cards. Can I use the credit cards for my divorce?"*

The prudent use of credit cards can provide an abundance of advantages.

Voodoo Tip 3.2

MAKE YOUR SPOUSE PAY YOUR LEGAL FEES BY USING CREDIT CARDS IN BOTH OF YOUR NAMES

Many aggressive attorneys take credit cards such a Visa, Mastercard, Discover, and American Express. You may have joint credit cards with your spouse. If so, use your joint credit card instead of paying with cash or by check. Pay as much on the card as possible. Make sure that you have a firm agreement with your attorney of how much of the fee paid is refundable if not used for legal services. Check with your credit card company, you may be told that as long as you sign the actual credit card receipt, then your spouse likely will not be able to successfully defeat the charge. Often your spouse will be the credit card company's primary contact regarding the card, and the credit card bill will be directed to his or her attention. You will put your spouse in a position of either having to pay the billed charges or jeopardizing the credit rating of both of you. In a worst case scenario, you will have to pay the minimal monthly balance required by the credit card company. By using this method, you have increased the available cash that can be used elsewhere.

> **Real Life Experience:** *Wendy M.*
> Age 25, Married, One Child
> Receptionist; Mobile, Alabama
>
> *"I'm short on cash right now after putting a deposit down on a new apartment. What can I do to survive until my next pay check?"*

Voodoo Tip 3.3

BUY OTHER NECESSITIES WITH JOINT CREDIT CARDS

You also may use your credit cards to buy items that you may need during the tendency of your divorce case. If you have left your residence, you may need sheets, pillows, additional clothes, nonperishable food stuffs, diapers, etc. Don't forget that most grocery stores now take credit cards. It is often a race to use the plastic before your spouse closes the credit card accounts. Be sure that you have secured enough valued items to get you through the potentially hard times ahead. Like a squirrel gathering nuts, be prepared for the harsh divorce winter. By having bought the essential goods that you will need until you get alimony, child support or other relief, you will have prevented your spouse from being able to use undue financial duress to force you into a less than favorable money settlement regarding alimony, child support or property division.

Don't forget that someone will ultimately have to pay the credit card bills, so judge what is most appropriate for your individual financial circumstance. You may not want to jeopardize your credit worthiness; however, sometimes a less than perfect credit rating is better than not eating.

> **Real Life Experience:** *Sandy C.*
> Age 34, Married, Two Children
> Police Officer; Indianapolis, Indiana
>
> *"Tom took all the money out of the bank. I have a credit card, but no cash. I'm afraid that he's going to cancel the credit card at any minute."*

Voodoo Tip 3.4

USE CREDIT CARDS AND/OR "ATM's" FOR CASH ADVANCES

Getting cash advances from your credit cards and automatic teller machines ("ATM's") gives you the control over your money and credit lines before the accounts are closed by your spouse. If you act fast, you can always put the money back into an account. It's always better to be the possessor, than the beggar (refer to Number 4 on "Get Possession of Everyone and Everything" for more details on the importance of control of money, property, and documents).

> **Real Life Experience:** *Ray M.*
> Age 53, Second Marriage, No Children
> Pilot; Long Beach, California
>
> *"I plan on canceling the joint credit cards as soon as my new separate card arrives."*

Voodoo Tip 3.5

GET YOUR OWN INDIVIDUAL CREDIT CARDS

Whether you are preparing for a future divorce or in the midst of a divorce lawsuit, apply for your own credit cards which are *only in your name*. It is best that the credit card accounts are opened with you using a post office box or a confidant's residence as the mailing and billing address for the credit card account. These separate (non-joint) credit cards will give you future freedom to have uninterrupted credit and provide you with greater spending flexibility. If your spouse cancels the joint accounts, you have your new accounts to protect you from unfair financial pressures from your spouse.

It often is easier to have your credit application accepted by a company while you are still married. If you are laying the ground work for a future divorce, be aware that information regarding applications and individual credit cards may be placed in a credit report that your spouse could get his or her hands on. It also is prudent not to apply to the same credit card company that you are presently using. Your spouse could call the company about the joint account and a credit card company representative could inadvertently inform your spouse about the other individual account.

> **Real Life Experience:** *Julie M.*
> Age 42, One Child
> Divorce Attorney; Trenton, New Jersey
>
> *"I have seven credit cards. Two cards are just mine."*

Voodoo Tip 3.6

TRANSFER THE BALANCES OF YOUR SEPARATE INDIVIDUAL CREDIT CARD ACCOUNTS INTO JOINT CREDIT CARD ACCOUNTS

Many credit card companies are more than pleased to allow you to transfer the balances of another credit card onto their account. They love the additional interest that they will earn.

> **Real Life Experience:** *Monica P.*
> Age 37, Two Children
> Plumber; Lexington, Kentucky
>
> *"I paid my attorney a $5,000 retainer with a credit card."*

Voodoo Tip 3.7

USE CREDIT CARD AND GET CASH REFUND AT THE END OF CASE

If you used a credit card to pay for your legal services and you have a credit balance at the end of your case, ask the lawyer to pay you the outstanding credit by check instead of crediting the credit card account. After a property division between spouses, a spouse may inadvertently overlook the overpayment of attorney fees. You might be able to keep the entire refund.

On the other hand, if your spouse paid his or her attorney with a credit card or a large retainer fee, make sure that you get your share of the refunded fees. Alert your attorney of this possibility.

Voodoo Tip 3.8

USE A CREDIT CARD THAT WILL SAVE YOU
INTEREST CHARGES ON UNPAID BALANCES

By using a credit card to pay your attorney, you may also benefit from not having to pay interest on unpaid balances to the attorney. With the favorable introductory terms that many credit cards are providing, your interest rate on outstanding balances may be significantly less through the credit card offer as compared to the interest charged by your attorney. Also, if a lawyer knows that you have paid your retainer and have a credit balance with him, with human nature, he has a greater incentive to devote valuable time and effort on your case.

> **Real Life Experience:** Donna E.
> Age 42, Two Children
> Secretary; Metairie, Louisiana
>
> *"After paying my attorney, I used my cards to stock up on everything that I thought I might need for the next several months. The cards are maxed out!"*

Voodoo Tip 3.9

CLOSE USED JOINT CREDIT CARDS

Once you have gained the maximum benefit from the joint credit cards, notify each credit card company and department store that you are canceling the account. Make sure that you notify them in writing, and send the letter by certified mail. Be sure to keep copies of these letters.

> **Real Life Experience:** Will T.
> Age 36, Married, Three Children
> Rancher; Butte, Montana
>
> *"I have no idea how many credit cards we have. Janet has always been in charge of paying the family bills."*

Voodoo Tip 3.10

GET YOUR CREDIT REPORTS

Call or write one or more credit reporting bureau's to get a full record of your and your spouse's credit history. You may find information regarding debt/credit that you in which you were not aware.

The three main credit reporting bureaus are listed here:

EQUIFAX 1-800-685-1111
EXPERIAN (Formerly TRW) 1-800-682-7654
TRANS UNION 1-800-961-8800

Real Life Experience: *Denise F.*
Age 41, Married, One Child
Sales Associate; Simi Valley, California

"I have several department store credit cards. Are they of any use?"

Voodoo Tip 3.11

GIFT CERTIFICATE HEAVEN!

Spouses often are quick to close joint major credit card accounts with Visa, Mastercard, Discover and American Express, but spouses frequently forget to close the department store credit card accounts. With a Macy's, J.C. Penny, or Sears credit card you can make charges or buy gift certificates made out to yourself with the cards. Once you have the gift certificates, even if your spouse gets around to closing the account, your certificate can be used just like money at the store. Remember, you can always use the unused gift certificate later to pay the department store's credit card bill. The key is to maintain control of your financial resources.

Another nifty use of gift certificates is to pay your attorney fees with them. Many lawyers will entertain taking the gift certificates in lieu of cash. After all, who doesn't need a set of craftsman tools from Sears or nice flatware from Macy's.

CASH IS KING!

Real Life Experience: *Alexis F.*
Age 29, Married, One Child
Retail Manager; Savannah, Georgia

"I still don't know if I want to get divorced. We have a son to think about. My husband is in pharmaceutical sales. He makes more money than I do. I don't know if I can make it on only my salary. I definitely don't have enough money for an attorney."

Voodoo Tip 3.12

SIPHON MONEY TO BUILD UP RESEREVES FOR ATTORNEY FEES AND OTHER EXPENSES

If time is on your side, and you have the ability to hold off on filing for your divorce, consider siphoning off a few dollars here and there and build up a nest egg of cash that can be secreted from your spouse. A safety deposit box at a new bank is an excellent place to keep these funds.

> **Real Life Experience:** *Erin A.*
> Age 28, Married, One Child
> Bookkeeper; Lansing, Michigan
>
> *"Shouldn't I leave money in the checking account so that he can pay all of his bills?"*

Voodoo Tip 3.13

DON'T GET PAID WITH "OLD MONEY"; AND PAY WITH "OLD MONEY"

Halloween can come once or twice a month if you have the shocking experience of being paid child support or alimony with money that was quickly seized by your spouse from a prior joint bank account ("Old Money"). Likewise, the payer spouse has a greater ability to pay his or her obligations if he uses the "Old Money."

The goal of the recipient of the funds is to be paid with money recently earned by the payer ("New Money"), versus the funds from both spouses' prior savings ("Old Money").

Whether the payment is a trick or a treat often depends on where the money came from in the first place. The wisdom of having control of the funds is ever more apparent upon reflection of this principle.

> **Real Life Experience:** *Lisa M.*
> Age 59, Married, Three Adult Children
> Housewife; Pittsburgh, Pennsylvania
>
> *"What in the world am I to do with our bank accounts?"*

Voodoo Tip 3.14

TAKE MONEY FROM JOINT CHECKING AND/OR SAVINGS ACCOUNTS

A rush to the bank may be the only action that prevents you from being at the financial mercy of your spouse. Look at the checking account register and insure that there is enough money to cover previously written checks, then consider removing the balance of the money. In grave financial circumstances, you may consider cashing in any certificate of deposit accounts ("CD's"); however, in doing so, you may have significant penalties and/or loss of interest.

Put the funds into a new checking, savings, and/or money market account, solely in your name, at a different bank. Also, consider putting some or all of the funds in other investments and/or a safety deposit box.

COURT FEES, SERVICE COSTS, AND EXPERT FEES

> **Real Life Experience:** *Amber C.*
> Age 30, Married, One Child
> Unemployed; St. Louis, Missouri
>
> *"The filing fees are so high! I can't afford a lawyer if I have to pay the clerk of court as well."*

Voodoo Tip 3.15

TRY AN *IN FORMA PAUPERIS* APPLICATION

Divorce courts throughout the nation have forms that you can fill out asking the court to allow you to file your domestic papers without paying filing fees up front. These forms are usually called *"In Forma Pauperis"* applications or motions. The forms require you to report your income, expenses, as well as the various assets and liabilities that you have. If the court grants your application, you have saved an average of one to two hundred dollars.

You can usually obtain a copy of an *In Forma Pauperis* application or motion through your attorney or through the clerk of court's office at your local courthouse. You can file this application even if you have paid for an attorney. Typically, with a gross income of $1,000 or less, a court may likely grant your application. There are no hard and fast rules as to how much income, expenses, assets and liabilities a court deems are appropriate for granting this application. It is usually at the judge's discretion.

As a worst case scenario, the judge will not grant your application, and you will have to pay the filing fees. Another down side of filing this application is that, if the motion is denied, then the court may not serve your spouse with the pleadings and/or hear your case until the filing fees are paid in full.

Be accurate in your representations regarding the amount of your income and expenses that you are claiming to the court in your *In Forma*

Pauperis application. A skillful domestic lawyer can hold your feet to the fire as to these representations in a later hearing on child support or alimony.

Some courts allow a party to pay the filing fees and service charges in monthly installment payments. Look into this, it can help your cash flow.

> **Real Life Experience:** *Stephen S.*
> Age 55, Divorced, Two Adult Children
> Professor; Grand Rapids, Michigan
>
> "*My divorce is finally over. Hoorah!*"

Voodoo Tip 3.16

GET REFUND OF UNUSED COURT COST DEPOSIT FROM THE CLERK OF COURT AFTER CASE IS FINISHED

Usually, your initial filing fees are a deposit for the initial pleadings and for future filings. Once the domestic case is over it's major battles, a vast majority of lawyers and clients forget to inquire with the clerk of court's office as to whether any filing fees are unused. These excess funds usually can be refunded to you. Simply ask the clerk of court's office for their procedure on obtaining a refund of these unused filing fees.

> **Real Life Experience:** *Ashley R.*
> Age 33, Married, Two Children
> Real Estate Agent; Little Rock, Arkansas
>
> "*I paid the attorney fees and court costs. What other expenses can I expect?*"

Voodoo Tip 3.17

ANTICIPATE POSSIBLE FEES FOR EXPERTS, MEDIATORS, APPRAISERS, DNA TESTS, DEPOSITIONS AND EVALUATORS

It is not uncommon for many domestic cases to require additional costs for experts, mediators, appraisers, evaluators, DNA paternity tests and/or depositions. Ask your attorney whether any of these costs are expected. Additionally, ask him to provide you with an estimate of these costs. Many times a lawyer can give you a good sense on when these expense will have to be paid. Knowledge that these expenses exist will enable you to better budget and manage your cash flow.

> **Real Life Experience:** *Latesha O.*
> *Age 31, Divorced, Two Children*
> *Office Manager; Columbus, Ohio*
>
> "*My ex has not paid child support for the last three months. Now I have to pay a lawyer to make him pay.*"

Voodoo Tip 3.18

REIMBURSEMENT OF ATTORNEY FEES, COURT COSTS AND SERVICE FEES ASSOCIATED WITH SEEKING PAST DUE CHILD SUPPORT OR ALIMONY

Most states allow you to get reimbursed for the attorney fees, court costs and service fees that were expended by a spouse seeking past due child support or alimony. This general rule only applies where there is a prior judgment awarding the spouse child support or alimony. Unfortunately, in many cases, the court will order an amount of attorney fee reimbursement that is less than what the seeking spouse has actually expended. Ask your attorney to request the court to order the other spouse to pay the actual attorney fees paid by you.

MORE MONEY MATTERS

> **Real Life Experience:** *Bob A.*
> *Age 43, Married, One Child*
> *Plumber; Phoenix, Arizona*
>
> "*My best friend is a great personal injury attorney. I can save a lot of money by using him.*"

Voodoo Tip 3.19

DON'T USE FRIEND ATTORNEY FOR FREE SERVICES

In a domestic proceeding, the chances are high that using a friend to represent you will put a strain on the friendship.

> **Real Life Experience:** *Rebecca F.*
> *Age 45, Divorced, One Adult Child*
> *Accountant; Olympia Washington*
>
> "*My lawyer sent me a bill. I was surprised to see several errors in it.*"

Voodoo Tip 3.20

CHECK YOUR LEGAL BILL FOR ERRORS

Always check your legal bill. Attorney's support staff usually produce your statement and errors can occur. Insist that your lawyer send you a statement of legal services on a monthly basis, which itemizes his work and the related expenses. Never hesitate to question a charge. A good attorney should welcome your billing inquires.

> **Real Life Experience:** *Gary F.*
> Age 41, Married, One Child
> Photocopier Sales Associate; Ithaca, New York
>
> *"I want to sell my boat to my buddy at a "discount" so that my wife won't get it in the divorce."*

Voodoo Tip 3.21

SELL ITEMS TO FRIENDS AND GET NOTARIZED BILL OF SALE

Further financial discussions regarding child support, alimony, property, taxes, and bankruptcy are found in subsequent chapters.

Summary of Voodoo Tips from Number 3

CONTROL YOUR LEGAL FEES, COURT COSTS, AND OTHER LEGAL EXPENSES

Voodoo Tip 3.1	Contrary to popular opinion, payment of legal fees can be a sound financial investment.
Voodoo Tip 3.2	Make your spouse pay your fees by using credit cards in both of your names.
Voodoo Tip 3.3	Buy other necessities with joint credit cards.
Voodoo Tip 3.4	Use credit cards and/or "ATM's" for cash advances.
Voodoo Tip 3.5	Get your own individual credit cards.
Voodoo Tip 3.6	Transfer the balances of your separate individual credit card accounts into joint credit card accounts.
Voodoo Tip 3.7	Use credit card and get cash refund at the end of case.
Voodoo Tip 3.8	Use a credit card that will save you interest on unpaid balances.

Voodoo Tip 3.9   Close used joint credit cards.

Voodoo Tip 3.10   Get your credit reports.

Voodoo Tip 3.11   Gift certificate heaven!

Voodoo Tip 3.12   Siphon money to build up reserves for attorney fees and other expenses.

Voodoo Tip 3.13   Don't get paid with "old money"; and pay with "old money."

Voodoo Tip 3.14   Take money from joint checking and/or savings accounts.

Voodoo Tip 3.15   Try an *In Forma Pauperis* application.

Voodoo Tip 3.16   Get a refund on unused court costs/deposit from the clerk of court after the case is finished.

Voodoo Tip 3.17   Anticipate possible fees for experts, mediators, appraisers, DNA tests, depositions and/or evaluators.

Voodoo Tip 3.18   Reimbursement of attorney fees, court costs, and service fees associated with seeking past due child support or alimony.

Voodoo Tip 3.19   Don't use friend attorney for free services.

Voodoo Tip 3.20   Check your legal bill for errors.

Voodoo Tip 3.21   Sell items to friends and get notarized bill of sale.

**VOODOO SPELL
TO REDUCE YOUR LEGAL FEES**

Dip a purple candle in white vinegar. Light the purple candle. Place seven shiny pennies around the lit candle. Put the following ingredients in your gris-gris bag: Alfalfa, Allspice, Almond, Bayberry, Buckwheat, Chamomile, Honeysuckle, Irish Moss, Lucky Hand Root, Pine, and Trillium. Fold a one dollar bill and pin it to your voodoo doll's left hand.

Go to your lawyer's office. Take out your joint credit card that is billed to your spouse. Say three magical words to your attorney, *"Please charge it!"*

VOODOO INGREDIENT NUMBER 4

Get Possessed!
Get Possession of Everyone and Everything

> **Real Life Experience:** *Paula G.*
> Age 44, Married, One Child
> Flight Attendant; Richmond, Virginia
>
> *"I know that there are many things to do, but I don't know what to do first."*

Voodoo Tip 4.1

GET POSSESSED!

In a divorce case, possession of children and property is everything. Get and keep the physical custody of your children, money, documents, and property. Safeguard everyone and everything. You must protect your monetary assets during a divorce. You and your spouse have conflicting financial interests.

> **Real Life Experience:** *Adelle P.*
> Age 27, Married, Two Children
> Nurse; San Jose, California
>
> *"There is no way that I would allow my husband to take my little boy and girl from me."*

1. CHILDREN

Without a court order indicating which parent has temporary physical custody of your children, both parents have equal rights to the kids. If you want custody of your children, go get your children. If you have possession of your children, keep them. Immediately have your attorney file a motion asking for the temporary custody of your children and a restraining order preventing your spouse from taking them without your written permission.

> **Real Life Experience:** *Laura S.*
> *Age 27, No Children, One Dog, Two Cats*
> *Computer Consultant; Atlanta, Georgia*
>
> *"My schnauzer and two Persians are my children. I have had Fritzy since he was a puppy. I've had Chops and Suey for four years."*

2. PETS

Despite popular sentiment, pets are "property." If you want your pets, keep them. When you hire an attorney, tell him of your concerns regarding your pets. The facts regarding how you acquired them are very important.

> **Real Life Experience:** *Carla N.*
> *Age 36, No Children*
> *Television Producer; Los Angeles, California*
>
> *"We have thousands of dollars in a joint checking account. We also have several credit cards in both of our names."*

3. MONEY

Get cash from all available sources. Make sure enough money is kept in accounts to pay for previously written checks. Also speak to your attorney, CPA, and certified financial planner about other legal, tax and financial consequences.

> **Real Life Experience:** *Robin E.*
> Age 36, One Child
> Housewife; Charleston, West Virginia
>
> *"My home is beautiful. The renovation has been a labor of love. It's part of me. I've painstakingly found the most beautiful pieces to complement the decor.*
> *The house is my home—my daughter's home. I want to do everything that I can do to keep it."*

4. THE HOUSE/APARTMENT/FURNISHINGS

If you want possession of your house or apartment, remain there. If you are battered or otherwise abused, immediately refer to the chapter on abuse for further insights.

Voodoo Tip 4.2

BE THE QUEEN OR KING OF THE CASTLE

After consulting with your attorney, consider changing the locks of your house or apartment. Be sure to get the approval of your lawyer because in many states, to prohibit a spouse from entering their own house/apartment without a court order, may be considered "constructive abandonment."

> **Real Life Experience:** *Henry A.*
> Age 44, No Children
> Architect; Peoria, Illinois
>
> *"I came back from a business trip to Detroit. My wife changed all of the locks on the house and left me a note that she wants a divorce."*

Voodoo Tip 4.3

DON'T GET LOCKED OUT OF YOUR HOUSE/APARTMENT

If your spouse changes the locks at your house or apartment, immediately call your attorney, your spouse, and the police to see if your spouse has a legal right to prohibit you from being in your house/apartment.

Ask your lawyer to file a motion seeking a restraining order against your spouse from locking you out of your residence.

5. THE VOODOO DIVORCE BOOK

Voodoo Tip 4.4

KEEP VOODOO DIVORCE BOOK HIDDEN FROM SPOUSE!

You certainly don't want your spouse to take advantage of the insights and forms found in this book.

Real Life Experience: *Michael. R.*

Age 50, Married Twice
One Minor Child, One Adult Child
Bankruptcy Attorney; Lancaster, Pennsylvania

"I spoke to my present wife about getting a divorce. Although this is my second marriage and I've gone through this before, this marriage is quite different; we've accumulated a lot of assets in the past nineteen years.

I want to be as civil as possible; however, Kelley is quite angry about the new woman in my life. There's no telling what she may do. I want to protect my belongings. She has threatened to burn my stuff. She is a very wicked woman."

Real Life Experience: *Nicole H.*

Age 32, Three Children
Artist; Waterbury, Vermont

"He has all of the paperwork. He pays all of the bills. I am deeply concerned that he is going to get a moving van and take all of the furniture out of the house."

Voodoo Tip 4.5

INVENTORY EVERYTHING

You can prevent trying to rely solely on your memory by inventorying your property. Once you have a good inventory of these items, consider photographing and/or videotaping them. Additionally, get a friend to view all of the items and provide the date and his initials next to each item that he inspects so that he later may testify as a witness as to the existence and condition of your property, should the property disappear.

When listing all of your financial records, including credit card accounts, car titles, and insurance policies, be sure to be as specific as possible by including the account number and account balances at the time that you make your list. Get the originals or copies of all documents.

You may use the VOODOO FORM found in the Appendix (Voodoo Spice Number 32) to assist you in this inventory process. As an additional mental reminder, use the following list to assist you in your quest to locate, inventory, possess, and/or photocopy.

DOCUMENTS AND THINGS TO LOCATE, INVENTORY, POSSESS, AND/OR COPY

Gather documents and things regarding you, your spouse and your children as to the following:

Income Information:
- Pay checks
- Payroll stubs
- Federal and state income tax returns and refunds
- Cash register receipts
- Receipt records
- Deferred, retirement, and/or savings plans such as IRAs, 401Ks, profit sharing, and stock options
- Severance pay
- "Golden parachute" retirement plans
- Documents evidencing any company or employer reimbursement for entertainment, travel, automobile, and/or other expenses
- Other employment benefits such as sick pay, vacation pay, bonuses, health club and country club memberships, and frequent flier programs
- Financial statements, balance sheets, profit and loss statements, and income statements
- Records regarding rental income
- Bank accounts: checking, savings, money market, and line of credit accounts
- Scholastic and vocational diplomas, awards, and/or degrees

Investment Information:
- Stocks, bonds, mutual funds, promissory notes, options, certificates of deposit, purchase agreements, and other investments
- All financial statements
- Trust agreements
- Custodial accounts

Bank Records:
- Checkbook registers
- Canceled checks
- Savings accounts
- Christmas club accounts
- Loan applications
- Documents in safety deposit boxes

Insurance Information:
- Insurance policies, whether life, health, auto, disability, or other.

Cars, Boats, Motorcycles, Motor Homes, Trailers, and Airplanes:
- Titles and registrations
- Keys
- Actual vehicles
- Appraisals on all vehicles

Marriage Related Documents:
- Present and prior marriage licenses, divorce papers, adoption papers
- Inheritance documents, judgments regarding child support
- Prenuptial, antenuptial agreements

Real Estate and Furniture:
- Titles or deeds to all property
- Appraisals of property
- Evaluations of furniture, furnishings, etc.
- Time-share units agreements
- Household furniture and furnishings

Other Business Records:
- Articles of incorporation, initial and annual reports, minute books, stockholder subscriptions, partnership agreements, and other documentation concerning the financial condition of any legal entity in which your spouse has or had a legal or equitable interest

Medical Records:
- Medical records
- Counseling and/or psychological evaluations of any party to this litigation and/or of the minor child
- Medical insurance cards
- Dental and orthodontic records
- Prescriptions

Other Monthly Expenses:
- All current invoices/bills
- Housing (Rent or mortgage note payment)
- Property insurance and taxes
- Premises/yard maintenance and repair
- Condominium charges
- Furniture payments
- Household supplies and repairs
- Utilities
    - Electricity
    - Gas
    - Water
- Telephone
    - Home
    - Car
    - Beeper
- Cable
- Food
    - Groceries
    - Meals eaten out/including work lunches
- Automobile/Transportation
    - Car note
    - Gasoline
    - Car maintenance
    - Parking
    - Other transportation expenses

- Clothing
- Average new purchases/replacements
    - Dry cleaning and laundry
- Personal and grooming (haircuts/nails)
- Education
    - School/lessons/tutoring
    - Books
    - Miscellaneous education expenses
- Day-care/baby sitting
- Pet/pet supplies
- Maid
- Union dues
- Recreation
- Gifts, donations, religious tithes
- Vacation
- Other debts

Miscellaneous Documents and Things:
- The *Voodoo Divorce* book
- Your Completed VOODOO FORMS
- Pets
- Jewelry
- Artwork
- Antiques and collectibles
- Birth certificates
- Passports/Visas/Green cards
- Vaccination records

Real Life Experience: *Catherine W.*

Age 37, Married, Two Children
Physician and Co-owner of Nursery
Indianapolis, Indiana

"My husband is the manager of our family owned nursery business. We review all of the books on a monthly basis. The company bookkeeper pays all of the company bills. I pay our personal monthly bills."

Voodoo Tip 4.6

YOUR FINANCIAL FIGURES ARE YOUR FRIENDS

If your spouse is not anticipating your move towards a divorce, then methodically and discreetly get originals or copies of all financial records regarding your spouse's business affairs and income as well as both of your expenses. Safeguard these documents with your attorney, a confidant, or in a new safety deposit box at a new bank. Refer to the above list and the VOODOO FORMS found in the Appendix to guide you to seek all of the various types of documents to find.

> **Real Life Experience:** *Lena P.*
> Age 55, Married, Two Children
> Part-Time Retail Sales Clerk
> Bismarck; North Dakota
>
> *"We have been using Quicken software program to keep track of our bills and investments. Lately, I have noticed some strange e-mails sent to George."*

Voodoo Tip 4.7

GET INFORMATION FROM COMPUTERS

Make a backup tape or diskette of the information on your computer. Give the tape and or diskette to your attorney. Also consider making a print out of any particularly revealing data.

> **Real Life Experience:** *Faye W.*
> Age 48, Married, One Child
> Jeweler; Jackson, Mississippi
>
> *"He has always prepared the state and federal tax returns."*

Voodoo Tip 4.8

GET POSSESSION OF ALL DOCUMENTS THAT YOU NEED TO PREPARE YOUR TAXES

Accumulate all documents that you will need to prepare your taxes.

Voodoo Tip 4.9

GET MONEY (REFER TO NUMBER 3)

> **Real Life Experience:** *Tammy T.*
> Age 22, Married, No Children
> Unemployed; Cambridge, Massachusetts
>
> "I am leaving my husband and moving out of the apartment this weekend. I don't have a place to move the furniture."

Voodoo Tip 4.10

VIDEOTAPE AND/OR PHOTOGRAPH EACH ROOM OF YOUR HOUSE/APARTMENT

> **Real Life Experience:** *Aimee C.*
> Age 28, Married, One Child
> Court Reporter; Orlando, Florida
>
> "I have taken the money out of our checking account. I've put the money in my separate safety deposit box at my new bank. Tomorrow I am changing the locks on the house while Richard is at work. My daughter is going to stay at my mother's house tomorrow night."

Voodoo Tip 4.11

FILE *EX PARTE* MOTIONS

Often the test on who gets the immediate possession of children, money, homes, and property, depends on who wins the race to the courthouse and files *Ex Parte* motions. Please refer to the next chapter for an extensive overview of these special pleadings.

Summary of Voodoo Tips from Number 4

GET POSSESSED! GET POSSESSION OF EVERYONE AND EVERYTHING

Voodoo Tip 4.1   Get possessed!

Voodoo Tip 4.2   Be the queen or king of the castle.

Voodoo Tip 4.3   Don't get locked out of your house/apartment.

Voodoo Tip 4.4   Keep *Voodoo Divorce* hidden from your spouse!

Voodoo Tip 4.5   Inventory everything.

Voodoo Tip 4.6   Your financial figures are your friends.

Voodoo Tip 4.7   Get information from computers.

Voodoo Tip 4.8   Get possessions of all documents that you need to prepare your taxes.

Voodoo Tip 4.9   Get money.

Voodoo Tip 4.10   Video tape and/or photograph each room of your house/apartment.

Voodoo Tip 4.11   File *Ex Parte* motions.

**VOODOO SPELL
TO GET POSSESSED**

Get your kids and pets. Go to your bank. Take money out of any joint bank accounts. Use your joint credit cards to your full advantage. Stay in house (unless abuse exists). Keep your *Voodoo Divorce Book* in a safe place. Inventory and safeguard your possessions. Ask your lawyer to file requests for protective orders.

Light a red candle. Put the following ingredients in your gris-gris bag: Aloe, Angelica, Blood Root, Boldo Leaves, Cinquefoil, Cinnamon, Cowslip, Cypress, Lavender, and Orris Root.

Place a picture of your spouse and black mustard seed under your front door mat. You will start to feel the security that comes from being "possessed."

VOODOO INGREDIENT NUMBER 5

Injunctions and *Ex Parte* Relief

Acting swiftly to protect your rights is one of the most effective maneuvers in your divorce case. Insist that your lawyer file pleadings asking for *Ex Parte* Relief. *Ex Parte* Relief is simply a request for a judge to grant orders without a hearing or prior notice to your spouse. This is beneficial because your lawyer can ask for certain orders without your spouse or his or her lawyer being present in court to argue against your requests.

These *Ex Parte* requests seek temporary relief until a full blown hearing can occur. *Ex Parte* orders usually protect people and property.

> **Real Life Experience:** Mariel F.
>
> Age 30, Married, One Child
> Teacher; Nashville, Tennessee
>
> *"I want my lawyer to protect me as much as possible."*

Voodoo Tip 5.1

HAVE AN *EX PARTE* PARTY!

1. Ask for an order of temporary physical custody of your children.
2. If you suspect abuse or neglect, ask for an order temporarily terminating the other parent's visitation rights until an investigation into the allegations can be made.
3. Ask for an order preventing the other parent from taking the children out of your county (parish in Louisiana), state, or the jurisdiction of the court.

Quick Fact: According to the U.S. Census Bureau, the average American moves 11.7 times during his/her lifetime.

4. Ask for an order preventing the other parent from having someone of the opposite sex spend the night when he or she has physical custody of the children or are exercising his or her visitation rights.

5. Ask for an order requiring your spouse to stay a specified minimum distance from:
   a. You;
   b. Your children;
   c. Your residence;
   d. Your place of employment;
   e. Other family members that live with you;
   f. Your children's school;
   g. Your children's day care facility; and/or
   h. Any other place that your children may be found.

6. Protect your children and yourself by asking for an order prohibiting your spouse from:
   a. Any form of abuse;
   b. Harassment; and/or
   c. Alienation of your children's affection.

   (For further discussion regarding abuse and harassment, turn to Number 13 entitled "Don't Stand For Abuse and Avoid Being Falsely Accused.")

Real Life Experience: Chris M.

Age 35, Married Twice, Three Children
Caterer; Tallahassee, Florida

"My husband keeps calling. He yells profanities and tells me that I will lose everything."

Voodoo Tip 5.2

USE YOUR TELEPHONE AS A SHIELD AND A SWORD

Should your spouse start harassing you with repeated telephone calls and/or vulgar, threatening or emotional messages, consider the following:

   a. Screen your telephone calls by getting an answering machine or using a voice mail system provided by your local telephone company. If your spouse leaves an inappropriate message, save the recorded message and give it to your attorney so that he can present it to the judge;

b. Change your telephone number to an unpublished listing;
c. Keep a written log of the dates, times and content of each and every harassing telephone call.
d. Use "Caller ID" which is provided by your local telephone company.
e. Use "Call Blocking" which is provided by your local telephone company. This service allows you to block out or otherwise prevent your spouse from calling from specific telephone numbers.
f. Use "Call Forwarding" which is provided by your local telephone company. Should your spouse continue to call you late at night with harassing telephone calls, simply call forward your telephone calls to your attorneys' office or to a voice mail service.
g. Use "Call Tracing" which is provided by your local telephone company. The telephone company can provide documents that can prove calls were made from a certain location. You may need an appropriate person from the telephone company to come testify as to the accuracy and authenticity of these documents.
7. It's extremely wise to ask for an order preventing your spouse from alienating, hiding, or disposing of property without a court order or without your written permission (exceptions are usually made for necessary and ordinary living expenses and regular business expenditures).

Voodoo Tip 5.3

RECORD A NOTICE OF *LIS PENDENS*

If you own real estate with your spouse, ask your lawyer to consider filing and recording a document, in most states, called a "Notice of *Lis Pendens*," where the real estate records are properly kept in the courthouse. This document may assist you in preventing your spouse from transferring the property or putting another encumbrance on your real estate.

8. Likewise, you can ask for an order prohibiting your spouse from incurring greater debt which you might be responsible for, without a court order or your written permission (again, exceptions are

usually made for necessary and ordinary living expenses and regular business expenditures).

9. If you own a business with your spouse, you can ask for an order that will:
   a. Prohibit your spouse from firing or hiring certain critical employees;
   b. Limiting business expenditures over a certain sum of money without your written approval or a court order; and/or
   c. Compel a full accounting of all business operations.

Voodoo Tip 5.4

DON'T OVERDO YOUR "*EX PARTE*" PARTY!

Ex Parte requests should be made sparingly and wisely. You want to protect people and property without looking unreasonable or being overreaching. Your requests are limited only by your state's law, the judge's discretion, and your own imagination.

Summary of Voodoo Tips from Number 5

INJUNCTIONS AND *EX PARTE* RELIEF

Voodoo Tip 5.1	Have an *Ex Parte* party!
Voodoo Tip 5.2	Use your telephone as a shield and a sword.
Voodoo Tip 5.3	Record a notice of *Lis Pendens*.
Voodoo Tip 5.4	Don't overdo your *Ex Parte* party!

**VOODOO SPELL
FOR PROTECTION**

Call your attorney. If abuse occurs, call the National Domestic Violence Hotline at the following number:

1-800-799-SAFE.

Light white, blue, and brown candles. Your gris-gris bag should contain the following ingredients: Aloe, Angelica, Aspen, Boldo Leaves, Caraway Seed, Cinquefoil, Clover, Cowslip, Cypress, Garlic, Magnolia, Orris Root, Rose Buds, St. John's Wort, and Violet.

Pin a chicken's foot onto the chest of your voodoo doll.

VOODOO INGREDIENT NUMBER 6

Grounds for Divorce

> **Real Life Experience:** *Ellen B.*
> Age 45, Married, Two Children
> Housewife; Kenner, Louisiana
>
> *"I've tried for years to make things work out. Every couple has their share of problems. I've always thought that love was enough to get us through anything. I was wrong."*

Quick Facts:

Each year, approximately two million people get divorced. The divorce rate hovers around 4.4 to 4.6 divorces per every 1,000 in population. In the seventies and eighties, the divorce rate climbed from 2.5/1000 in 1966 to highs of 5.3/1000 in 1979 and 1981. The divorce rate has leveled off since the 1981 peak. The divorce rate since 1940 is found in the Appendix. Additionally, the state by state divorce statistics and rates are found in the Appendix.

The average length of a first marriage is 11 years. A woman remarries for an average of 7.1 years, while men remarry for an average of 7.4 years. The average duration of an American marriage is 9.8 years. The average age for a woman who marries and divorces several times is 33 for the first divorce, 39 for the second, and 42 for three or more. The average age for men of multiple divorces is 35 for the first, 42 for the second, and 46.5 for subsequent divorces.

Divorces are more prevalent during the time when men are, on average, 30–34 years old and for women 25–29 years old.

Women's divorce rate is highest between the very young ages of 15 and 19. Men's divorce rate is highest between the ages of 20 and 24.

At the time of their first marriage, the median age for women is 21.0 years and 23.1 years for men. The median age of spouses at the time of the first marriage divorce decree is 35.1 for women and 33.2 for men. For the median ages of individuals for subsequent divorces, refer to the Appendix.

Women commence the legal proceedings in more than 90 percent of all divorces.[1]

THE EVER CHANGING NATURE OF DIVORCE LAW

Divorce law has evolved to conform to the prevailing views of our time. In past decades, divorce laws were drafted to dissuade persons from divorcing. These restrictive laws were framed with the purpose of preserving the family unit. The state was our parent with the arrogant position that it knew what was best for us. Divorces were instituted based on a spouse's guilt or innocence ("Fault"). Fault was a major player in the determination of alimony and apportionment of property. Along with the age of fault, came the age of gender bias. This included the "tender years doctrine" which presumed that the mother should be the custodial parent of an infant or young child.

This rather antiquated system of family "justice" created bitter court fights and lingering anger and regret.

Today, divorce in America is taking a new direction. States are no longer as stringent in their role to maintain family units. Enlightened legislatures are realizing America's freedom of choice while preserving and enforcing the legal and moral parental obligation to raise and support a child. As a result of this changed focus, more states are permitting divorces on grounds other than fault. A no-fault divorce aids in lessening the stresses associated with torrid allegations of infidelity or intemperance. Such allegations still raise their ugly head in battles over alimony, child custody and the like; however, the system is slightly more civil and less combative as a whole. Accompanying a trend toward no-fault divorces, is the aspiring goal of the courts to be gender neutral. The goal truly has not been obtained, yet progress is being made.

With the emergence of the religious right, there has been a regression toward more restrictive laws regarding divorce. For example, Louisiana has implemented "covenant marriages" as an alternative to traditional marriages that we are used to seeing. In a "covenant marriage," the state

---

1. Source: Advance Report of Final Divorce Statistics, 1989 and 1990. *Monthly Vital Statistics Report*; Vol. 43 no.8, Supp. Hyattsville, Maryland; National Center for Health Statistics, 1995).

would recognize the spouses as contractual partners with much more restrictive grounds for divorce and an extended time period of separation that must be satisfied prior to being eligible for the divorce. Marriage counseling also may be a prerequisite to the divorce. Big brother is still alive.

As socio-economic and political influences change, so will our divorce laws. They will evolve, whether for good or bad, based on the will of the people. Hence, you have a vital role in molding the future of our domestic life. If you have a strong view on an issue surrounding marriage and divorce, write your local, state, and federal representatives. Find out their views on issues that affect you and your children. Advocate or you may succumb to the will and views of others.

> **Real Life Experience:** *Daniel C.*
> *Age 36, Married*
> *Just Served With Divorce Papers, Two Children*
> *Chiropractor; Miami, Florida*
>
> *"Last evening, I received papers from my wife's divorce lawyer. She wants a divorce, sole custody of my children, the house, my Volvo—everything."*

Voodoo Tip 6.1

IF YOU HAVE JUST BEEN SERVED WITH DIVORCE PAPERS, CONTACT YOUR LAWYER IMMEDIATELY!

WHAT IS A DIVORCE?

A divorce is a formal statement and a court's legal termination of the marriage contract between spouses. In order to be divorced , most states require one or both spouses to reside or be domiciled in the state for a certain length of time. Some states don't have a residency requirement. To be "domiciled" in a state simply means that the state is considered your primary residence.

Once you are divorced, you may change your name and/or remarry.

We have all heard that the divorce rate is at an alarming fifty (50%) percent of marriages.

Society is beginning to look at marriage as a contract. As a result of this sterile view of the union, judges are becoming more dispassionate towards particular litigants. Today a divorce is like going to the dentist and getting a tooth pulled. It may be painful, but it also can be quick.

Quick Fact: Approximately 95% of divorce proceedings do not result in a contested trial. (American Bar Association)

Real Life Experience: *Sue A.*

Age 29, Married, No Children
Pharmaceutical Sales Representative
Topeka, Kansas

"I was transferred to Topeka from Alabama. My husband stayed in Birmingham. How long do I have to wait in order to get divorced here?"

WHAT ARE THE RESIDENCY REQUIREMENTS OF YOUR STATE?

At the time of publication, the residency requirements of the states are listed below. Keep in mind that the state's legislatures can change the length of time required to be a resident for divorce purposes. In fact, they often do change. Check with your lawyer to see if the requirements have remained the same.

State Residency Requirement

State	Requirement
Alabama	Six months
Alaska	No residency requirement
Arizona	Ninety days
Arkansas	Sixty days
California	Six months
Colorado	Ninety days
Connecticut	One year
Delaware	Six months
Florida	Six months
Georgia	Six months
Hawaii	Six months
Idaho	Six weeks
Illinois	Ninety days
Indiana	Six months
Iowa	No residency requirement
Kansas	Sixty days
Kentucky	One hundred and eighty days
Louisiana	No residency requirement
Maine	Six months
Maryland	One year
Massachusetts	No residency requirement
Michigan	Six months

Minnesota	One hundred and eighty days
Mississippi	Six months
Missouri	Ninety days
Montana	Ninety days
Nebraska	One year
Nevada	Six weeks
New Hampshire	One year
New Jersey	One year
New Mexico	Six months
New York	One year
North Carolina	Six months
North Dakota	Six months
Ohio	Six months
Oklahoma	Six months
Oregon	Six months
Pennsylvania	Six months
Rhode Island	One year
South Carolina	Three months
South Dakota	No residency requirement
Tennessee	Six months
Texas	Six months
Utah	Ninety days
Vermont	Six months
Virginia	Six months
Washington	One year
Washington D.C.	Six months
West Virginia	One year
Wisconsin	Six months
Wyoming	Sixty days

Real Life Experience: *Barbara P.*
Age 34, Married, One Child
Waitress; Philadelphia, Pennsylvania

"How do I prove that I now live in Pennsylvania? I want to get divorced as soon as possible."

Voodoo Tip 6.2

PROVE YOUR RESIDENCY

You can help your lawyer prove your residency in the state by your ability to show your permanent or substantial connection to the state by:

1. Getting a drivers license in your state
2. Send a change of address form to the U.S. Post Office in your former state indicating your new address
3. Register to vote in the state
4. Purchasing a house or renting an apartment in the state
5. Any other act that establishes your intent and desire to remain in the state

"FAULT" AND "NO-FAULT" DIVORCES

All states provide a legal basis to get a divorce without the necessity of formally blaming your spouse with bad conduct that caused the break up of the marriage. These states are typically called "No-fault" states. Terms often found to describe the basis of seeking a "No-fault" divorce are "Irreconcilable differences," "Incompatibility," and/or "Irretrievable breakdown." Other "No-fault" trends include allowing a couple to get divorced after they have lived separate and apart for a requisite period of time, depending on the state, from six months up to three years. Usually, the separation of the parties must be accompanied by an intent of the parties to permanently be separated, without reconciliation.

Most "No-fault" states also provide grounds for divorce that are found in states that require a statement of fault.

In a divorce proceeding, a state may require you to cite reasons for divorce in your divorce pleading why you want the divorce. These states are called "Fault Divorce" states. In "Fault Divorce" states, the party seeking the divorce alleges that the other spouse is to blame for some conduct or omission that renders a valid reason for the state to grant a divorce. The actual grounds for a fault related divorce vary from state to state. Your attorney can tell you which grounds apply in your state; however, the following is an alphabetical listing of grounds found throughout the country:

Examples of Fault Grounds:

Abandonment
Adultery
Attempted murder of spouse

Bigamy
Conviction of a felony with imprisonment
Cruel treatment, physical or mental
Desertion
Habitual drunkenness or intemperance
Habitual use of narcotic drugs
Impotency and/or sterility not known at the time of marriage
Infection of a spouse with a venereal disease
Insanity

ADULTERY

Real Life Experience: Jane E.
Age 43, Married, Two Children
Certified Public Accountant; Omaha, Nebraska

"I listened in on Tom's telephone conversation with that woman from my bedroom phone. He had the nerve to call her from our house. I can't take this any more. He has hurt me enough."

Quick Fact: Although adultery may appear to be a common ground used in getting a fault divorce, only 3 percent of divorces in the United States are granted on the grounds of adultery.

A common defense for the allegation of adultery is that the spouses reconciled with an intent to resume their marriage after the faithful spouse became aware of the adulterous acts of the "fallen" spouse. In many states, if the parties reconcile, then the act or acts of adultery cannot be used as the fault ground for the divorce. States vary on their position of whether a single act of intercourse after knowledge of the other party's adulterous act(s) constitutes a reconciliation. A new act of adultery would have to occur in order to create a new cause of action for adultery. If adultery is a potential issue in your case, talk to your attorney on how reconciliation may affect your litigation.

Adultery can be proven by direct evidence such as eyewitness testimony of a reliable witness (i.e., an investigator) as well as by a video tape or photograph. Adultery is most often proven by inferential circumstantial (non-direct) evidence. In order to prove adultery by circumstantial evidence, motive and opportunity to commit adultery are crucial.

Circumstantial evidence can be found in all shapes and forms. Look at the following examples:

- Bambi's (paramour's) telephone number
- Calendars
- Cellular telephone bills
- Condom wrappers
- Credit card receipts and billings
- Discarded hose
- Hotel receipts
- Lingerie
- Lipstick
- Long distance telephone bills
- Match books
- Personal address books
- Perfume or lipstick on shirt, on other garments, or sheets (Do not wash or launder)
- Photographs
- Restaurant receipts
- Sworn testimony of eye witnesses
- Sworn testimony of guilty spouse
- Sworn testimony of Bambi (Paramour)
- Telephone calls on answering machine (Save and do not erase)
- Viagra bottle

Real Life Experience: *Helen U.*
Age 50, No Minor Children
Housewife; Lincoln, Nebraska

"My best friend used a private eye in her divorce. Her husband was caught having sex with an employee at the girl's apartment. I'm going to hire that same investigator. I'm going to catch him in the act!"

Voodoo Tip 6.3

TALK TO YOUR LAWYER BEFORE YOU HIRE A PRIVATE EYE

Most divorce cases do not require the use of a private investigator. Before you spend money for surveillance on your spouse, talk to your lawyer about the need for this expense. Furthermore, your spouse may suspect surveillance and dodge your efforts to catch him in the "Act."

> **Real Life Experience:** *Ellen E.*
> *Age 40, Married, Four Children*
> *Owner of Coffee Shop*
> *Manchester, New Hampshire*
>
> *"I've been recording his telephone conversations with his little girlfriend. It's sickening. He sounds like a child. My lawyer is going to eat his lunch!"*

Voodoo Tip 6.4

BE AWARE OF THE OMNIBUS CRIME CONTROL AND SAFE STREET ACT OF 1968

The Omnibus Crime Control and Safe Street Act of 1968 makes it a federal crime to do any of the following acts:

1. To listen in on a telephone conversation if one is not a party to the call and does not have permission to listen by at least one party to the call;
2. To record a telephone call if one is not a party to that call and/or does not have permission from the party to record the call.

We all have heard people before or during a divorce who have recorded their spouse's telephone conversation with a lover. Because it is done all the time does not make it legal. If you presently have unauthorized recordings of telephone calls of your spouse with his lover, or if you feel the need to record your spouse's telephone conversations, relax, but immediately consult your lawyer.

**VOODOO SPELL
TO STOP ADULTERY**

Place saltpeter in a pair of your spouse's underwear. Throw the underwear into a lit fireplace. Light one black and one pink candle. Pin a picture of your spouse, along with a red hot pepper, on the groin of the voodoo doll.

Put the following ingredients in your gris-gris bag: Cactus, Cinnamon, Clover, Damiana, Elder Bark, Heartsease, Lavender, Pistachio, Rye, Skullcap, and Walnut.

Write your spouse's name on a ripe banana. Step on it.

> **Real Life Experience:** *Jimmy S.*
> Age 47, Married, Two Children
> Banker; St. Petersburg, Florida
>
> *"I don't want a big fight. All I want is a simple divorce."*

Exclusively "No-Fault" Grounds States:

States that currently permit solely "No-fault" divorces are :
Arizona, California, Colorado, Delaware, Florida, Hawaii, Iowa, Kentucky, Michigan, Minnesota, Missouri, Montana, Nebraska, Oregon, Washington, Washington D.C., Wisconsin, and Wyoming.

States That Allow "Fault" Grounds for Divorce:

States that currently permit divorces based on "No-fault" and/or "Fault" grounds include the following:
Alabama, Alaska, Arkansas, Connecticut, Georgia, Idaho, Illinois, Indiana, Kansas, Louisiana, Maine, Maryland, Massachusetts, Mississippi, New Hampshire, Nevada, New Jersey, New Mexico, New York, North Carolina, North Dakota, Ohio, Oklahoma, Pennsylvania, Rhode Island, South Carolina, South Dakota, Tennessee, Texas, Utah, Vermont, and West Virginia.

*****

Regardless of the state in which the divorce proceeding is being conducted, or the grounds used for the divorce, you must also address applicable issues of child custody, child support, alimony, property division, and related matters.

> **Real Life Experience:** *Timothy E.*
> Age 44, Married
> Physically Separated for Five Months
> Oil Executive; Shreveport, Louisiana
>
> *"Do I have to file for a legal separation before I get a divorce?"*

SHOULD YOU GET A SEPARATION?

A legal separation is a court's decree and recognition that married persons are living separately while remaining married. This legal separation provides an increased opportunity for reconciliation. A legal separation and a divorce are different. If you are legally separated, you are still married. If you merely get a legal separation, you have not dissolved the marriage. If you are merely legally separated, you cannot remarry. If you are divorced you can. Talk to your lawyer and see whether your state offers a legal separation. If so, ask him how it might benefit you.

A legal separation may provide a period of time for you to evaluate your marriage. A legal separation also permits you to resolve any unresolved emotional conflicts.

During a legal separation, you may be entitled to temporary spousal support, often called "alimony pendente lite." You also may be entitled to child support and other relief. A marriage can only be dissolved through a divorce decree or an annulment.

> **Real Life Experience:** *David H.*
> Age 37, Married One Month Ago, No Children
> Hotel Concierge; Hilo, Hawaii
>
> *"I made a huge mistake! I married her for the wrong reasons."*

CAN YOU GET AN ANNULMENT?

A legal annulment is a court's official decree that the marriage was not valid, thus somewhat eliminating the alleged trauma or stigma of divorce. Grounds for an annulment include circumstances where the marriage occurred due to fraud or duress, or in instances of bigamy, marriage of a person under the age of consent, or marrying a close relative.

Annulments are uncommon because State legislatures have narrowly defined circumstances where a legal annulment would be appropriate. Consult your attorney to see if this would be a viable or desired option for you.

Legal annulments and religious annulments are different. Usually, your legal annulment must be decreed before a religious annulment can occur. Consult your attorney and religious leader.

> **Real Life Experience:** *Kay Q.*
> Age 54, Married, Three Adult Children
> Retail Sales Associate; New York, New York
>
> *"I want my maiden name back."*

Voodoo Tip 6.5

IF DESIRED, DON'T FORGET TO ASK FOR YOUR NAME CHANGE

If you wish to return to the use of your maiden name, ask your lawyer to seek it at the time of your divorce. You can ask the court to change your name back to you maiden name, another unmarried name, or any other new name that you choose.

Your spouse cannot force you to change your married name.

> **Real Life Experience:** Charlotte L.
> Age 38, One Child
> Model; Durham, North Carolina
>
> *"My lawyer is doing a fine job. Is there anything else that I need to do while he is at work on my case?"*

You should notify all pertinent persons and companies of your name change and/or change in address and telephone number. Remember to contact the following entities:

- Banks
- Credit card companies
- Doctors
- Drivers license bureau
- Employer
- Friends
- Internal Revenue Service
- Landlord
- Lawyers
- Mortgage companies
- Post Office
- Professional associations
- Registrar of voters
- Schools
- Social Security Administration
- State tax department
- Telephone company
- United States State Department (for name change on passport)
- Utility company

> **Real Life Experience:** Angela A.
> Age 31, Married, No Children
> Newspaper Reporter; Washington, D.C.
>
> *"I don't want him to have anything of mine."*

Voodoo Tip 6.6

ONCE DIVORCED, MAKE A NEW WILL

Once you are divorced, you should consider making a new will that accounts for your current desires.

Summary of Voodoo Tips from Number 6

GROUNDS FOR DIVORCE

Voodoo Tip 6.1   If you have just been served with divorce papers, contact your lawyer immediately!

Voodoo Tip 6.2   Prove your residency.

Voodoo Tip 6.3   Talk to your lawyer before you hire a private eye.

Voodoo Tip 6.4   Be aware of the Omnibus Crime Control and Safe Street Act of 1968.

Voodoo Tip 6.5   If desired, don't forget to ask for your name change.

Voodoo Tip 6.6   Once divorced, make a new will.

VOODOO SPELL TO WIN YOUR DIVORCE

Safeguard *Voodoo Divorce*. Light a brown candle. Your red velvet gris-gris bag should contain the following: Ague Root, Alfalfa, Bayberry, Calendula, Cascara Sagrada, Catnip, Cedar, Clover, Cypress, Dill, Dog Grass, Dragon's Blood Reed, Elder Bark, Frankincense, Galangal Root, Garlic, Gilead Buds, Ginger, Goat's Leaves, Horseradish, Irish Moss, Job's Tears, Marigold, Myrrh, Orris Root, Poke Root, Rue, Sandalwood, Sumbul Root, Sweetpea, Vanilla, Violet, and Yarrow.

Write your spouse's name on a piece of paper, pin the piece of paper under your voodoo doll's left foot. Write your spouse's lawyer's name on another piece of paper, pin that piece of paper under your voodoo doll's right foot. Read the rest of this book.

VOODOO INGREDIENT NUMBER 7

Alimony

Alimony, also called spousal support or maintenance, is a payment from one spouse (the "breadwinner") to the other spouse who earns less income. The purpose of alimony is to allow the spouse of less means and/or abilities to pay for his or her living expenses and other needs. Permanent alimony may last the extent of the recipient's life. The underlying rationale for alimony is to assist the spouse of less fortune, opportunities, and/or abilities.

"Rehabilitative" or "Restitution" alimony is for a definitive period of time, with the goals of having the other spouse create sufficient finances, opportunities, and/or abilities to be self-sufficient. The reason for the need of "rehabilitation" may result from the recipient spouse's previous foregoing of educational and/or employment opportunities during the marriage that he or she would have reasonably expected to otherwise have experienced. Unlike child support, alimony is not calculated by using state guidelines, but rather the figure is derived by the agreement of the parties or at the discretion of the judge.

Alimony may be classified by the time period in which it is paid—either *before* or *after* the divorce.

PRE-DIVORCE ALIMONY (TEMPORARY ALIMONY)

Pre-divorce alimony, commonly called "temporary" alimony or "alimony pendente lite," is alimony established for the period of time from the date of filing a pleading asking for such relief, until the date of the divorce. Some states provide exceptions that permit the obligation of "temporary" alimony to extend beyond the date of the divorce. An extension in "temporary" alimony is most common where "permanent" alimony also is requested by a spouse and the court has not been able to have the trial regarding the issue of permanent alimony.

Although states vary in the application of factors that are used to determine whether and to what extent temporary alimony should be paid, generally, the courts will look at both partys' prior standard of living. Fault for the break up of the marriage, as well as each spouse's assets, are either not considered or given less consideration during the evaluation and calculations made for temporary spousal maintenance.

POST-DIVORCE ALIMONY ("PERMANENT" ALIMONY)

Post-Divorce Alimony, often simply referred to as alimony, is financial support of a spouse after the termination of the marriage. Like temporary alimony, states vary on the factors used in addressing such support. In order to determine whether "permanent" alimony is appropriate, and to what degree and duration, if any, that it should be paid, the court weighs the relative positions of each party.

> **Real Life Experience:** *Lauren F.*
>
> Age 58, Divorced Three Times
> Retired Postal Employee; Salem, Oregon
>
> *"I haven't worked in seven years. My ex is the manager at the ***** Department Store. My alimony trial is in two weeks. What are my chances of winning? How much can I expect to get?"*

Common factors considered in determining "permanent" alimony are as follows:

- Needs of each party
- Income of each party
- Expenses of each party
- Separate and marital assets of each party
- Debts/obligations of each party
- Earnings capacity of each party (including opportunities, education, and/or training)
- Proposed paying party's ability to pay
- Fault leading to the break up of the marriage (applicable in many states; see Appendix: Voodoo Spice Number 17)
- Length of the marriage

- Standard of living to which each party is accustomed (as well as station in life and social standing)
- Presence of young children in need of care that would make it difficult for the recipient of alimony to work
- Age of each party
- Physical and mental health of each party
- Intended use of the alimony payments
- Tax consequences of all court orders
- Distribution of separate and marital property and
- Any other factor that the judge deems appropriate.

Other factors that courts often consider, but should not, include the following:

- Punishment (the judge's particular dislike or disdain for a party)
- A means to indirectly increase the child support award over the state's guidelines and
- The sexual preference of the parties

> **Real Life Experience:** *Denis W.*
> Age 49, Divorced, No Children
> Algiers, Louisiana
>
> *"I can't seem to make ends meet. My former spouse is a very wealthy pediatrician. What can I do?"*

Voodoo Tip 7.1

DON'T BE EMBARRASSED TO ASK FOR ALIMONY

Regardless of your gender, if you have a reasonable basis to seek alimony, seek it.

ALIMONY IS AN ENDANGERED SPECIES

Throughout the country, we are seeing a shift in the view of courts towards permanent alimony. With an increasing number of women entering the work force, and the decreasing focus on gender, many states are moving away from the term "alimony" to the term "maintenance." The seemingly subtle shift in the use of terms is an example of the growing paradigmatic shift of today's courts. As a public policy, Texas has had no provisions for alimony (although it may in the near future). Other state courts are becoming more resistant to awarding alimony, except in cases where a spouse has been and remains financially dependent on the other spouse for a lengthy period of time.

Quick Fact: Approximately fifty three (53%) percent of women with children are in the labor force. (U.S. Census Bureau)

Real Life Experience: *Margo L.*
Age 61, Married, One Adult Child
Unemployed; Columbia, South Carolina

"I was diagnosed with breast cancer and fibromalgia. I'm deeply concerned about my ability to get health insurance when I get divorced."

Voodoo Tip 7.2

COBRA

A divorce usually terminates an ex's right to be covered under the former spouse's employer's medical insurance plan (unless each spouse works for the same employer and is covered under the same insurance plan.) Under the Consolidated Omnibus Budget Reconciliation Act of 1985 (COBRA), *upon request*, a non-employee former spouse can receive continued insurance coverage with the same insurance carrier for up to three years. This helps to eliminate the immediate post-divorce concerns of a potential lapse in medical insurance coverage. The insurance company (insurance agent) should be immediately notified of your desire to exercise your COBRA rights.

Real Life Experience: *Suzanne R.*
Age 28, Divorced, One Child
Actress; Los Angeles, California

"My husband is in the house painting contract business. It's a cash cow. He never reported all of his income to the IRS. I know that he is going to lie about his business profits and expenses."

MANIPULATION OF INCOME AND EXPENSES FOR PURPOSES OF AFFECTING ALIMONY AWARD

A manipulation of events can occur that directly affects the alimony award.

A spouse may attempt the following:
1. Control, possess, and/or hide assets
2. Decrease his income/earning capacity, while seeking to increase spouse's income/earnings capacity
3. Increase his expenses (allowing less disposable funds to be available to spouse); while decreasing spouse's expenses (thereby decreasing her "need" for alimony)
4. Attempt to withhold funds from spouse to a point where the spouse is under financial duress and is more likely to concede to a less favorable alimony award

In order to affect the numbers used in the calculation of alimony, a spouse may attempt to:
1. Change his standard of living
2. Postpone salary increases
3. Delay bonuses
4. Encourage the other spouse to get a job or change jobs
5. Reduce the number of hours worked
6. Reduce the overtime hours worked
7. Increase or decrease expenses
8. Fail to report actual income earned in tax returns
9. Put assets/income in someone else's name
10. Become "disabled"
11. Shelter money in corporations, partnerships, or trusts
12. Have personal expenses paid through family business
13. Get reimbursed on the side by employer for expenses (i.e., auto expense, meals, travel, etc.) and
14. Make misrepresentations to the court about his income or expenses

(The same acts can occur in an attempt to manipulate a *child support award*.)

Prior to or during the divorce process, a "breadwinning" spouse may encourage the other "spouse" to do the following:
1. Seek employment and/or training
2. Increase hours worked
3. Seek higher pay

4. Seek a second job
5. Decrease expenses and/or
6. Sign a consent agreement to waive alimony or to accept a less favorable alimony award

> **Real Life Experience:** *Eugenia W.*
> Age 43, Divorced, Two Children
> Unemployed; Jefferson City, Missouri
>
> *"My ex-husband has one of the best divorce lawyers in town. His attorney has filed papers seeking custody. He told me that he will fight for full custody unless I drop my claim for alimony."*

Voodoo Tip 7.3

WATCH OUT FOR "ALIMONY BLACKMAIL"

Unfortunately and frequently, a spouse threatens a custody battle unless the other spouse concedes to waiving alimony or receiving a lower alimony and/or child support award. Report any such threats to your attorney. Any evidence of these threats should be tendered to your lawyer.

> **Real Life Experience:** *Bill M.*
> Age 43, Divorced, One Child
> Insurance Agent; Oklahoma City, Oklahoma
>
> *"My ex-wife stopped working when we had our boy. She keeps on telling me that she is unable to get a good paying job because of her lack of experience."*

Voodoo Tip 7.4

GET OR ENCOURAGE EDUCATIONAL AND VOCATIONAL REHABILITATION

Although often used to lessen an alimony award, educational and/or vocational training and rehabilitation can have a long term benefit to both spouses. The spouse paying alimony may receive the benefit of having the payment period shortened or terminated and the spouse receiving alimony will achieve a point of rehabilitation to allow him to become financially independent.

Vocational experts can assist in the evaluation and placement of training and/or employment in the job market.

> **Real Life Experience:** *Isabelle T.*
> Age 55, Divorced, Three Adult Children
> Carson City, Nevada
>
> "Matt will do whatever he can to hide his money from my lawyer."

Voodoo Tip 7.5

WATCH FOR HIDDEN ASSETS OR INCOME

There are many ways that spouses attempt to hide assets and income. An attorney can propound discovery pleadings that seek to find what is hidden. Refer to Number 17 for examples of these pleadings (see Appendix: Voodoo Spice Numbers 31 and 32).

> **Real Life Experience:** *Abe J.*
> Age 36, Divorced, No Children
> Paralegal; New Orleans, Louisiana
>
> "I put my ex through medical school. She started sleeping with a resident doctor. Now she is making loads of money."

Voodoo Tip 7.6

SEEK REIMBURSEMENT FOR OTHER SPOUSE'S EDUCATION, TRAINING, AND/OR INCREASED EARNINGS CAPACITY

Many states allow a financial award, generally considered separate and apart from an award of alimony or of a property division, that permits a spouse to receive money for her contribution to the other spouse's education, training, and/or increased earnings capacity that was not realized and benefited from during the marriage. See your attorney for more details. This award is found in cases such as where a spouse has put the other through medical or law school and was divorced soon after the degree was earned.

> **Real Life Experience:** *Karina R.*
> Age 48, Divorced Twice, One Child
> Office Manager; Raleigh, North Carolina
>
> "I received a settlement offer from my ex's attorney that was composed of a combination of child support payments and a lump sum payment for an alimony and property settlement."

Voodoo Tip 7.7

KNOW THE TAX CONSEQUENCES AND REQUIREMENTS OF ALIMONY

Alimony creates a tax deduction for the payer in the year paid and is taxable as income to the recipient in the year received. The Internal Revenue Service considers alimony completely different from its treatment of child support. The payment of child support is neither deductible nor treated as income to either the payer or the recipient. For an extensive discussion of the tax consequences and requirements of alimony refer to the Tax Chapter of this book.

> **Real Life Experience:** Courtney K.
> Age 39, Married, Three Children
> Advertising Representative
> Montgomery, Alabama
>
> *"I found out that he slept with several women and I kicked him out. Now he says that he's sorry and wants to come back home."*

Voodoo Tip 7.7

BE WARY OF RECONCILIATION

As previously noted, reconciliation may defeat prior grounds of fault. Be wary of your spouse's attempts to reconcile for the sole purpose of eliminating a crucial consideration used in the determination of permanent alimony.

> **Real Life Experience:** *Gordon W.*
> Age 52, Divorced, One Child
> Meteorologist; Long Beach, California
>
> *"My ex-wife is engaged to be married. She has been living with her fiancé. When can I stop paying her alimony?"*

WHEN DOES "PERMANENT" ALIMONY/SPOUSAL SUPPORT END?

In most states, "permanent" alimony usually ends when one or more of the following events occurs:

- Death of either party
- Remarriage of the recipient of alimony
- Recipient of alimony lives (cohabits) with an adult of the opposite sex
- By expiration of the terms of the payment schedule

Summary of Voodoo Tips from Number 7

ALIMONY

Voodoo Tip 7.1	Don't be embarrassed to ask for alimony.
Voodoo Tip 7.2	COBRA
Voodoo Tip 7.3	Watch out for "Alimony Blackmail."
Voodoo Tip 7.4	Get or encourage educational and vocational rehabilitation.
Voodoo Tip 7.5	Watch for hidden assets or income.
Voodoo Tip 7.6	Seek reimbursement for other spouse's education, training, and/or increased earnings capacity.
Voodoo Tip 7.7	Know the tax consequences and requirements of alimony.
Voodoo Tip 7.8	Be wary of reconciliation.

VOODOO SPELL TO GET ALIMONY

Fasten a dollar bill around a green candle. Light the green candle. Place the following ingredients in your gris-gris bag: Alfalfa, Almond, Ash Tree Leaves, Basil, Buckwheat, Calendula, Cascara Sagrada, Catnip, Gravel Root, Lucky Hand Root, Marigold, Mint, Pine, and Trillium. Place a magnet in the gris-gris bag. Place your blank checking account deposit slip in a spider's web. Take the dollar bill that had been wrapped around the lit green candle and attach a feather to it.

VOODOO SPELL TO NOT PAY ALIMONY

Fasten a dollar bill around a green candle. Light the green candle. Place the following ingredients in your gris-gris bag: Alfalfa, Almond, Ash Tree Leaves, Basil, Buckwheat, Calendula, Cascara Sagrada, Catnip, Gravel Root, Lucky Hand Root, Marigold, Mint, Pine, and Trillium. Place a weight for a fishing line in the gris-gris bag. Place your blank check under an alligator foot. Take the dollar bill that had been wrapped around the lit green candle and keep it in your wallet throughout the litigation.

VOODOO INGREDIENT NUMBER 8

Paternity/Maternity

A prerequisite to the establishment of child custody or support is the determination of paternity and maternity. In most cases, the matter is not disputed and both parents have their names on the child's birth certificate. However, in a growing number of cases, the paternity of the child is in dispute. The majority of the time, the biological mother is trying to prove that a certain man is the biological father of a child. In other instances, the presumed father is in doubt of his paternity because of reservations about the mother's fidelity. Regardless of the reason, the matter may come into dispute. When it does, the courts have created a body of law and testing procedures to deal with these concerns.

THE LAWS OF PRESUMPTION

Most states have enacted laws that provide that if a couple is married during the conception or birth of a child, then the couple is "presumed" to be the biological parents of the child. Since the chief goal of these laws is to establish paternity, many state laws address this issue in terms of the "husband" being the "father" of the child. In these states, the laws provide a "rebuttable presumption" in which the parent can go to court, within a limited time period, and attempt to prove that he is not the parent of the child.

Other states have a more narrow stance on paternity/maternity. These state laws provide that if a couple is married during the conception or birth of a child, then it is "conclusive" that the couple are the parents of the child.

Whether "rebuttable presumptions" or "conclusive presumptions" exist, the states have taken the parental policy of making it difficult to make a child illegitimate.

If a couple is not married, no presumptions are applicable. A mother may be able to prove paternity by the following evidence:

- The man's name listed as the father on the child's birth certificate
- The alleged father's signature on a notarized act of acknowledgment
- Testimony that the alleged father has claimed himself to the community as the child's father; blood tests/DNA tests and other evidence of parenthood

TIME LIMITS TO DISAVOW OR ESTABLISH PATERNITY

States have established narrow time limits (usually less than one year from birth) for a father to attempt to legally disavow a child. Again, the policy is intended to prevent the child from becoming legally illegitimate, regardless as to whether the husband is the father. On the other hand, states have established much broader time frames to allow the establishment of paternity. The Appendix (Voodoo Spice Number 18) provides the time limits of each state for a parent to establish paternity.

In many states, after a child reaches the "age of majority," he has another one to five years to seek the establishment of paternity.

> **Real Life Experience:**   *John B.*
> Age 25, Married, One Alleged Child
> Waiter; Des Moines, Iowa
>
> *"My wife and I just had a baby. He's beautiful; however, I have heard rumors that Cody is not my child. I have several friends who believe that Holly is fooling around."*

Voodoo Tip 8.1

TIME IS OF THE ESSENCE WHEN ESTABLISHING OR DISAVOWING PATERNITY

Whether you wish to establish or disavow paternity, the time allowed to bring the matter before a court is passing (it may have already passed). Immediately seek your attorney's assistance if paternity or maternity is at issue.

Voodoo Tip 8.2
GENETIC TESTING IS THE MOTHER OF ALL PROOFS

Science has advanced to a point where most of the guess work is taken out of a paternity dispute. Genetic DNA testing has become the norm for disputed paternity cases. Each state has established a "threshold" (percentage requirement) for genetic test results in which a rebuttable or conclusive presumption of paternity is created if the probability of paternity is equal to or greater than a threshold percentage (i.e., alleged father's probability of being the child's biological father is a 99% likelihood according to DNA test results). The threshold percentage for each state is provided in the Appendix (see Voodoo Spice Number 19).

DNA testing can be accomplished as early as nine to ten weeks of pregnancy. Tests can be taken of the fetus through chronic villis sampling (CVS). Although rarely used, this technique is available and may be valuable in assisting your attorney in seeking the establishment of paternity at the earliest time allowed by state law.

Summary of Voodoo Tips from Number 8
PATERNITY/MATERNITY

Voodoo Tip 8.1   Time is of the essence when establishing or disavowing paternity.

Voodoo Tip 8.2   Genetic testing is the mother of all proofs.

**VOODOO SPELL
TO ESTABLISH PATERNITY**

Light a green and pink candle. Items to be placed in your gris-gris bag include the following: Adam and Eve Root, Basil, Caraway Seed, Corn Flower, Couch Grass, Damiana, Heartsease, Goat's Leaves, Jasmine, Mistletoe, Musk, Pistachio, Primrose, Rose Petals, Rye, Skullcap, and Venus Flytrap.

Pin your child's name on the groin of your voodoo doll. Place a strand of the other parent's pubic hair under your pillow.

VOODOO INGREDIENT NUMBER 9

Custody and Visitation

> **Real Life Experience:** *Myra I.*
> Age 31, Married, Three Children
> Computer Consultant
> Salt Lake City, Utah
>
> *"What's the best way to get custody of my children?"*

Voodoo Tip 9.1

BE A GOOD PARENT!

Quick Facts:

There are 11.5 million single, never married custodial parents in America that have children under 21 whose other parent does not live in the same home. The 11.5 million American divorced custodial parents are comprised of 9.9 million women and 1.6 million men (U.S. Census Bureau).

According to national statistics, for each divorce decree granted, an average of one minor child (under the age of 18) is involved (0.9 per divorce decree in 1990). Thus, under the current divorce rate, more than one million additional children are directly affected by a divorce each year (1,075,000 in 1990).

Throughout America, mothers are awarded sole custody of their children 71 percent of the time. Joint custody awards occur 15.5 percent of the time. Fathers receive the sole custody award 8.5 percent of the time. And friends and other relatives receive custody in 5 percent of all custody decrees.[1]

---

1. Source: *Monthly Vital Statistics Report*, Vol. 43, No. 9, Supplement, March 22, 1995, Centers for disease Control and Prevention, National Center for Health Statistics.

WHAT IS CUSTODY?

Custody can be defined in terms of physical possession or in terms of legal responsibilities. Custody may be temporary or permanent.

Temporary / Permanent

Temporary custody (also referred to as "Provisional Custody") generally means that the person possessing temporary/provisional custody has legal possession and control of a child until a court rules otherwise or until an event occurs that would trigger a change or termination in custody (i.e., the child reaching the age of majority, the child being emancipated, etc.). The child will live with a particular parent while the court proceedings are under way. Getting temporary custody has great advantages that are discussed in this chapter.

Permanent custody means, as the name suggests, a continued possession and control of a child after the custody matter has been resolved in court or agreed upon by the parties.

Joint / Shared / Sole

Legal and physical custody may be either joint, shared, or sole. Joint or shared (also referred to as "Split" custody) is generally highly preferred with courts throughout the nation. When both parents seek custody of a child, courts rarely award one parent sole custody because of the harsh deprivation of parental rights to the "loser." Sole custody is more readily seen in cases where one parent is found to be neglectful, abusive, or mentally/physically incapable of taking care of a child.

When parents have joint and/or shared custody, both parents have rights on crucial decisions such as the child's moral and spiritual upbringing, choices of schools, and choices regarding medical care. When one parent has sole custody, these vital decisions are left to that parent.

The heart and soul of "legal custody" is in the ability of a parent to make these crucial decisions regarding the child, including the day to day decisions of child rearing.

The ultimate criteria used in determining which parent gets primary custody of a child is the court's evaluation of what is in the "best interest" of the minor child. In general terms, the "best interest" test inquires into the safety, health, happiness, and well-being of the child.

Quick Fact: Of the 19 states that reported to the National Center for Health Statistics, the mother received custody 71% of the cases, with the father getting custody 8.5% of the time. Shared custody was awarded in only 16% of these cases.

A child's relationship with both parents is very important to the child's future. Children who do not have an active relationship with a parent are more likely to commit crimes, do poorly in school, drop out of school, and have greater psychological health concerns.

Real Life Experience: *Sabrina D.*

Age 38, Married, Four Children
Unemployed; Madison, Wisconsin

"I took the kids to their grandparents' house. I met with my lawyer yesterday and I've asked him to do whatever he can to insure that my husband does not get custody of the kids."

Voodoo Tip 9.2

GET TEMPORARY CUSTODY

As previously stated in the "Get Possessed!" section of this book, your immediate and continued physical possession and custody of your children will significantly increase your chances of getting permanent custody. If at all possible, do the following:

1. Keep the kids!
2. Stay in your house with your children.
3. Get a court order of temporary custody, pending the custody trial.

This is often a race to the courthouse so—Do it now!

Real Life Experience: *Carl M.*

Age 34, Married, Two Children
Retail Sales Associate; Wilmington, Delaware

"The judge gave my wife temporary custody of my girls. My lawyer told me it will be three months before we go to court for the custody trial."

Voodoo Tip 9.3

IF YOU POSSESS THE CHILDREN—CONTINUE THE TRIAL; IF YOU DON'T—PRESS FOR A QUICK TRIAL DATE

If you have an order of temporary custody of your children, it is to your advantage to prolong the date of the custody trial which determines the permanent custody arrangements. Judges do not like to disturb the status quo of the children's existence. The continuity of the children's living environment is an important factor in the ultimate custody determination. Remember that when the children are accustomed to the neighborhood of friends, certain schools, and churches, a judge will be hesitant to usurp then from the familiar living arrangements. Hence, ask your attorney to file for a continuance of the custody trial date.

If you are on the other side of the temporary custody fence, where you do not have the physical custody of the children, ask your attorney to expedite a trial date. Have the attorney emphasize to the judge that any undue delays in trying the custody issues shall be unfairly prejudicial to your case.

The bottom line is that temporary custody often leads to permanent custody!

> **Real Life Experience:** *Allen A.*
> Age 34, Married, One Child
> Lobbyist; Washington, D.C.
>
> *"I will never let my wife take my boy from me. I want custody. I travel a lot, but I know that I can handle it."*

Voodoo Tip 9.4

SINCERELY ACT IN THE "BEST INTEREST" OF YOUR CHILDREN

If you are truly a good parent, you are going to want what is best for your children. The "Best Interest" test is the pivotal legal standard used in custody disputes. The court will inquire into the quality of your relationship with your children, as well as the emotional, spiritual, educational, and health needs of each child. The court also will weigh the positive and negative attributes of each parent.

The most impressive characteristic of a parent that transcends all other aspects of custody determinations is whether a parent is sincerely acting in the best interest of his or her child.

> **Real Life Experience:** *Valerie D.*
>
> Age 24, Married, One Child
> Secretary; Newcastle, Wyoming
>
> "I take care of my girl, Elizabeth. My husband saw her in the morning and before her bed time. Shouldn't I get custody?"

Voodoo Tip 9.5

FACTORS USED IN DETERMINING CUSTODY AND VISITATION

States have adopted general guidelines to aid the courts in determining what custody and visitation arrangements are in the "best interest of the children." Your state will have guidelines extremely similar to those found as follows:

1. The love, affection, and other emotional ties between each party and the child
2. The capacity and disposition of each party to give the child love, affection, and spiritual guidance and to continue the education and rearing of the child
3. The capacity and disposition of each party to provide the child with food, clothing, medical care, and other material needs
4. The length of time the child has lived in a stable environment, and the desirability of maintaining continuity of that environment
5. The permanence, as a family unit, of the existing or proposed custodial home or home.
6. The moral fitness of each party, insofar as it affects the welfare of the child
7. The mental and physical health of each party
8. The home, school, and community history of the child
9. The reasonable preference of the child, if the court deems the child to be of sufficient age to express a preference
10. The willingness and ability of each party to facilitate and encourage a close and continuing relationship between the child and the other party
11. The distance between the respective residences of the parties
12. The responsibility for the care and rearing of the child previously exercised by each party

Louisiana Civil Code Article 134. (All states have similar provisions.)

Other often unspoken variables that influence a judge's custody decision include the following:

1. The gender of the child and parent (maternal/paternal preferences)
2. The age of the child and parent
3. The sexual preference of the parent
4. The "significant others" of a parent (i.e., new spouse, boyfriend, girlfriend, other relatives, etc.)
5. The criminal and/or driving record of a parent
6. The race of the child and parent
7. The religious orientation of a parent
8. The temporary custody arrangements currently in effect
9. Keeping children together
10. The work schedules of the parents
11. The financial resources of a parent
12. Alcohol or drug abuse of a parent
13. History of neglect or abuse and
14. Which parent lives in the state, county (parish), and city ("Home Cooking!").

> **Real Life Experience:** *Yvonne H.*
> Age 36, Married, One Child
> Teacher; Anchorage, Alaska
>
> *"My twelve year old boy wants to live with me. Will this make the difference?"*

Voodoo Tip 9.6

YOUR CHILD'S PREFERENCE

One of the most commonly asked questions that lawyers receive in custody disputes is whether their child's preference shall be considered by the judge. There is no set age for a minor child to testify; however, if your child is mature, a judge might allow him to testify in open court or in the judge's chambers.

The judge may consider your child's maturity, intelligence, willingness to testify, his emotional stability, and the child's susceptibility to be bribed or unduly persuaded ("brainwashed").

Children may testify against the "better" parent because of the lack of discipline and rules of the other parent, the bribes of the other parent, the other parent's lies told about you. Children often change their minds on a regular basis. It is not surprising to see that a child tells each parent, in private, that he or she wishes to reside with that parent.

Having the child testify can be very stressful on the child and may lead to psychological problems such a guilt regarding having to choose one parent over the other. You should first ask yourself whether your child should provide any testimony.

As a rule of thumb, most children thirteen (13) or older, will be allowed to testify as to their preferences and any other material facts that he or she has observed. Often a child's preference is revealed to the judge through the report of an evaluator. The child talks to the evaluator and this information is often related to the judge and is often a significant factor in the evaluator's custody recommendation to the court. Usually, children under thirteen (13) years old can tell their preference to the evaluator.

Please be very cautious about bringing your children to court. The event can be very traumatic.

Quick Facts:

Custodial mothers are more likely than custodial fathers to have never been married. Custodial fathers are more likely to be currently married than their female counterparts; and both parents are equally likely to have been divorced or separated.

Generally, fathers with custody are older than mothers with custody. Approximately 46% of custodial fathers are over forty years old. Only 11% of custodial fathers are 30 years old or younger.

Custodial fathers have more education than the average custodial mother. Men with custody are twice as likely to have a college degree (National Center for Health Statistics).

Children who have fathers that are actively involved in their school lives receive improved grades and are less likely to fail a grade and/or be expelled.[2]

The judge will consider your involvement in the child's life. Do you know all of the following information. If not, get to know these individuals and become very involved in your child's life.

For each child, who is the following person after you in your child's life? What is your relationship with this person? How can you develop a better relationship with that person? Will he or she be a good witness for your custody case?

---

2. U.S. Department of Education, and *Child Support Bulletin*, December, 1997, The Children's Foundation.

What are the names, addresses, and telephone numbers of the following persons:

1. Teachers
2. Day-care providers/baby-sitters/nanny
3. Coaches
4. Doctors
5. Dentist
6. Priest/pastor/rabbi/spiritual leader
7. Neighbors
8. Child's best friends
9. Boy scout/cub scout/girl scout/brownie leaders
10. School principal
11. PTA members
12. Sunday school teachers
13. Guidance counselor
14. Relatives actively involved in child's life
15. Other persons actively involved in child's life
16. Police officers summoned to any domestic dispute
17. Housekeeper
18. Psychiatrist/sociologist/social worker
19. School nurse
20. Instructors of extracurricular activities

Voodoo Tip 9.7

FILL OUT A CUSTODY/VISITATION RESOURCE VOODOO WORKSHEET FOR EACH CHILD

The worksheet is found in the Appendix.

> **Real Life Experience:** *Tiffany R.*
>
> Age 23, Married, One Child
> Health Club Receptionist; Augusta, Maine
>
> *"I want my girl's father to have an active role in her life; however, I have been the parent who has been there on a day-to-day basis—morning, noon, and night. We both work, but I end up taking care of Karen each morning and night."*

Voodoo Tip 9.8

FIND OUT WHO IS THE PRIMARY CARETAKER OF YOUR CHILD

An excellent way to assist your attorney and the judge is to establish which parent is actively involved in the day-to-day activities of your child's life. Ask yourself and tell your attorney—who does (or doesn't do) the following tasks:

1. Who wakes up your child?
2. Who bathes your child?
3. Who grooms your child?
4. Who dresses your child?
5. Who buys the groceries for your child?
6. Who prepares the meals/cooks for your child?
7. Who buys your child's clothing?
8. Who buys your child's books and uniforms?
9. Who takes your child to and from school and/or daycare?
10. Who prepares the school lunches for your child?
11. Who takes your child to and from extracurricular activities?
12. Who coaches or attends the extracurricular activities of your child?
13. Who participates in the boy scout or girl scout activities of your child?
14. Who attends the PTA meetings?
15. Who takes your child to the doctor?
16. Who takes your child to the dentist or orthodontist?
17. Who keeps the medical records?
18. Who stays home from work in order to take care of your sick child?
19. Who takes your child to church or synagogue?
20. Who takes your child to Sunday school?
21. Who assists your child with his or her homework?
22. Who attends parent-teacher conferences?

23. Who monitors what your child watches on television or at the movies?
24. Who changes the diapers?
25. Who toilet trains your child?
26. Who disciplines your child?
27. Who knows your child's friends?
28. Who speaks to your child's guidance counselor?
29. Who cleans your child's house or bedroom?
30. Who cleans your child's clothes?
31. Who tucks your child into bed at night?
32. Who reads your child bedtime stories?
33. Who keeps the house safe for your child?
34. Who takes your child to birthday parties?
35. Who takes the child "trick or treating"?
36. Who regularly communicates with your child?
37. Who has custody of any other siblings?
38. What else do you do for your child?

> **Real Life Experience:** Lee N.
>
> Age 32, Married, Two Children
> Postal Worker; Oklahoma City, Oklahoma
>
> *"How do I show that I spend more time and effort with my kids?"*

Voodoo Tip 9.9

KEEP RECEIPTS AND DOCUMENTS REGARDING ALL OF THE ABOVE ACTIVITIES

While loving and helping your child, you will inevitably incur expenses, receive receipts, receive documents, and take photographs. These documents and things can assist you in proving your active participation in your child's life.

> **Real Life Experience:** Jack F.
> Age 46, Second Divorce, Three Children
> Corporate Attorney; New Haven, Connecticut
>
> *"I did not have the chance to have a good relationship with my son from my first marriage. I've tried much harder with my second marriage. I want to make sure that I stay active in their lives. I love the children very much."*

Voodoo Tip 9.10

SOUL SEARCH AND DO A PERSONAL INVENTORY OF WHY YOU WANT CUSTODY

By answering the above questions you will be able to come to grips with your actual involvement in your child's life. If you score yourself high on your personal involvement with your child, then you should move to the next inquiry as to why you want the primary physical custody of your child.

If you scored yourself low or less involved in the day-to-day activities of your child's life, be honest with yourself and evaluate what is in the best interest of your child.

Regardless of how you scored yourself or your spouse as a parent, please re-visit your shortcomings and evaluate how you can become more involved as a parent. This constructive criticism and the acting upon it should compel you to be a better parent and significantly improve your chances of becoming the primary custodial parent of your child.

> **Real Life Experience:** *Don S.*
> Age 38, Married, One Child
> Psychiatrist; Cincinnati, Ohio
>
> *"Admittedly, I haven't been as involved in my girl's life as I should be. What can I do to increase my chances of getting custody?"*

Voodoo Tip 9.11

BECOME INVOLVED IN YOUR CHILD'S LIFE, KNOW THE PEOPLE IN YOUR CHILD'S LIFE, AND CREATE MORE FAVORABLE WITNESSES

> **Real Life Experience:** *Maria K.*
> Age 36, Married, Two Children
> Insurance Agent; Pierre, South Dakota
>
> *"I have been smoking marijuana since I was in high school. I never smoke in front of the girls. Jose use to smoke, but, now he drinks a lot, mainly on weekends."*

Voodoo Tip 9.12

CORRECT YOUR BAD HABITS

We all have bad habits. Realize and work on them.

Voodoo Tip 9.13

GO TO CO-PARENTING CLASSES

A child is often the victim and pawn in a couple's emotionally charged turmoil. Co-parenting courses are designed to bring parents back to the core of their responsibility to love, communicate, and take care of their child. Another goal of co-parenting classes is to emphasize the importance that although a couple no longer will be husband and wife, they will remain parents of that child. Creating a level of harmony is important for the sake of the child. Go to a co-parenting course. Every parent can be enriched by the experience.

> **Real Life Experience:** *Patricia R.*
> Age 32, Married, Two Children
> Artist; Newport, Rhode Island
>
> *"I have finally come to the realization that a divorce is inevitable. I have scheduled an appointment with a lawyer this Monday. The kids sense that something is going on."*

Voodoo Tip 9.14

KNOW WHEN AND WHAT TO TELL YOUR CHILDREN

It is a difficult thing to tell your children that you are divorcing. No matter how hard it is to do, it must be done. Once the decision has been made to divorce, the children should be told. If possible, both parents should talk with the children together. The meeting with the children-should be an honest discussion of your separation. Emphasize that the break up is not their fault and that the decision to divorce is made and that they cannot change it. Do not degrade or cast blame or fault on the other parent. Frequently reassure the children that both of you are still their parents and that they are loved and will not be abandoned. Tell them that you will take care of them and keep them safe.

After you have comforted and reassured your children, inform them, as well as you can, of the proposed living arrangements, such as where each parent and child shall reside.

If one parent is absent and/or not willing to cooperate in a joint meeting with the children, speak to your children with the same honest love and affection. Continually remember to "divorce yourself from your emotions" and not degrade or blame the other parent in the presence of the children.

Anticipate that regardless of how well your discussions with your children have gone, they will likely experience some feelings of abandonment, fear, guilt, and despair. It is natural. Perhaps the best advice is to continue to communicate with your children. Tell and show them that they are loved. To some degree, they too are going through stress of the divorce process, as well.

> **Real Life Experience:** *Eli E.*
> Age 39, New York, New York
>
> *"What's the point of even fighting for my kids? The judge is going to give them to my wife anyway. Women have the edge from the very beginning. It's just a waste of money to fight it."*

Voodoo Tip 9.15

DO NOT UNDERESTIMATE THE MATERNAL PREFERENCE

In the seventies, gender based presumptions in the law were declared unconstitutional by the United States Supreme Court. *Orr v. Orr*, 440 U.S. 268 (U.S. Supreme Court, 1979). Prior to this decision, "the tender years doctrine," which provided that the mother should have custody of infants and toddlers in their "tender years," was routinely cited as the basis of custody decisions. Mothers had to be found "unfit" to lose custody of their very young children.

Judges throughout the nation are slowly coming into the twenty-first century. Unfortunately, gender bias still exits. For generations, young children, regardless of their age, were thought to be best served by being with their mother. Various psychological and sociological studies have varied results on what is in the "best interest" of children based on their gender and age. Many courts provide preferences towards fathers for male children in their teens. As the maternal/paternal debate races on, children are being placed with a certain parent, with significant consideration given to the gender of the parent. The best way to overcome gender bias hurdles is to show the court your overwhelming involvement in your child's life.

> **Real Life Experience:** *Deborah H.*
> Age 40, Married, Two Children
> Retail Sales Manager; Kenner, Louisiana
>
> *"I don't think that my husband and I can work out most of our differences regarding custody and visitation. He also won't pay for the boys to go to private school."*

Voodoo Tip 9.16

MEDIATION

Many courts require medication in a custody dispute. Please refer to Number 18 on Mediation for further discussion.

Voodoo Tip 9.17

CUSTODY/VISITATION EVALUATIONS—GET EXPERTS AND USE TESTS

Make sure that the evaluator interviews the children, the parents and any other person that can shed light on your attributes as a parent, your spouses' deficits as a parent, or your child's needs. The failure to request that the evaluator interview third parties is often a tragic flaw that can effect the evaluator's custody recommendation. Use your list of favorable witnesses that you outlined in your Custody/Visitation Worksheet found in the Appendix(Voodoo Spice Number 13).

Voodoo Tip 9.18

**PREPARE FOR A POTENTIAL VISIT FROM
THE DEPARTMENT OF SOCIAL SERVICES**

In many custody disputes where a private sector evaluator is not used, the Department of Social Services, also referred in many states as "Family Services," provide a social worker that conducts interviews of the parents, the children, and other relevant parties. The social worker also may visit your house to inspect your living environment. Make sure that your house is clean and tidy. Traces that you are a member of the local cult or paramilitary group should be removed.

Real Life Experience: *Owen E.*
Age 37, Married, One Child
Physician; Eugene, Oregon

"Since she filed for the divorce, she has had custody of the children. She took all the money out of my accounts and has hired a bulldog lawyer. The lawyer is the best known divorce lawyer in town. I bet he's been dealing with these evaluators for years."

Voodoo Tip 9.19

WATCH OUT FOR UNDUE INFLUENCES ON THE EVALUATION PROCESS

Some attorneys and/or parents attempt to unfairly influence the evaluation process by attempting to select or recommend an evaluator who may be prone to side with a particular gender or a particular attorney. Ask your attorney to inquire into the past personal and professional relationships between the opposing attorney and the evaluator.

Another grave concern in the evaluation process is the tendency of many parents to lie about the other parent in an attempt to gain favor with the evaluator. If you believe that your spouse might stoop to such despicable tactics, anticipate any potential lies and provide the evaluator with evidence, including other witnesses, that would impeach your spouse's false statements. If your spouse is caught in a lie, you can gain significant advantage over the liar.

Voodoo Tip 9.20

FIND OUT THE TRACK RECORD OF THE EVALUATOR

If you reasonably believe that the evaluator is unfairly biased towards the other side, ask your lawyer to request that the evaluator send copies of all correspondences to or from any attorney or party in your case.

> **Real Life Experience:** *Roger S.*
> Age 40, Married, Two Children
> Pilot; Pensacola, Florida
>
> *"The court appointed evaluator is absurd. She hasn't listened to anything that I have to say. All she wants to do is agree with my wife. I totally disagree with her one-sided recommendation about the custody schedule."*

Voodoo Tip 9.21

GET AN INDEPENDENT EXPERT/EVALUATOR

If you reasonably believe that the evaluator's bias is overwhelming, ask your attorney to seek appointment of another evaluator. If the court refuses to change the court appointed evaluator, your attorney can request that an additional independent evaluation be conducted by your own privately retained expert. This may be very expensive; however, in a hotly contested custody battle, your own expert evaluator could make all the difference.

Voodoo Tip 9.22

**IF THE ODDS ARE STACKED AGAINST YOU,
ASK THAT VARIOUS TESTS BE CONDUCTED**

Many psychological tools are now available to custody evaluators. These tests are used to evaluate whether a parent has any significant psychological disorders or personality flaws that would substantially interfere with parenting.

The MMPIT (Minnesota Multiphase Personality Inventory Test) is widely used to diagnose objectively various personality traits and abnormalities of parents and children that assist an evaluator in a custody evaluation. Without going into the details of each test, it is important to know that most psychological tests involve the evaluator's administration of the test and his or her subjective scoring and interpretation.

Tests on the children also can be used to see whether the child has any emotional, behavioral, or learning disorders that need to be addressed. Psychiatrists, sociologists and social workers conduct various tests that are used to evaluate behavior patterns and characteristics of children.

> **Real Life Experience:** Sarah H.
>
> Age 30, Married, One Child
> Physical Therapist; Buffalo, New York
>
> *"Stephen's grades have been great. I'm very proud of him. His homeroom teacher is very fond of him."*

Voodoo Tip 9.23

USE THE CHILD'S SCHOOL GRADES TO YOUR ADVANTAGE

Be sure to get a copy of your child's grades and attendance record. A good grade point average and high attendance are persuasive exhibits for the parent that had the physical custody of the child during the relevant period of school. Likewise, records of poor grades and/or low school attendance may be valuable exhibits if you did not possess the child during these poor academic endeavors. Hence, school records can be used as a sword or a shield. See how these records may affect you.

> **Real Life Experience:** Isaac J.
> Age 45, Divorced, Two Children
> Bank Manager; Fresno, California
>
> *"The school refuses to send me my kids' grades and notices about school activities."*

Voodoo Tip 9.24

BOTH PARENTS ARE ENTITLED TO SCHOOL RECORDS

Pursuant to the U.S. Family Educational Rights and Privacy Act, either parent, whether custodial or noncustodial, is entitled to full access of his child's school records. Upon request, noncustodial parents are allowed to receive written documents normally sent to the custodial parent such as grades/report cards and notices of parent-teacher conferences.

Additionally, insist on notification if any health or medical conditions arise concerning your children.

> **Real Life Experience:** *Vince V.*
> Age 43, Divorced, One Child
> Trucker; Kansas City, Missouri
>
> *"Alexis has been with my ex-wife since we divorced. She enrolled her in a private high school. I simply can't afford it."*

Voodoo Tip 9.25

HAVE PROVISION IN COURT ORDER/CUSTODY PLAN THAT YOUR CHILD SHALL NOT BE PLACED IN ANY SCHOOL OR CAMP WITHOUT A COURT ORDER OR WITHOUT YOUR WRITTEN PERMISSION

> **Real Life Experience:** *Susan T.*
> Age 35, Married, One Child
> Retail Sales Associate
> Atlantic City, New Jersey
>
> *"Henry has been an alcoholic for years. I don't want him around Skip when he's drunk."*

Voodoo Tip 9.26

IF THE OTHER PARENT HAS A DRUG OR ALCOHOL PROBLEM, ASK THE COURT TO CONDUCT RANDOM DRUG TESTS AND/OR ORDERS THAT THE ADDICTED PARENT GO TO *ALCOHOLICS ANONYMOUS* OR *NARCOTICS ANONYMOUS*

It is beneficial to all concerned for a parent to seek assistance with their drug or alcohol problems. It is also important that the judge address the problem because of the potentially devastating results that could occur if the substance abuse is left unattended.

Additionally, bringing to the court's attention the legitimate substance abuse problems of the other parent, sgives you a competitive advantage in the custody dispute.

Ask your attorney to seek injunctions prohibiting your spouse from drinking, being intoxicated, and/or using drugs in the presence of the children.

Voodoo Tip 9.27

IN CASES OF SUBSTANCE ABUSE, INSIST ON SUPERVISED VISITATION

When your spouse has a substance abuse problem, the health and welfare of your children are in jeopardy. Your attorney should request the court to restrict the other parent's visitation privileges to supervised visitation, if not to terminate visitation.

The person supervising visitation should be trustworthy and reliable. Courts frequently order supervised visitation and believe that the children are being adequately protected. Too often, the person ordered to supervise the visitation is irresponsible and/or is not even present at the time of the visitation sessions. Insist on a responsible party to conduct the supervision of the visitation.

> **Real Life Experience:** *Kathy E.*
> Age 40, Married, Two Children
> Caterer; San Francisco, California
>
> *"He has threatened to move out of the state and take the children."*

Voodoo Tip 9.28

STOP SPOUSE FROM TAKING CHILDREN OUT OF THE STATE OR COUNTRY

Until a court has issued a ruling regarding temporary or permanent custody of the acknowledged children, either parent is free to take the child out of the state and/or even the country. Hence, you see the importance in rushing to the courthouse and request temporary custody and a temporary restraining order prohibiting the other parent from removing the child from the state and country, as well as from secreting the child in any manner.

When a custody and visitation plan is being created by the judge or the parties, insist that the order reads that neither parent shall be able to remove the child outside of the United States without an order of the court and/or without the written notarized authorization of both parties.

Also use the enclosed VOODOO FORMS (found in the Appendix: Voodoo Spice Number 1) to collect as much information as possible about the other parent. (i.e., his social security number, his state drivers license number, the numbers of all of his credit cards). This information shall be helpful to law enforcement agencies and private investigators in tracking down the other parent if he "kidnaps" your child.

Voodoo Tip 9.29

GET THE PASSPORT

If you have reason to be alarmed that the other parent might attempt to take your child to another country, ask the court to order the other parent to surrender his passport.

Voodoo Tip 9.30

KNOW THE UNIFORM CHILD CUSTODY JURISDICTION ACT

The Uniform Child Custody Jurisdiction Act (UCCJA) has been adopted throughout the country. This legislation establishes jurisdiction across state lines.

Under the act, a state has jurisdiction for a custody dispute if the child lives in the state or has lived in the state for at least six months before one files a pleading regarding custody. Additionally, a state may have jurisdiction for a custody dispute if the child and one or more parents have a "significant connection" with the state.

A powerful tool of the UCCJA is that it allows "Emergency" jurisdiction for child custody if the child is physically present in the state and an emergency order is required to protect the child from abuse or neglect. The "Emergency" provision of the UCCJA can be a valuable shield to help protect a child from harm, yet it also provides an avenue to abuse the system in order to find a more favorable forum for a custody dispute in another state.

> **Real Life Experience:** *Mary W.*
> Age 32, Married, One Child
> High School Coach; Athens, Georgia
>
> *"He has already fired two attorneys. After each hearing, he fires his lawyer."*

Voodoo Tip 9.31

BE CAREFUL IF YOUR SPOUSE'S LAWYER IS FIRED

On occasion a person will fire his lawyer and instruct him to immediately withdraw from the court record, in order to avoid being served pleadings and orders through the attorney. If you have concerns that your spouse may fire his attorney, ask your lawyer to request the sheriff to serve both the attorney and the other parent.

> **Real Life Experience:** *Paul C.*
>
> Age 41, Married, One Child
> Car Salesman; Katy, Texas
>
> *"My wife won't put my boy on the telephone when I call. She also is making it difficult to see him."*

Voodoo Tip 9.32

WHAT TO DO IF SPOUSE DENIES YOU ACCESS TO YOUR CHILDREN

The best action is to anticipate a problem before it arises so that your lawyer can address the possibility with the court. Hopefully, admonitions and restraining orders can be placed to prevent the denial of access to your children. If all else fails, the following are potential actions:

1. File a motion for visitation
2. File a motion to have other parent held in contempt of court if a prior order exists awarding you custody/visitation
3. Seek a reduction or suspension in child support until the other parent obeys the custody/visitation order
4. File a motion to modify the prior custody/visitation order
5. File a motion for sole custody
6. File a motion seeking the other party to post a bond to insure your custody/visitation rights
7. Ask your attorney for other advice and/or
8. Seek assistance from law enforcement officers to enforce a custody/visitation order

Regrettably, sometimes there are reasons to deny access, i.e., for abuse, neglect and/or substance abuse problems that affect the children. Courts, counselors, child protection agencies, battered womens' shelters, and law enforcement agencies are prepared to deal with these problems.

> **Real Life Experience:** *Claude P.*
> Age 24, Married, One Child
> Butcher; Denver, Colorado
>
> *"She says that I can have reasonable visitation."*

Voodoo Tip 9.33

SPECIFY THE VISITATION RIGHTS

When working on a visitation plan for both parents, it is usually a great error to simply allow for "reasonable" or "liberal" visitation. A custody and visitation plan or order that merely contains this language is a plan or order that does not address the real world problems of visitation disputes. If the term "reasonable" is used in the visitation plan, the parent seeking visitation is subject to the whims of the primary custodial parent. What is "reasonable" to one parent may be quite "unreasonable" to the other.

The best way to avoid the nightmares that can exist with a lazy visitation plan, is to insist on specified visitation. A visitation plan that explicitly identifies the dates and times of visitation will not be subject to the whims of one parent or the interpretation of either parent.

> **Real Life Experience:** *Jay C.*
> Age 25, Divorced, One Child
> Cook; Chicago, Illinois
>
> *"I want to see my girl as much as possible."*

Voodoo Tip 9.34

MAXIMIZE YOUR VISITATION RIGHTS

A child has the general right to continue his relationship with both parents. Parents seeking visitation should consider maximizing their specified dates of visitation. Remember to design a visitation plan that will be compatible with your work schedule.

Your imagination may be the limit to what days you may seek. Consider the following:

Any holiday recognized by your local, state or federal government

- Any holiday that the judge takes off
- April Fool's Day
- Arbor Day
- Armed Forces Day
- Ash Wednesday
- Boss' Day
- Christmas
- Christmas Eve
- Columbus Day
- Days during the week
- Days during the weekend
- Days when the teachers have conferences or workshops
- Easter
- Father's Day
- Flag Day
- Fourth of July
- Frank Sinatra's Birthday
- Graduations
- Grandparent's Day
- Halloween
- Hanukkah
- Labor Day
- Mardi Gras
- Martin Luther King's Birthday
- Memorial Day
- Mother's Day
- New Years Day
- New Years Eve
- Palm Sunday
- Passover
- President's Day
- Rosh Hashanah
- School Vacations
- Secretary's Day
- Special sporting events (i.e., Super Bowl, World Series)
- St. Joseph's Day
- St. Patrick's Day
- Summer vacation
- Thanksgiving
- Uncle Bob's Birthday
- Valentine's Day
- Veterans Day
- Washington's Birthday
- Yom Kippur
- Your Birthday
- Your Children's Birthdays
- Your Deceased Great Grandmother's Birthday

(Ask a florist—they have holidays for everything under the sun!)

Real Life Experience: Beverly G.
Age 29, Divorced, Remarried, One Child
Housewife; Reno, Nevada

"We moved from Menlo Park, California when I got remarried. Shouldn't Tim pay for the plane tickets for his summer visitation?"

Voodoo Tip 9.35

FORMALLY AGREE ON COST ARRANGEMENTS INVOLVED WITH VISITATION AND TRAVEL

Often parties agree to visitation schedules without having a formal agreement as to who pays the cost of any travel involved. Have a written agreement and/or order that sets forth the financial responsibilities associated with any travel involved in the visitation process.

> **Real Life Experience:** *Cathy F.*
> Age 34, Divorced, Three Children
> Retail District Sales Manager
> Seattle, Washington
>
> *"I'm a good mom, but I also want to feel like I am a woman again. I would love to be able to date someone who will make me feel special."*

Voodoo Tip 9.36

ALLOWING VISITATION CREATES A FREE BABY-SITTER

Many people that are in a heated contested custody or visitation dispute often forget that allowing visitation allows for a free baby-sitter. The thirst for your spouse's blood often clouds one's view of your future needs and desires. Months down the road, you may want a break from your children to go to the beach or take a vacation with a new lover.

> **Real Life Experience:** *Bob H.*
> Age 33, Divorced, Two Children
> Deputy Sheriff; Gretna, Louisiana
>
> *"I have the kids for almost forty percent of the time, but I pay a lot of child support. It's not fair. What can I do?"*

Voodoo Tip 9.37

GET MORE VISITATION AND PAY LESS CHILD SUPPORT

In most states, child support guidelines and schedules are based on the parent receiving visitation having average visitation rights such as having the children on alternating weekends, alternating major holidays and several weeks during the summer. If you receive visitation rights that are greater than the visitation rights normally given by the court, ask your lawyer to seek for a decrease in your child support obligation as you are incurring expenses in support of your children when they are in your custody that was not envisioned by the child support schedule.

> **Real Life Experience:** *Gretchen S.*
> Age 34, Divorced, Remarried, Three Children
> Housewife; Auburn, California
>
> *"My ex-husband is supposed to have the children every other weekend, but he never comes and gets them."*

Voodoo Tip 9.38

IF YOUR SPOUSE DOES NOT USE HIS VISITATION RIGHTS, ASK FOR MORE CHILD SUPPORT AND/OR PAYMENT FOR BABY-SITTING

Again, if your child support guidelines envision average visitation, and the other parent is not taking the children during his scheduled visitation days, then ask your attorney to seek an increase in child support for the extra days and nights that you have custody of your children. An alternative is to ask the court to order the other parent to pay or reimburse for extra food, utilities, daycare or baby-sitting expenses incurred because he did not pick up the children pursuant to the visitation plan.

Most courts will not compel a parent to exercise his visitation rights; however, a court is much more likely to award you money for the extra expenses incurred because of your unanticipated cost of keeping the children when the other parent should have.

> **Real Life Experience:** *Shelly S.*
> Age 38, Divorced, Two Children
> Nurse; Fort Worth, Texas
>
> *"My eldest daughter defiantly insists that she does not want to see her father. She is extremely bitter."*

Voodoo Tip 9.39

IF YOUR CHILD DOES NOT WANT TO SEE THE OTHER PARENT, INFORM YOUR ATTORNEY AND THE COURT

Frequently, children do not wish to have visitation with the non-custodial parent. When this occurs, immediately inform your attorney. Whether or not your child's hesitancy has any valid basis may ultimately be determined by the judge. By informing your attorney and allowing him to inform the court of the problem, then you have diminished the chances that the court would sanction you for interfering in the other parent's visitation rights. If you do not inform your attorney of the problem, then the other parent might allege that you are persuading your child to resist visitation. Let the court and/or the court's evaluator to get to the heart of the problem.

> **Real Life Experience:** *Joe C.*
> Age 44, Divorced, Two Children
> Accountant; Long Island, New York
>
> "My ex-wife has moved four times since our divorce. She never informs me of her new address and telephone number."

Voodoo Tip 9.40

INSIST ON ADDRESSES AND TELEPHONE NUMBERS AND MAXIMIZE TELEPHONE ACCESS

The parent with the physical custody of the children may attempt to prohibit or restrict your physical or telephone access to your children. Insist that you have the addresses and telephone numbers of each place where the children shall be residing. Additionally, you may wish to have an agreement on the minimum and maximum telephone calls the noncustodial parent can have with the children. A court order delineating the agreement shall assist in eliminating future problems.

If the parents are cooperative, reasonable open access to the children is preferable.

> **Real Life Experience:** *Cindy T.*
> Age 61, Material Grandmother
> Housewife; Hattiesburg, Mississippi
>
> "It pains me to say that my own child is an unfit parent. I cannot abide by her behavior. I want to take care of my grand-baby!"

Voodoo Tip 9.41

GRANDPARENT CUSTODY/VISITATION RIGHTS

Custody is seldom awarded to grandparents when one or more of the parents are alive. Most states will allow grandparents the opportunity to file for custody or visitation. In the evaluation process of the grandparent custody/visitation requests, the courts will turn to the "best interest of the child" standard, as well as look at the general preference to award custody to the parents.

The basic ways that grandparents get legal custody of children are as follows:

1. One or both parents have died
2. One or both parents are incarcerated
3. One or both parents have a substance abuse problem and/or
4. One or both parents have been neglectful and/or abusive

Grandparent visitation can be quite beneficial to a child—if the grandparent does not play mind games with the child in an attempt to "brainwash" the child into taking sides with a particular parent or grandparent.

Courts will review the appropriateness of grandparent custody or visitation on a case by case basis. Most courts do recognize the importance of an extended family and the advantages of positive role models.

Voodoo Tip 9.42

KNOW WHEN TO REQUEST A MODIFICATION IN VISITATION

The custodial parent may wish to request a change in the visitation schedule if the other parent routinely refuses to honor the visitation plan and/or refuses to return the child at the designated time and place.

> **Real Life Experience:** *Faith B.*
>
> Age 37, Married, Two Children
> Unemployed; Anchorage, Alaska
>
> *"He said that he will fight for the children unless I agree to sell the house."*

Voodoo Tip 9.43

WATCH OUT FOR "CUSTODY BLACKMAIL"

As stated in the alimony and child support chapters of this book, be aware of any attempts on the part of your spouse to threaten a custody battle when he or she really does not want physical custody, but merely seeks financial advantage in another area of dispute. These threats of a custody battle are often used in a hidden or blatant agenda for a spouse to make monetary concessions. If this occurs, speak to your attorney about these attempts to intimidate.

Summary of Voodoo Tips from Number 9

CUSTODY AND VISITATION

Voodoo Tip 9.1   Be a good parent!

Voodoo Tip 9.2   Get temporary custody.

Voodoo Tip 9.3   If you possess the children—continue the trial; if you don't—press for a quick trial date.

Voodoo Tip 9.4   Sincerely act in the "best interest" of your children.

Voodoo Tip 9.5   Factors used in determining custody and visitation.

Voodoo Tip 9.6   Your child's preference.

Voodoo Tip 9.7   Fill out a custody/visitation worksheet for each child.

Voodoo Tip 9.8   Find out who is the primary caretaker of your child.

Voodoo Tip 9.9   Keep receipts and documents regarding all of your activities with your child.

Voodoo Tip 9.10   Soul search and do a personal inventory of why you want custody.

Voodoo Tip 9.11   Become involved in your child's life, know the people in your child's life, and create more favorable witnesses.

Voodoo Tip 9.12   Correct your bad habits.

Voodoo Tip 9.13   Go to co-parenting classes.

Voodoo Tip 9.14   Know when and what to tell your children.

Voodoo Tip 9.15   Do not underestimate the maternal preference.

Voodoo Tip 9.16   Mediation.

Voodoo Tip 9.17   Custody/visitation evaluations—get experts and use tests.

Voodoo Tip 9.18   Prepare for a potential visit from the Department of Social Services.

Voodoo Tip 9.19   Watch out for undue influence on the evaluation process.

Voodoo Tip 9.20   Find out the track record of the evaluator.

Voodoo Tip 9.21   Get an independent expert/evaluator.

Voodoo Tip 9.22 If the odds are stacked against you, ask that various tests be conducted.

Voodoo Tip 9.23 Use the child's school grades to your advantage.

Voodoo Tip 9.24 Both parents are entitled to school records.

Voodoo Tip 9.25 Have provision in court order/custody plan that your child shall not be placed in any school or camp without a court order or without your written permission.

Voodoo Tip 9.26 If the other parent has a drug or alcohol problem, ask the court to conduct random drug tests and/or order that the addicted parent attend *Alcoholics Anonymous* or *Narcotics Anonymous*.

Voodoo Tip 9.27 In cases if substance abuse, insist on supervised visitation.

Voodoo Tip 9.28 Stop spouse from taking children out of the state or country.

Voodoo Tip 9.29 Get the passport.

Voodoo Tip 9.30 Know the Uniform Child Custody Jurisdiction Act.

Voodoo Tip 9.31 Be careful if your spouse's lawyer is fired.

Voodoo Tip 9.32 What to do if your spouse denies you access to your children.

Voodoo Tip 9.33 Specify the visitation rights.

Voodoo Tip 9.34 Maximize your visitation rights.

Voodoo Tip 9.35 Formally agree on cost arrangements regarding visitation and travel.

Voodoo Tip 9.36 Allowing visitation creates a free baby-sitter.

Voodoo Tip 9.37 Get more visitation and pay less child support.

Voodoo Tip 9.38 If your spouse does not use his visitation rights, ask for more child support and/or payment for baby-sitting.

Voodoo Tip 9.39 If your child does not want to see the other parent, inform your attorney and the court.

Voodoo Tip 9.40 Insist on addresses and telephone numbers and maximize telephone access.

Voodoo Tip 9.41 Grandparent custody/visitation rights.

Voodoo Tip 9.42 Know when to request a modification on visitation.

Voodoo Tip 9.43 Watch out for "Custody Blackmail."

**VOODOO SPELL
TO GET CUSTODY OR VISITATION**

Light one white and one orange candle. Put Catnip, Jasmine, and Peppermint in your red flannel gris-gris bag. Place copies of your children's birth certificates, or pictures of your children, under your bed.

Take a piece of paper that contains your children's names and pin the paper on the heart of the voodoo doll.

VOODOO INGREDIENT NUMBER 10

Child Support

The purpose of a child support award is to provide financial assistance for a child based on the average monthly expenses associated with that child. The child support award should be based on the proportionate income or earnings capacity of the parents.

Each state has implemented child support guidelines to assist the courts with a means of calculating what is legislatively presumed to be sufficient for the child's needs and which is fair relative to the parents' earnings.

> **Real Life Experience:** *Nikki F.*
> Age 32, Divorced, Two Children
> Paralegal; Brunswick, Maine
>
> *"I'm always fighting to get the child support that we deserve."*

Quick Facts:

Only 6.2 million (approximately half) of the 11.5 million custodial parents have a child support award or agreement. Mothers receive child support awards at a higher rate than fathers. Annually, over 5 million custodial parents live without any award of child support from the other parent. Reasons for not seeking a child support award include that the custodial parent does not want child support and that the other parent can not afford to pay child support. Approximately one-third of the 5 million parents without child support awards decided not to seek child support. 1996 statistics show that a mere sixty-seven (67%)

percent (or $11.9 billion dollars) of the $17.7 billion dollars of child support due to custodial parents is paid. (U.S. Census Bureau).

Only half of custodial parents that have an order or agreement for child support receive payment in full. Unfortunately, approximately 25 percent of all custodial parents receive only partial payment. Worst of all, another 25 percent of custodial parents don't receive any child support at all.

Approximately, 90 percent of fathers who have joint custody pay child support, while 80 percent of fathers who receive visitation pay child support. (The U. S. Census Bureau; American Bar Association).

State prosecutors report that approximately 2 to 5 percent of their child support cases involve mothers who owe past due child support. (American Bar Association).

Before a child support order can be made, paternity/maternity must be established. Paternity/maternity is discussed in a separate chapter.

STANDARD OF LIVING

Quick Facts:

Mothers who receive child support have a lower annual income (Average $18,144 per year) versus their male counterparts receiving child support who have an average income of $33,579 per year. Less than 5 percent of divorced or separated women raising children of the marriage receive alimony. Approximately 42 percent receive child support, and the average amount received by them is approximately $125 per child per month. (U.S. Census Bureau)

A widely cited study discovered that a year after a divorce, the standard of living of women and children drops by an average 73 percent, while men's standard of living actually increases an average of 42 percent. (Lenore Weitzman, "The Economics of Divorce: Social and Economic Consequences of Property, Alimony, and Child Support Awards," UCLA Law Review 28:1181, 1245 (1981).) Approximately one-third of all female headed families with children live in poverty.

CHILD SUPPORT MODELS

There are two basic models for child support:

1. Fixed child support payments that have no provisions for future modifications

2. Escalator Clause/Variable child support payments that periodically change proportionate to actual changes in the parents' income, the consumer price index (CPI), or some other variable

CHILD SUPPORT GUIDELINES

Federal law requires each state to create child support guidelines. (42 U.S.C. 667) Child support guidelines presume that parents with similar incomes should be required to pay relatively equal amounts in child support. Likewise, a further goal of the implementation of child support guidelines is to prevent large variability in the child support awards under similar circumstances. Unfortunately, our national and state systems are seriously flawed as they operate under a false premise that people can accurately calculate child support figures and that parents will not misrepresent their income and/or earnings capacity. A significant danger for you lies in a haphazard implementation of your state's child support guidelines as your child may suffer financially from the miscalculations and/or misrepresentations. The only key to safeguard you and your child from such neglect and abuse is to know the pitfalls and to benefit from the knowledge that you will gain from the following information.

MANIPULATION OF THE NUMBERS:

Lawyers may add "two plus two" and come up with "three."

There are no national or statewide criteria on determining how much a person earns. Nor are there any uniform standards regarding what period of time should be used to examine a parent's income. Many jobs are cyclical such as construction, lawn care, Christmas tree sales, etc.; hence, the more cyclical the business, the more important it is to have an examination of income over a twelve month (or more) period of time.

Voodoo Tip 10.1

CHECK THE CALCULATION OF EACH PARENT'S INCOME

Be leery of anyone who quickly estimates and/or calculates what the other parent makes in an average month. People have wide and diverse payment methods. Many people get paid by the hour, by the week, by the job, every two weeks, get paid overtime, get reimbursed for travel expenses, have expense accounts, etc.

Since child support guidelines provide formulas for calculations based on average actual income and/or earnings capacity, the time period from which the "average" is taken becomes critical.

For example, if parent one ("Darth") earned the following income for the last year and one-half, the time period used to determine his average monthly income and/or earnings capacity could create significantly varied results.

Darth's "Declared" Income:

Last year:	January	$3,000.00
	February	3,000.00
	March	3,000.00
	April	3,000.00
	May	3,000.00
	June	3,000.00
	July	3,000.00
	August	3,000.00
	September	3,000.00
	October	3,000.00
	November	3,000.00
	December	3,000.00
	Bonus (Paid in December)	6,000.00
This year:	January	2,000.00
	February	2,000.00
	March	2,000.00
	April	2,000.00
	May	2,000.00
	June	2,000.00

According to the above example, Darth made $42,000 last year. If your attorney did not discover that Darth made a $6,000.00 bonus, then he may incorrectly believe that Darth's income last year was only $36,000.

Additionally, if your attorney only calculated Darth's average income based on his recent pay stub for the current year, your attorney would assume that Darth made an average of only $2,000.00 per month.

If your attorney calculates Darth's income based on last year's income of $42,000, Darth's average monthly declared income would be $3,500.

If your attorney calculates Darth's income based on the last eighteen months, Darth's average monthly declared income would be $3,000.

As you can see from the above example, lawyers can use the figures that are available (through proper discovery) and come up with entirely different answers to the question of what a parent's monthly income is.

Have a talk with your attorney and ask him how he is calculating the declared income of each parent.

Instruct your attorney to subpoena the other parent's federal tax returns (and W-2 and/or 1099) for the past several years, as well as the payroll records and personnel files from his employer(s).

(Sample Questions: Did your attorney know that Darth would receive a bonus and reimbursement for travel expenses at the end of the year? Did your attorney know that Darth made an arrangement with his boss to defer his earned compensation until after the court resolved the child support issues?)

> **Real Life Experience:** *Ebony C.*
> Age 23, Divorced, One Child
> Secretary; Baltimore, Maryland
>
> *"Jeff gets paid each week. I get paid on the first and fifteenth of each month."*

Voodoo Tip 10.2

THERE ARE 4.3 WEEKS IN EACH MONTH

1. Use the "4.3 Factor" when calculating a parent's income.

Mistakes are continually made in calculating a parent's income by the assumption that there are four weeks in a month. There are not. Each year contains 52 weeks in a twelve-month period. Fifty-two divided by twelve equals 4.3. Hence, if the other parent is claiming to earn $1,000 per week, he may be declaring only $4,000 in income per month. His actual monthly income may be $4,300.

2. Apply the "4.3 Factor" when calculating a child support award.

Similar mistakes can be made in calculating the child support award. An award of $100 per week does not equal $400 per month. There are 52 weeks in a year. If child support is ordered at $100 per week, the recipient of the child support would get $5,200 per year. If child support is ordered at $400 per month, the recipient gets only $4,800 that year.

The above example shows how easy it can be for a party to manipulate the child support calculations using your state's guidelines.

Quick Fact: In 1991, women custodial parents received an average of $3,011 in annual child support payments. Male custodial parents received average annual child support payments of $2,292. (U.S. Census Bureau)

Your state's child support guidelines shall be presumed to be fair; however, most states allow for deviation from the standard guideline formulas based on the special circumstances of a parent or child.

> **Real Life Experience:** *Cheryl T.*
> Age 33, Divorced, One Child
> Restaurant Manager; Galveston, Texas
>
> *"My ex-husband is in cahoots with his boss. He usually gets a salary increase and a bonus at the end of each year."*

Voodoo Tip 10.3

WATCH FOR MANIPULATION OF THE NUMBERS

It is worth repeating in this chapter: In order to effect the numbers used in the calculation of child support and/or alimony, a spouse may attempt to:

1. Change his standard of living
2. Postpone salary increases
3. Delay bonuses
4. Encourage the other spouse to get a job or change jobs
5. Reduce the number of hours worked
6. Reduce overtime hours worked
7. Increase or decrease child care expenses
8. Fail to report actual income earned in tax returns
9. Put assets/income in someone else's name (including new spouse)
10. Become "disabled"
11. Shelter money in corporations, partnerships, or trusts
12. Have personal expenses paid through family business
13. Get reimbursed by employer for personal expenses (i.e., auto expenses, meals, travel) and
14. Make misrepresentations to the court on required financial affidavits

> **Real Life Experience:** Bob F.
> Age 45, Divorced, Two Children
> Electrician; New York, New York
>
> *"Now that she is getting married, she will be living a very comfortable life with her new husband. She clearly will not need as much child support. What can I do to reduce my child support obligation?"*

Voodoo Tip 10.4

LOOKING AT THE INCOME OF YOUR EX'S NEW SPOUSE

States view your Ex's new spouse's income in various ways. Some states prohibit any consideration of this income. Many states allow consideration of the income, but do not provide guidelines to the court on how to consider it. Other states allow the courts to consider the income of the new spouse only to the extent that your Ex has shared living expenses with his new spouse and as such should have more disposable income available for child support.

Generally, the new spouse's income will not be considered until or unless your attorney pushes for it (where allowed) and he has propounded discovery pleadings seeking the information about the new spouse.

> **Real Life Experience:** Terry E.
> Age 31, Married, One Child
> Actor; Los Angeles, California
>
> *"She asked the court to waive her filing fees, but she lied. She did not report all the money that she makes in tips."*

Voodoo Tip 10.5

LOOK AT FINANCIAL AFFIDAVITS AND *IN FORMA PAUPERUS* APPLICATION

Whether called a "financial affidavit," "financial declaration," or an "income and expense declaration," representations made by a party on these pleadings often are the primary basis in the court's determination of a child support award. Misrepresentation on these pleadings is rampant. Gone unchecked and/or without requests for supporting documentation, abuse can and likely will occur.

Additionally, many parties request the courts to waive the filing fees because of their reported inability to pay. These financial affidavits, often called *"In Forma Pauperus"* Applications are sworn representations of the applying party's income and expenses. Once the form is filed it is often forgotten. A sharp opponent will compare the representations made on this initial affidavit with the sworn representations made at the time of the child support hearing. On occasion you will discover grave inconsistencies that will aid in the impeachment of your spouse's credibility.

DEVIATIONS FOR THE CHILD SUPPORT GUIDELINES

The court may allow a deviation for the child support guidelines if the court finds that there are special needs of the child or extraordinary earnings of the parent. Generally, it is purely at the discretion of your judge as to whether he will permit a deviation from the guidelines.

Examples of grounds for deviation from the guidelines that might translate into a greater child support award are as follows:

- The health condition and related medical expenses of a child
- The extraordinary medical expenses relating to the child, not covered by insurance
- The special educational needs and related expenses of the child
- The extraordinary expenses of the child
- The extraordinary length of time that a child spends with the parent receiving child support

Examples of grounds for deviation from the guidelines that might translate into a smaller child support award are as follows:

- The income of a parent far exceeds the financial needs of a child
- The medical limitations and disabilities of a parent
- The wages earned and received by a child
- The extraordinary length of time that a child spends with the parent paying child support

Quick Facts:

The Federal Office of Child Support Enforcement compiled a list of the most common reasons that deviations from the guidelines were allowed. Throughout America, reasons for deviation in child support awards are as follows:
- Agreement between the parents (21%)
- Needs of second households (14%)
- Extended or extraordinary visitation/custody expenses (13%)
- Non-custodial parent's low income (11%)
- An otherwise unjust result
- Extraordinary needs of the parent

Other common excuses heard in courts throughout the country for parents seeking to pay less child support include the following:

- Payer's physical or mental disabilities
- Payer's irregular or cyclical employment
- Custodial parent's interference with visitation rights
- Child support payments not benefiting children
- Payer paid for other items for children
- Not biological children
- Child is working or
- Payer's incarceration

> **Real Life Experience:** *Kim P.*
> Age 38, Married, Three Children
> Housewife; Covington, Louisiana
>
> *"Two of my children go to an orthodontist. All of the kids go to private school."*

Voodoo Tip 10.6

ASK FOR CONTRIBUTIONS FOR "EXTRAS"

In order to insure that each parent is financially responsible for his proportionate share of all child-related expenses, instruct your attorney to seek contributions for the other parent's proportionate share of all insurance deductibles, co-payments, and payments not covered by insurance. These "Extra" expenses can quickly add up. Don't let these dollars slip through the hands that help your child.

- Medical expenses/medical insurance
- Dental expenses/dental insurance
- Extraordinary medical expenses (orthodontic/psychiatrist/ counseling/miscellaneous health-related expenses)
- Day-care expenses
- Tuition/educational expenses
- Extraordinary non-medical related expenses

MEDICAL AND DENTAL EXPENSES/MEDICAL AND DENTAL INSURANCE

Quick Fact: Only about 40% of child support awards include medical insurance benefits as part of that award. Unfortunately, another 31% of those parents who were ordered to provide health insurance for their children failed or refused to provide it. Likewise, of the non-custodial parents who were not ordered to provide health insurance, 18% provided such insurance without an order. (U.S. Census Bureau)

Medical and dental expenses associated with your child should be included in the calculation and implementation of a child support award and related child care obligations. All orthodontic, psychiatric, and related needs of your child should be brought to the attention of your attorney.

If you anticipate certain future expenses for your child that have not yet arisen, ask your attorney to seek provisions in the child support order that compel the other parent to pay for a proportionate share of these expenses as they arise. This shall prevent you from having to pay your attorney to go back into court at a later date to seek this relief.

Real Life Experience: *Cindy C.*
Age 28, Married, One Child
Bank Teller; Chicago, Illinois

"Rick continues to threaten to take me off of his medical insurance policy."

Voodoo Tip 10.7

WATCH OUT FOR CANCELLATION OF INSURANCE POLICIES

Occasionally, upon the filing of a divorce action, a spouse may cancel the health, life and/or homeowner's insurance that covers you, your children, and your property. Ask your lawyer to file an *"Ex Parte"* motion for a temporary restraining order/injunction prohibiting these actions.

If your spouse cancels the insurance, your attorney should ask the court to compel him to re-instate the insurance and pay for any expenses that were incurred that would have been covered by the insurance had you or your child had been covered under the policy. Once again, ask your lawyer to file a motion for a temporary restraining order/injunction prohibiting the use of the policy.

Voodoo Tip 10.8

WHOLE LIFE INSURANCE POLICIES ARE A SOURCE OF QUICK CASH

Whole life insurance policies may have an cash value/equity value that can be taken or borrowed against for quick cash. If you want to prevent your spouse from having access to the liquidation or alienation of this policy, ask for a restraining order.

Warning: The liquidation of the whole life insurance policy can have detrimental financial consequences if an insured party dies or becomes disabled during the applicable term of the policy.

> **Real Life Experience:** *Ann L.*
> Age 27, Married, One Child
> Unemployed; Boston, Massachusetts
>
> *"I'm going to have to go back to work. The school has an excellent after-school program."*

Voodoo Tip 10.9

GET DAY-CARE

Day-care is a common and important expense that significantly can add to a parent's child support obligation. Inquire with your attorney as to whether day-care expenses are included in the basic child support award or whether you should request it as an additional child-related expense.

The actual day-care expense incurred is usually under the discretion of the primary domiciliary parent. That parent usually chooses the day-care facility and resulting costs.

> **Real Life Experience:** *Chip H.*
> Age 41, Married, Two Children
> Stock Broker; Atlanta, Georgia
>
> *"Sandy wants to put the kids in day-care near her work. This is totally unacceptable. I have the girls quite often and I don't want to drive to the other side of the city for the mere convenience of Sandy."*

Voodoo Tip 10.10

ASK THE COURT FOR PARTICIPATION IN THE DECISION REGARDING WHICH DAY-CARE FACILITY IS USED

By assisting in the choice of the day-care facility, you also participate in cost control.

Voodoo Tip 10.11

REPLACE DAY-CARE WITH SELF OR RELATIVES

A parent may be able to significantly decrease the day-care expense by asking relatives to baby-sit. Grandparents and adult siblings often are more than willing to assist with this supervision. Your own physical care of your child can decrease the cost of day-care. Ask for the "right of first refusal" of having the physical possession of the child in events when the child would otherwise be at the day-care center or with a baby-sitter.

A parent may argue that having relatives provide baby-sitting services is inferior to a day-care facility as the day-care center may allow the child to gain socialization skills.

> **Real Life Experience:** *Stephanie B.*
> Age 30, Married, One Child
> Human Resource Manager; Miami, Florida
>
> *"There is a particular day-care center where I would like to place my child."*

Voodoo Tip 10.12

PLACE CHILD IN CHOSEN DAY-CARE FACILITY PRIOR TO COURT DATE

Judges are quite hesitant to remove a child from a day-care facility once the child has commenced attending the center. Many attorneys believe that it is prudent to register and put your child into a day-care facility prior to the child support and/or custody trial date as the parent shall be able to show stability in the child's life and provide evidence of actual day-care expenses. If a parent does not have the child in previously registered and/or attending a day-care facility, then the other parent will have greater chances to impeach the need for day-care, the choice of day-care, and the expense of day-care.

TUITION

Like day-care, school tuition is an expense that can be quite costly. Inquire with your attorney as to your rights associated with school expenses. Your attorney should ask for the other parent's contribution toward tuition, school loan interest payments, uniforms, school books, supplies, and school extracurricular expenses.

Judges generally have the discretion to determine whether a parent should be obligated to pay the additional expense for a child to attend a private or parochial school instead of a public institution. Many judges require a parent to prove that the child has a special need which would require the child to attend the private or parochial school. Yet, judges are reluctant to remove a child who already attends the private or parochial school. The court will look to the "best interest of the child" standard. Continuity of the child's life is very important.

Quick Fact: Thirty four (34%) percent of America's three- and four-year-olds are enrolled in nursery schools. (U.S. Census Bureau)

Real Life Experience: *Seth H.*

Age 44, Married, Three Children
Farmer; Twin Falls, Idaho

"My wife makes more money than I do and she suggests that we split the school and day-care costs."

Voodoo Tip 10.13

WATCH OUT FOR 50-50 SPLIT OF OTHER CHILD RELATED EXPENSES

Lawyers and judges often suggest a 50-50 split of medical insurance, extraordinary medical expenses, day-care expenses, tuition, and the like. Whether such a proposal benefits you depends on what percentage of the two parents' combined gross income belongs to you.

DEPENDENCY TAX CREDIT

All tax consequences shall be discussed in Number 15 of this book.

Voodoo Tip 10.14

**TEMPORARY AWARD OF CHILD SUPPORT
SETS THE TONE FOR REGULAR CHILD SUPPORT**

A temporary award of child support and related child care expenses often later becomes a permanent award. A child support award is rarely reduced from the original temporary award. "Temporary" should not be equated to "not important" or "temporary" at all!

ALIMONY VS. CHILD SUPPORT

Whether a payment is considered alimony or child support has significant tax consequences. Please refer to Number 15 for an in-depth discussion of these distinctions.

Voodoo Tip 10.15

WATCH FOR THESE TAXING WORDS: "FAMILY SUPPORT"

Some states allow for the payment of a commingled combination of child support and alimony called "family support." Be cautious of any proposal regarding "family support." There shall be tax consequences to such a transaction. Federal law allows alimony to be deductible to the payer and taxable to the recipient. Child support is neither deductible nor taxable to either party. Certain rules apply to the deductibility of "family support." Before you entertain such a proposal, consult your attorney and tax advisor.

MODIFICATION OF CHILD SUPPORT

As long as the court maintains jurisdiction of the case and the child is eligible to receive the benefits of child support, the judge has the discretion to modify the child support award.

At the request of either party, the court can review the propriety of the child support award in effect. A party may seek a change in child support based on a "substantial" and/or "material" change of circumstance (either increase or decrease) in a party's income, financial needs of the child, when one child becomes ineligible by age or other factors such as emancipation, or where medical support has not been considered.

Many states have no criteria to determine what dollar change is required to be considered "substantial." Other states have provided standards to provide pecuniary measures as to whether a change is "substantial." Some states require a change in a party's average gross income, while others look to the proposed change in the actual child support award. "Substantial" could be defined as, as little as $50.00 or a ten (10%) percent change or as much of a minimum requirement of $100.00 or a thirty (30%) percent change. In many cases, the criteria established to allow a modification in child support are not rigidly followed.

As a recipient or payer of child support who has not sought a review in the award within the last several years, you should inquire as to whether an increase or decrease is in order. Your attorney's request for various income and expense documents may assist you in this evaluation. Child support cases that involve AFDC, Title IV-E Foster Care and/or Non-AFDC Medicaid should be reviewed every three years.

> **Real Life Experience:** *Jimmy G.*
>
> *Age 45, Divorced, One Child: Age 17*
> *Computer Consultant; Dallas, Texas*
>
> *"My boy becomes 18 in August. When can I stop paying child support?"*

WHEN CHILD SUPPORT ENDS

Child support usually ends when a child reaches the "age of majority." Society deems the age of majority as the point in a child's life when he is able to be legally independent from his parents. To be declared legally and financially independent is referred to as being "emancipated." Emancipation is an event that generally terminates a child support obligation.

The "age of majority" of a child, in reference to the termination of child support, varies from state to state. The following states generally terminate child support upon the child reaching the age of 18:

Alaska, Arkansas, Arizona, Connecticut, Delaware, Florida, Georgia, Idaho, Iowa, Kansas, Kentucky, Louisiana, Massachusetts, Maine, Maryland, Michigan, Minnesota, Missouri, Nevada, New Mexico, North Carolina, North Dakota, Ohio, Oklahoma, Oregon, Pennsylvania, Rhode Island, South Carolina, South Dakota, Tennessee, Texas, Utah, Vermont, Virgin Islands, Virginia, Washington, West Virginia, Wisconsin, and Wyoming.

Of the above referenced states, most states have provisions for the continuation of child support beyond a specified age based on extraordinary medical or educational circumstances (generally until the age of 19).

States such as Hawaii and Massachusetts allow the extension of the obligation of child support through to the age of 23, if the child is enrolled in full-time higher education.

Washington D.C., Mississippi, New York, and Puerto Rico consider the age of majority as being 21.

As there are currently no uniform laws as to the definition of the "age of majority" throughout the United States, theoretically a custodial parent with a child could move from one state that defines the "age of majority" as 18 to a state that has an "age of majority" as 21, and extend the child support obligation for another three years.

Events that may create a basis to terminate child support are the following:

1. Obtaining the "age of majority"
2. Marriage of the child
3. Death of the child
4. Completion of the child's education
5. The child entering the military
6. The child's full-time employment and
7. The incarceration of the child (going to jail)

BASIS FOR EXTENDING CHILD SUPPORT OBLIGATION BEYOND THE "AGE OF MAJORITY"

There are two basic reasons that a child support obligation could extend beyond the child reaching his "age of majority":

1. The child has serious medical problems
2. The child remains in secondary school

Each state has laws that control one's eligibility to extend child support payments beyond the child's "age of majority." One thought is extremely prudent:

If a parent wants an extension of child support payments beyond the "age of majority," then the parent should formally seek an extension from the court prior to the child reaching that age.

When one or more children reach the "age of majority," the entire child support obligation may be affected.

When parents have two or more minor children, a critical question arises as to what happens to the child support obligation when one of the children reaches the age of majority (or the child support obligation related to that child otherwise ends).

One of two circumstances can occur:

1. The amount of the child support obligation continues unchanged
2. The amount of the child support obligation is reduced

Prior to any of your children reaching the age of majority, consult your attorney and see how that event will effect you. A child support agreement or order can have provisions for a change in the child support award upon the occurrence of certain events (i.e., a child reaching the "age of majority"). Furthermore, a child support award can be calculated in increments based on a "per child" basis.

File for modifications, termination, or extension in child support in advance of event.

Although a change or termination in a child support obligation may be automatic by the occurrence of an event such as the child's attainment of the "age of majority," it is inadvisable to assume that a modification, termination or extension in the obligation occurs without a formal request to the court. Speak with your lawyer to determine whether an action with the court is required. Failure to check with your lawyer, prior to the event, could be a costly mistake.

WHEN PAYMENTS OF CHILD SUPPORT SHOULD BE MADE

Although a moral obligation to pay child support begins at the child's birth, in most states, a legal obligation to pay child support does not begin until it is requested by filing a pleading in court. In some states, the child support obligation is only retroactive to the date of filing for child support. Hence, it is important for the custodial parent to file for child support as soon as possible after the child is born.

Once a legal obligation of child support is created by law and/or by a judgment of a court, then the timing of the payments must be established. Courts often require payments each month, each week, every two weeks, or on the payer's paycheck cycle.

A payer of child support may not get credit for payments made to the custodial parent that were made prior to the custodial parent's formal request to the court for the support. Likewise, a payer of child support may not get credit against his child support obligation for the payment of child-related goods, such as diapers, food, and clothing.

> **Real Life Experience:** *Phil R.*
> Age 28, Divorced, Two Children
> Graphic Designer; Washington, D.C.
>
> "*I spend a lot of money on the children's clothes, food, and toys. I should be able to deduct these expenses from my child support payments.*"

Can the payer deduct for his expenses? Generally—no

For the payer to receive full credit for each cent that is paid in child support, the payments should be made directly to the recipient custodial parent.

Real Life Experience: *Charlie N.*
Age 37, Divorced, One Child
Investment Advisor
Fort Washington, Pennsylvania

"I don't trust Nancy. I want proof that I paid my child support."

Voodoo Tip 10.16

GET PROOF OF PAYMENT

A payer should be able to prove payment of child support for a specified time period (i.e., month) by specifying in the memo of the check the following:

1. Payment of "Child Support"
2. Date (include period covered—i.e., "January of 1999")

Example:
"Memo: Child Support for January of 1999"

The burden of proof that a child support payment was made generally falls on the payer. Regardless of whether you are the recipient or payer of child support, you should keep records and copies of all child support payments. This shall assist you if a dispute occurs at a later date.

Best Methods of Payment:
1. Pay by personal check (Keep canceled checks and check registry)
   The payer should keep photocopies of checks in case the bank does not return canceled checks.
2. Pay by money orders or cashier's checks (keep copies)
3. Mail by "Certified Mail, Return Receipt Requested"
4. Pay through the child support enforcement agency or the clerk of the court
5. Pay through an income assignment

> **Real Life Experience:** *Andy F.*
> Age 39, Divorced, Two Children
> Engineer; Scottsdale, Arizona
>
> *"I've always paid my child support in cash until she took me to court and testified that I never paid her for seven months. I had no way to prove that she was lying."*

Voodoo Tip 10.17

A PAYER SHOULD NEVER PAY IN CASH

Cash is the worst method of payment of child support. Unless a receipt is made and signed by both parties, proof becomes a swearing match. Furthermore, receipts may become suspect in cases where a spouse has threatened violence unless the custodial parent signed a fake receipt.

Payment should be made on or before the due date.

Make sure that the payment is received by the recipient on or before the date ordered. If the payment is due on the first of each month, then it should be mailed before and not on the first day of the month.

> **Real Life Experience:** *Price M.*
> Age 43, Married, Two Children
> Insurance Defense Attorney; Antioch, Illinois
>
> *"Since I left my wife, I have been routinely sending her more than sufficient money to take care of the children."*

Be careful of setting a precedent in child support.

Many people who pay child support make the personal mistake of paying child support to the recipient parent in an amount much greater than the amount reasonably expected to be ordered to pay at the child support hearing. Many times, these "excessive" payments are made out of guilt or other emotions. The payer should realize that the continual excessive payment of child support could set a precedent which the court feels is appropriate at the time of the hearing.

A more safe and accurate approach to paying the appropriate amount of child support is with the help of your lawyer. Your attorney can use your state's guidelines and suggest a figure that is fair.

It should be noted that any parent who has the ability and the desire to pay more child support than would be ordered should be commended.

> **Real Life Experience:** Eric H.
> Age 39, Divorced, One Child
> Police Officer; Charlotte, North Carolina
>
> *"I pay much more money in child support than what Melinda spends on Campbell."*

Does the child support money have to go toward the children?

Many parents who are ordered to pay child support complain that the other parent is not spending the child support money on the children. Most courts will not entertain discussions in this area unless the payer can prove that the custodial parent is neglecting to pay for the necessities of the children.

BANKRUPTCY AND CHILD SUPPORT

The payer of child support cannot interrupt his legal obligation to pay child support by filing bankruptcy. Furthermore, past-due child support is not dischargable in bankruptcy. See Chapter 16 on Bankruptcy.

Late payments may subject the payer to penalties and sanctions.

A payer of child support may be subject to many court sanctions if he is continually late in his payment of child support. The penalties and sanctions are listed below.

COLLECTION OF CHILD SUPPORT

> **Quick Fact:** According to the Federal Office of Child Support Enforcement, in excess of 30% of child support claims involve parents who live in different states than their children.

> **Real Life Experience:** Meg E.
> Age 36, Divorced, Three Children
> Chef; Madison, South Dakota
>
> *"How can I increase my chances that he will pay on time?"*

Voodoo Tip 10.18

CHILD SUPPORT ORDERS SHOULD INCLUDE A LATE PAYMENT FEE PROVISION

If you are the recipient of child support, suggest that your attorney propose a provision in the agreement or order of child support that calls for a late payment fee if the payer is delinquent in his child support payment (the same principal can apply for alimony payments). You can argue that if the payer is sincere in his intent to pay timely, then he should not complain about a late payment provision as the event would never arise. The payer would only have an objection if he had concerns or an intent to not pay timely.

> **Real Life Experience:** *Sal S.*
> Age 33, Divorced, Two Children
> Pet Shop Owner; Green Bay, Wisconsin
>
> *"Last month, I was late on paying the child support. Now Gina won't let me see the children on my weekends."*

Voodoo Tip 10.19

DON'T RESTRICT VISITATION BECAUSE OF A REFUSAL TO PAY CHILD SUPPORT

It is commonly tempting to refuse or restrict visitation if the payer is not providing child support payments as ordered. Unless a refusal or restriction of visitation is pursuant a "linkage order" (discussed later in this chapter), then the custodial parent is exposing himself to contempt of court sanctions. Also remember that the custodial parent must be a "good parent" for the child's sake. Let the judge do his job, and deal with the non-paying parent. Let the wrath of the court come down only on the delinquent payer; otherwise, the wrath of the court may come down on both of you.

Another unintended result might occur. A few courts have ordered that child support payments are suspended where a custodial parent has intentionally refused and/or interfered with visitation rights.

Always remember that the child suffers by a refusal or restriction of visitation rights (unless the visiting parent is neglectful or abusive). The payment of child support and visitation generally are separate issues.

Quick Fact: Non-custodial parents who have joint custody and/or visitation rights are more likely to pay child support than those parents that do not have these rights. Of the 11.5 million non-custodial parents, 6.9 million have joint custody of their children. (U.S. Census Bureau)

> **Real Life Experience:** Rebecca O.
> Age 37, Divorced, One Child
> Hair Stylist; York, Maine
>
> "I think that it's a good time to ask Ron if he will agree to pay for Bobby's college tuition. He feels very guilty about leaving me."

Voodoo Tip 10.20

TRY TO ENTER INTO CONSENT AGREEMENT AND ORDER WHEREBY THE PARENTS AGREE TO PAY FOR COLLEGE EDUCATION

Although it may not be otherwise enforceable, if both parents are agreeable to the general child support provisions, it may be a good time to propose an agreement regarding the payment of your child's college education. If both parents enter into such an agreement and it is converted into a judgment of the court, it may be enforceable at a later date. There does not appear to be any harm in trying to get an agreement that benefits the future of your child.

ENFORCING CHILD SUPPORT OBLIGATIONS

> **Real Life Experience:** Taylor V.
> Age 39, Divorced, Two Children
> Librarian; San Fernando, California
>
> "David owes $3,750 in past due child support. His wages are being garnished, but it's not enough. It seems that I'm never able to get what I deserve. David is not making any effort to pay the arrearage. He's very angry that his pay is being deducted. He claims that he doesn't have the money to pay, but he can still take a vacation and routinely take his girlfriend out to dinner."

Voodoo Tip 10.21

SUMMARY OF TWENTY WAYS TO COLLECT CHILD SUPPORT

1. Income Withholding/Wage Assignment/Garnishment/Payroll Deduction
2. Contempt of Court
3. Collect Attorney Fees, Court Costs and Related Expenses
4. Intercept of Federal and State Income Tax Refunds
5. Property Seizure and Sale/Restraining Notices and Orders to Prohibit Transfer of Property

6. Suspension/Revocation of State Licenses
7. Arrest Warrants and Jail
8. "Most Wanted" Lists
9. New Hire Reporting
10. Intercept of Unemployment Benefits, Worker's Compensation Benefits, Social Security and Disability Benefits, State Lottery Winnings, and Pensions/Benefits of State Employees
11. Appointment of Receiver
12. Require a Bond/Security
13. Judicial and Administrative Liens
14. Report to Credit Bureaus
15. File Creditors Suit
16. Private Collection Agencies
17. Linkage Order
18. Collect from the Military
19. Private Attorney
20. Child Support Enforcement Office

Real Life Experience: *Maxine B.*

Age 28, Divorced, One Child
Teacher; Bowling Green, Kentucky

"It's been much easier to get my child support through the garnishment. I now know that I am going to get the check on the fourth or fifth of each month."

---

1. *Income Withholding/Wage Assignment/Garnishment/Payroll Deduction*

Quick Fact: Two-thirds of all child support dollars collected by state child support agencies come from income withholding.

Courts can order that the non-custodial parent pay child support through an income assignment. This forces payment of part or all of the support obligation with the assistance of the obligor's employer. In many states, failure of an employer to withhold to the extent ordered and/or allowed by law could result in the employer becoming liable for the amount of child support that should have been properly withheld.

If an employer fails to withhold earnings pursuant to a garnishment order, the failure of the employer to garnish does not excuse or relinquish the payer's obligation to pay the support.

Pursuant to the FAMILY SUPPORT ACT OF 1988 (Title IV, Part D of the Social Security Act), states should impose automatic income assignments to all new or modified child support decrees. Although mandated by the federal government, many courts are lax in the application of this law.

Quick Fact: When Congress first enacted legislation to garnish the wages of federal employees for child support in the late 1970s, fewer than 1,000 federal employees were affected annually. Now the federal government garnishes over 3,500 federal employee checks per month. (Defense Finance and Accounting Service)

Real Life Experience: *Elsa C.*
Age 35, Divorced, Two Children
Nurse; Madison, New Jersey

"I want Monty to pay for the pain that he has put me through. I need the child support to make it through each month."

2. *Contempt of Court*

The court will consider several factors in determining whether a party is in contempt of court. The factors include the following:
1. The existence of a valid written order
2. The payer's knowledge of the order
3. The payer's ability to comply with the order
4. The payer's willful disobedience of the order

Each state has different penalties for being held in contempt of court. Speak to your lawyer to find what penalties apply in your state.

Real Life Experience: *Jeremy C.*
Age 42, Divorced, Two Children
Chiropractor; Hershey, Pennsylvania

"She left me with the kids and wanted to have a fresh start. Despite the fact that she has abandoned the children, I refuse to let her abandon her financial and legal obligation to the boys."

3. *Collect Attorney Fees, Court Costs and Related Expenses*

> **Real Life Experience:** Pam L.
>
> Age 29, Divorced, One Child
> Waitress; Essex, Connecticut
>
> *"Frank owes me four months of back child support. He always gets a tax refund. Can I get it?"*

4. *Intercept of Federal and State Income Tax Refunds*

Your state can intercept the noncustodial parent's state income tax return for past due child support. Often the noncustodial parent will be more willing to allow the entire tax refund to be intercepted as payment for past due support as the noncustodial parent has never seen the money; therefore, it seems to hurt less.

> **Quick Fact:** For the 1995 tax year, the federal government collected over one billion dollars in past due child support payments through intercepts of income tax refunds. Since 1982, over 6 billion dollars has been collected from approximately 10 million intercepted federal tax refunds.

Every year the state child support enforcement agencies contact the Internal Revenue Service with the names of parents who owe past due child support.

Voodoo Tip 10.22

PROMPTLY NOTIFY THE STATE CHILD SUPPORT ENFORCEMENT OFFICE

Contact your state's child support enforcement agency as soon as possible in order to begin the process of seeking a federal tax refund offset, as tax returns are filed only once a year. You want to make sure that your state agency has enough time to properly submit your claim to the IRS before the refund is sent to the delinquent parent.

> **Real Life Experience:** Mary H.
>
> Age 46, Divorced, Remarried
> One Adult Child and One Minor Child
> Architect; New Town, North Dakota
>
> *"I have a judgment against Saul for over twelve thousand dollars in past due child support. Saul has several rental properties in New Town. As I suspected, my lawyer has confirmed that they are his separate property."*

5. *Property Seizure and Sale/Restraining Notices and Orders to Prohibit Transfer of Property*

Courts have procedures that allow a recipient of child support to seize property of a non-supporter to collect a support debt. A variety of assets can be seized ranging from real estate, automobiles, boats, jewelry, money in checking and savings accounts, and cash.

> **Real Life Experience:** Samantha W.
>
> Age 41, Divorced, Three Children
> Oral Hygienist; Houma, Louisiana
>
> *"Michael needs his drivers license for work. He owes me a couple thousand dollars. I know that the state can yank his license, but if he loses his license then he will lose his job. It's a big catch 22!"*

6. *Suspension/Revocation of State Licenses*

Many states allow the suspension and/or revocation of driver's licenses, hunting licenses, fishing licenses, and professional licenses such as license to practice law, medicine and the like.

> **Real Life Experience:** Jennifer P.
>
> Age 36, Never Married, One Child
> Insurance Agent; El Paso, Texas
>
> *"He has been found in contempt of court on two separate occasions. He still refuses to pay. I finally think that the judge has had enough of his antics."*

7. *Arrest Warrants and Jail*

Many states have criminal sweeps called "round-up days." In these cases, an arrest warrant has been issued and the deadbeat is a fugitive from justice.

Voodoo Tip 10.23

WHEN ALL ELSE FAILS, CONSIDER RELIEF PURSUANT TO THE CHILD SUPPORT RECOVERY ACT OF 1992

The Child Support Recovery Act of 1992 makes it a federal crime to willfully fail to pay arrearages in a child support award if the child lives in another state than the payer. For the law to apply, the past due child support must remain unpaid for in excess of one year or the past due child support is greater than $5,000. The United States Attorneys Office shall look at various factors in deciding whether to prosecute a case under the act. Factors include whether the non-paying parent is moving from state to state to avoid paying the child support, whether the parent is using deceit to avoid payment (such as using a fictitious name or social security number, whether the parent has refused to pay child support after being held in contempt of court by a state court, and whether the failure or refusal to pay is related to another federal crime such as bankruptcy or mail fraud.

Penalties for violation of this federal law include the following:
First Offense—Six months in prison and/or a fine
Subsequent Offense—Two years in prison and/or a fine

8. *"Most Wanted" Lists*

The United States Post Office displays "Wanted Lists" of persons who owe child support. States are encouraged to create and maintain a similar program. Private organizations have also considered using "Wanted Lists"; however, much of the private participation in this program has been stifled by concerns regarding defamation lawsuits.

Many states have "most wanted lists" that provide the picture, name and other information on the deadbeat parent.

Real Life Experience: *Hope B.*

Age 25, Divorced, One Child
Unemployed; Springfield, Illinois

"Dennis has been jumping from job to job. Every time that we start a garnishment, he changes jobs. He tries to stay one step ahead of me. My boy suffers from his father's gross irresponsibility."

---

9. *New Hire Reporting*

Under the Personal Responsibility and Work Opportunity Act of 1996 (HR 3734), all states must establish a Directory of New Hires. States have implemented a "New Hire Reporting" policy which requires employers to provide data to the state on the employment and/or re-employment of individuals. The data is sent to the state's Office of Child Support Enforcement. All states must have complied with this federal law by October 1, 1998.

This federal "New Hire Reporting" law requires that all employers must report the hiring/re-hiring of all new/re-hired workers within twenty days of the hire. The employer's report must include the following information:

1. The full name of the employee
2. The employee's social security number
3. The employee's home address
4. Date of employee's first day at work
5. The employer's name, address, and Federal Employer Identification Number (FEIN)
6. The employer's state identification number

Reports can be submitted by using the employee's W-4 form.

After the information is registered in the state and federal system, the information is processed to see if there is a match to a person who owes back due child support. If a match is found, an order is sent to the employer that compels the employer to withhold wages for the payment of child support.

Quick Fact: According to the United States Department of Health and Human Services, within the next ten years, the New Hire Reporting Program is expected to increase child support collections by 6.4 billion dollars.

Real Life Experience: *Patty K.*

Age 33, Divorced, One Child
Social Worker; Juneau, Alaska

"Frank hurt his back at work. He's receiving worker's compensation."

10. *Intercept of Unemployment Benefits; Worker's Compensation Benefits; State Lottery Winnings; and Pensions/Benefits of State Employees*

Federal law mandates that all states have procedures for withholding unemployment compensation benefits for payment of past due child support obligations.

States are particularly strict on their own employees.

Real Life Experience: *Carla B.*

Age 44, Divorced, Two Children
Co-Owner of Restaurant with Former Spouse
Cape Cod, Massachusetts

"Elliot has essentially kicked me out of the restaurant. He won't let me see the books and I trust him as far as I can throw him. It looks like the place is doing better than ever. He's probably taking all the profits out the back door."

11. Appointment of Receiver

> **Real Life Experience:** Ashley B.
> Age 35, Divorced, One Child
> Certified Public Accountant
> Bennington, Vermont
>
> "He continues disobey the judge. How can the court force him to pay?"

12. Require a Bond/Security

Courts may require the delinquent payer to provide a cash bond and/or other security to insure that the child support obligation is paid.

A few courts have directed property of a payer to be placed in a trust. States that allow such a trust include the following: Indiana, Iowa, Kansas, Michigan, New Mexico, North Carolina, Oklahoma, Oregon, Vermont, Washington, Wisconsin, and Wyoming.

> **Real Life Experience:** Brian B.
> Age 34, Divorced, One Child
> Real Estate Agent; Coral Gables, Florida
>
> "She has a personal injury case pending. I want to place a lien on any judgment that she might get."

13. Judicial and Administrative Liens

> **Real Life Experience:** Lane R.
> Age 25, Divorced, Two Children
> Retail Sales Associate
> Columbia, South Carolina
>
> "I want the world to know that he doesn't pay his child support."

14. Report to Credit Bureaus

The noncustodial parent will not want to have a poor credit rating on his report.

15. File a Creditor's Suit

If you become aware of property in the hands of third parties that belong to the delinquent payer of child support, your attorney may be able to file a creditor's suit against the other party with the intent to retrieve the asset(s) as partial or full payment of the past due child support debt.

16. *Private Collection Agencies*

17. *Linkage Order*

Although not uniformly favored throughout the country, some courts have made "Linkage Orders" that link a parent's ability to have visitation rights with his compliance with the payment of child support.

> **Real Life Experience:** *Jim R.*
> Age 29, Divorced, One Child
> Waiter; Cincinnati, Ohio
>
> *"Elena is stationed in Florida. Will the Air Force help me get my child support?"*

18. *Collect from the Military*

The United States Armed Forces makes a concerted effort to have their soldiers pay the child support obligation. If the noncustodial parent is in the military, contact the appropriate branches office found in the Appendix. (Voodoo Spice Number 23: Collecting Child Support From the Military)

> **Real Life Experience:** *Monique D.*
> Age 30, Divorced, Two Children
> Day Care Assistant; Kansas City, Missouri
>
> *"I frankly don't have any faith in the state to do a good job for me. I'm just a number to them. I need a shark!"*

19. *Private Attorney*

Whether you seek to collect child support through a private attorney or the state office of child support enforcement, the information requested in the appendices shall be of significant value to your attorney. Be sure to answer the questions, keep the information in a safe place, and provide your attorney with a copy of the information.

Also see the Number 2 on hiring the right attorney.

20. *Child Support Enforcement Office*

Voodoo Tip 10.24

REPORT PROBLEMS TO THE FEDERAL OFFICE OF CHILD SUPPORT ENFORCEMENT

If you find that a certain agency or court is failing to pursue the enforcement of your order awarding child support, you may seek assistance by reporting the problems, via certified mail, to the following federal office:

> Federal Office of Child Support Enforcement
> c/o Director
> 370 L'Enfant Promenade S.W.
> Washington D.C. 20447

The Office of Child Support Enforcement (OCSE) is an agency of the United Stated Department of Health and Human Services which works in conjunction with state agencies. The OCSE assists in locating missing parents, establishing paternity, and establishing and collecting collect support. The OCSE also may assist in the collection of alimony if the past due alimony is due pursuant to a prior order establishing both alimony and child support.

The OCSE will not assist a party in obtaining a divorce, property settlement, and/or the pursuit of a new order for alimony.

Quick Facts: In 1995, state child support enforcement agencies established over a million new child support orders, enforced and/or modified over five million child support orders, and collected $10.8 billion dollars in child support payments. In 1995, the state agencies also established paternity for 903,400 children.

Voodoo Tip 10.25

CALL STATE CHILD SUPPORT ENFORCEMENT OFFICES

State Child Support Offices assist in the following:
1. Locating non-custodial parents
2. Establishing paternity
3. Establishing child support orders and /or
4. Enforcing child support orders/collecting child support

The state office of child support enforcement telephone numbers and Internet addresses are listed below: (Also see the Appendix, Voodoo Spice Number 22: State Child Support Enforcement Agencies and Enforcement Support Groups)

Alabama	(205) 242-9300	http://www.state.al.us/
Alaska	(907) 276-3441	http://www.revenue.state.ak.us/csed/csed.htm.
Arizona	(602) 252-0236	http://aztec.asu.edu/cirs/alpha/1360.html
Arkansas	(501) 682-8398	http://www.state.ar.us/
California	(916) 654-1556	http://www.childsup.cahwnet.gov.
Colorado	(303) 866-5994	http://www.dss.state.ct.us/svcs/csupp.htm
Connecticut	(203) 566-3053	http://www.dss.state.ct.us/svcs/csupp.htm
Delaware	(302) 577-4863	http:www.state.de.us/govern/agencies/dhss/irm/dcse/dcsehome.htm
Florida	(904) 488-9900	http:fcn.state.fl.us/dor/cse.html
Georgia	(404) 657-3851	http://www.state.ga.us/Departments/dhr/cse/
Guam	(671) 475-3360	
Hawaii	(808) 587-3700	http://www.hawaii.gov/csea/csea.htm
Idaho	(208) 334-5710	http://www.state.id.us/
Illinois	(217) 782-8768	http://www.state.il.us/dpa/cse.htm
Indiana	(317) 232-4894	http://www.ai.org/fssa/cse/
Iowa	(515) 281-5580	http://www2.legis.state.ia.us/ga/76ga/legislation/sf/02300/sf02344/current.htl
Kansas	(913) 296-3237	http://www.ink.org/public/srs/srswanted.html
Kentucky	(502) 564-2285	http://www.state.ky.us/oag/childs.htm
Louisiana	(504) 342-4780	http://www.dss.state.la.us/mainfram.htm
Maine	(207) 287-2886	http://www.state.me.us/
Maryland	(410) 333-3979	http://www.state.md.us/srv_csea.htm
Massachusetts	(617) 727-4200	http://www.mst,oa.net:8002/macse.html
Michigan	(517) 373-7570	http://www.mfia.state.mi.us/1996 fact.htm#6-10
Minnesota	(612) 296-2542	http://www.co.hennnepin.mnus/weapsupp.html
Mississippi	(601) 359-4500	http://www.mdhs.state.ms.us/cse.html
Missouri	(314) 751-4301	http://services.state.mo.us/dss/cse/cse.htm

Montana	(406) 444-4614	http://www.dphhs.mt.gov/whowhat/csed.htm
Nebraska	(402) 471-9125	http://www.unl.edu/ccfl/cse.htm
Nevada	(702) 687-4744	http://state.mv.us/
New Hampshire	(603) 271-4426	http://little.nhlink.net/nhlink/governme/county/dhs/chld_sup.htm
New Jersey	(609) 588-2361	http://www.state.nj.us/judiciary/prob01.htm
New Mexico	(505) 827-7200	http://www.mostwanted.com/nh/support.html
New York	(518) 474-9081	http://www.state.ny.us/dss/
North Carolina	(919) 571-4120	http://www.state.nc.us/cse/
North Dakota	(701) 224-3582	http://www.state.nd.us/hms/oea.htm#child support
Ohio	(614) 752-6561	http://www.ohiogov/odhs/wanted/wanted.html
Oklahoma	(405) 424-5871	http://www.acf.dhhs.gov/acfprograms/cse/fct/sp_ok.html
Oregon	(503) 986-2417	http://170.104.17.50/rss/rogues.html
Pennsylvania	(717) 787-3672	http://www.state.pa.us/pa_exec/public_welfare/overview.html
Puerto Rico	(809) 722-4731	
Rhode Island	(401) 277-2409	http:www.state.ri.us/
South Carolina	(803) 737-5870	http://www.state.sc.us/
South Dakota	(605) 773-3641	http://www.state.sd.us/state/executive/social/social.html
Tennessee	(615) 741-1820	http://www.state.tn.us/humanserv/
Texas	(512) 463-2181	http://www.oag.state.tx.us/website/childsup.htm
Utah	(801) 538-4400	http://www.state.ut.us/
Vermont	(802) 241-2319	http://www.dsw.state.vt.us/ahs/ahs.htm
Virgin Islands	(809) 774-5666	
Virginia	(804) 692-2458	http://www.state.va.us/-dss/childspt.html
Washington	(206) 586-3162	http://www.wa.gov/dshs/csrc.html
Washington D.C.	(202) 724-8800	
West Virginia	(304) 558-3780	http://www.state.wv.us/
Wisconsin	(608) 266-9909	http://dhss.state.wi.us/dhss/pubs/html/childsp.html
Wyoming	(307) 777-6948	http://www.dfsweb.state.wy.us/csehome/wybody1.htm

INFORMATION AND DOCUMENTS TO BRING TO YOUR OFFICE OF CHILD SUPPORT ENFORCEMENT

1. Name of noncustodial parent
2. Last known address of noncustodial parent
3. Child's birth certificate
4. Any child support order
5. Any divorce decree (if applicable)
6. Last known name and address of noncustodial parent's employer
7. Any other information regarding the whereabouts and/or income/assets of the noncustodial parent

---

Real Life Experience: *Regan K.*

Age 37, Divorced, Three Children
Advertising Agent; Hartford, Connecticut

"I heard that John is on the west coast. I've been raising the kids without any help from him. Thank god, I have a judgment against him. Now, all I need to do is find him."

Voodoo Tip 10.26

LOCATE DEADBEATS

The PARENT LOCATOR SERVICE is one of the most effective methods to track down non-custodial parents who live in or out of your state. The computerized system locates parents by the use of drivers license numbers, security numbers, and other means of identification.

States differ in the extent of their ability to trace a person through their state agencies. States typically contact the following sources:

- Credit Bureau Contacts
- Department of Corrections
- Department of Human Services (Food Stamps and other programs)
- Department of Labor/Employment Security (Food Stamps and Unemployment Benefits)
- Department of Public Safety/Motor Vehicles/Transportation
- Department of Revenue/Taxation
- Department of Social Services
- Department of Vital Statistics (Birth Certificates)
- Department of Wildlife and Fisheries (Fish and Game Licenses)

- IV-A/Medicaid Database
- New Hire Reporting System
- Registrar of Voters/Department of Elections (Voter Registration)
- Secretary of State

> **Real Life Experience:** David I.
> Age 41, Divorced, Two Children
> Banker; Dallas, Texas
>
> *"I want to know my rights."*

THE UNIFORM RECIPROCAL ENFORCEMENT OF SUPPORT ACT (URESA)

This federal act was created in 1950 to assist in the uniform enforcement of child support orders across state lines. In 1968, the act was revised. States' use of URESA is decreasing as it has only marginal desirability and effectiveness. Under URESA, a person seeking child support would request the attorney to file a petition in their "initiating" state. The pleadings would be sent to the "responding" state where the noncustodial parent lives or owns property. It was the responsibility of the foreign responding state to establish and/or enforce a child support order. Under URESA, a noncustodial parent could argue before his or her home state ("responding state") that a reduction in the amount is sought. The possibility of more than one child support order could exist under URESA, thus creating a child support discrepancy between the "initiating" and "responding" state's orders.

Many states have repealed their URESA legislation in favor of the Uniform Interstate Family Support Act (UIFSA).

THE UNIFORM INTERSTATE FAMILY SUPPORT ACT (UIFSA)

Under UIFSA, the establishment and enforcement of a child support obligation is assisted with one order. Unless agreed by both parents, UIFSA provides that the state that originally makes the child support decree continues to have jurisdiction ("continuing exclusive jurisdiction") as long as one parent continues to reside in the state. This insures that only one child support order is in effect. Courts evaluate whether jurisdiction exists on a case by case basis. The court will consider the following factors in deciding whether jurisdiction exists:

1. Whether the noncustodial parent is personally served in the state
2. Whether the noncustodial parent consents to the jurisdiction of the state

3. Whether the noncustodial parent had resided with the child within the state

4. Whether the noncustodial parent had sexual intercourse in the state that lead to the conception of the child

5. Whether the child resides in the state as a result of any action of the noncustodial parent

6. Whether the noncustodial parent acknowledged the child in the state and/or

7. Any other facts that the court deems relevant

UIFSA legislation allows one state's income withholding order to be directly sent to an employer of the noncustodial parent in another UIFSA state.

Each state has a Central Registry for the collection of interstate child support orders. A listing of each state's Central Registry is found in the Appendix (see Voodoo Spice Number 22).

Your lawyer can give you more information on how these federal acts effect one's ability to collect child support.

> **Real Life Experience:** *Susan G.*
>
> Age 27, Married, Two Children, Store Owner
> Martha's Vineyard, Massachusetts
>
> *"He's offered me five hundred dollars less in monthly child support than he should pay. His family is very wealthy and they will spend all the money that they need to in order to destroy me. He's just playing games at the cost of the children. I'm scared to death."*

Voodoo Tip 10.27

WATCH OUT FOR CHILD SUPPORT BLACKMAIL

It is all too common for a spouse to threaten a custody battle unless the other spouse concedes to a lower child support, alimony, and/or property settlement. This blackmail should not be tolerated. Report these threats to your attorney. Any evidence of these threats also should be given to your attorney.

> **Real Life Experience:** *Ben T.*
> Age 36, Divorced, Two Children
> Stockbroker; St. Paul, Minnesota
>
> *"I'm now in the position to offer my ex-wife fifty cents on the dollar to pay off my past due child support because I know that she needs the money."*

Voodoo Tip 10.28

NEGOTIATE PAST DUE CHILD SUPPORT

Child support blackmail is despicable and should not be tolerated. On the other hand, a negotiation regarding the payment of past due child support is a common practice throughout the United States. Many proposals are accepted for a percentage of what is legally owed. It may be mutually beneficial to come to a compromise, rather than a lengthy and expensive court battle. Weigh your options and make an informed decision.

> **Real Life Experience:** *Blair S.*
> Age 46, Divorced, Remarried, One Adult Child
> Paramedic; Carlyle, Illinois
>
> "*My former husband has owed me over ten thousand dollars. The last time I went to court was in 1987. I know that I should have sought the money a long time ago. Can I still try to get it?*"

Voodoo Tip 10.29

STATUTE OF LIMITATIONS

A Statute of Limitations is the time period in which one can no longer seek enforcement of a former child support award. In many states, if a parent avoids payment of past due child support for a period of time longer than the state's statute of limitations, then that part of the child support obligation extending beyond the enforceable time period would be legally forgiven (exceptions do apply which your attorney can discuss with you in greater detail).

For example, State "A" has a statute of limitations of five years. If the payer owes six years of back child support, then only the last five years of back child support would be legally collectible.

Some states have taken the enlightened view that a child support obligation is never excused by the mere passage of time.

Many states allow the child to pursue the past due child support after he or she reaches the age of majority.

Voodoo Tip 10.30

**FOR FURTHER SUPPORT CONTACT A PARENTS WITHOUT PARTNERS GROUP
(Also see Appendix—Voodoo Spice Number 20)**

If you would like a support group to help you through these trying times, then contact a local Parents Without Partners support group by contacting their national toll free telephone number at 1-800-638-8078.

Other support groups for men and women are found in the Appendix.

HOW TO ENFORCE CHILD SUPPORT ABROAD

Although the United States does not have a treaty with any country regarding the enforcement of child support orders, many states have reciprocal arrangements with the following foreign countries:

Australia, Austria, Bermuda, Canada, Czech Republic, Fiji, Finland, France, Germany, Hungary, Ireland, Jamaica, Mexico, New Zealand, Norway, Poland, Slovak Republic, South Africa, Sweden, and the United Kingdom (England, Scotland, Northern Ireland, and Wales). Please see Appendix, Voodoo Spice Number 24, for the addresses and telephone numbers of proper contact for these countries.

Your first step in an attempt to get foreign enforcement of your child support award is to contact your state's office of child support enforcement found in the Appendix.

If the parent who owes the child support lives and/or works abroad, yet works for a company based in the United States, or for the United States government, then you likely will be able to enforce your support order through your state's office of child support enforcement or a private attorney in order to garnish wages.

Voodoo Tip 10.31

**IF NO RECIPROCAL AGREEMENT EXISTS WITH YOUR STATE
AND THE FOREIGN COUNTRY, RETAIN A FOREIGN ATTORNEY**

You may be able to retain a foreign attorney on a contingency basis. The United States Department Office of American Citizens Services can provide you with a listing of English speaking foreign attorneys. Furthermore, many countries have "Legal Aid" services. Call and/or write for the address and telephone number of the applicable foreign embassy in Washington, D.C. Additionally, the International Social Service (ISS) may be able to lend you assistance. The ISS can be contacted at the following:

International Social Service
10 W. 40th Street
New York, NY 10018
(212) 532-6350

Voodoo Tip 10.32

CONTACT THE FOREIGN-BASED EMPLOYER

Additional pressure can be levied by sending a certified translated copy of outstanding child support orders to the deadbeat's employer. A list of company presidents and other individuals in the corporate hierarchy may be found by consulting with a branch of the company and by using business directories such as *Standard and Poor's* and *Dunn & Bradstreet*.

Standards and Poors (http://www.stockinfo.standardpoor.com/)
Dunn & Bradstreet (http://dbisna.com/dbis/dbishome.htm)

Real Life Experience: *Elizabeth D.*
Age 24, Never Married, One Child
Military; Camp LeJeune, North Carolina

"*My child's father is also in the military. He's stationed in the Mid-East.*"

Voodoo Tip 10.33

COLLECT SUPPORT FROM A PARENT WHO IS SERVING ABOARD IN THE UNITED STATES MILITARY OR WHO IS A U.S. MILITARY RETIREE RESIDING ABROAD

Your state child support enforcement office or private attorney can contact the United States Armed Forces.

For Garnishment: Contact the Pentagon at (703) 545-6700 and you will be directed to the appropriate Judge Advocate General's office. Please refer to: http://www.jagc.army.mil/jagc2.htm

For Service of Process on Military Personnel: contact the Judge Advocate General's office for the appropriate branch of the armed forces.

Contact the following:

Air Force Judge Advocate General's Office:	http://www.ja.hq.af.mil
Army Judge Advocate General's Office:	http://21taacom.army.mil/aerja/
Navy Judge Advocate General's Office:	http://www.jag.navy.mil

Voodoo Tip 10.34

LOCATE MILITARY PERSONNEL

To locate a person in the United States Armed Forces contact the following:

Air Force
Headquarters
AFMPC/DPMD003
Attn: Worldwide Locator
Randolph Air Force Base, TX 78150-6001
(210) 652-5774

Army
Commander
U.S. Army EREC
Army Worldwide Locator Service
Fort Benjamin Harrison, Indiana 46249-5301
(317) 542-4211

Coast Guard
Commandant
United States Coast Guard
Coast Guard Locator Service
GPE 3-45 (Enlisted Personnel)
GPE-42 (Officers)
2100 2nd Street, S.W.
Washington, D.C. 20593
(202) 267-1615 (Enlisted Personnel)
(202) 267-1667 (Officers)

Marine Corps
Commander of the Marine Corps
Code MMRB-10
Attn: Locator Service
Washington, D.C. 20380-0001
(202) 694-1610

Navy
Naval Military Personnel Command
Navy Annex
Washington, D.C. 20370
(202) 694-3155

Summary of Voodoo Tips from Number 10

CHILD SUPPORT

Voodoo Tip 10.1   Check the calculations of each parent's income.

Voodoo Tip 10.2   There are 4.3 weeks in each month.

Voodoo Tip 10.3   Watch for manipulation of the numbers.

Voodoo Tip 10.4   Look at the income of your ex's new spouse.

Voodoo Tip 10.5   Look at financial affidavits and *in forma pauperis* application.

Voodoo Tip 10.6   Ask for contributions for "extras."

Voodoo Tip 10.7   Watch out for cancellation of insurance policies.

Voodoo Tip 10.8   Whole Life insurance policies are a source of quick cash.

Voodoo Tip 10.9   Get day-care.

Voodoo Tip 10.10 Ask the court for participation in the decision regarding which day-care facility is used.

Voodoo Tip 10.11 Replace day-care with self or relatives.

Voodoo Tip 10.12 Place child in chosen day-care facility prior to court date.

Voodoo Tip 10.13 Watch out for 50-50 split of other child-related expenses.

Voodoo Tip 10.14 Temporary award of child support sets the tone for regular child support.

Voodoo Tip 10.15 Watch out for these taxing words: "Family Support."

Voodoo Tip 10.16 Get proof of payment.

Voodoo Tip 10.17 A payer should never pay in cash.

Voodoo Tip 10.18 Child support order should include a late payment fee provision.

Voodoo Tip 10.19 Don't restrict visitation because of a refusal to pay child support.

Voodoo Tip 10.20 Try to enter into consent agreement and order whereby the parents agree to pay for college education.

Voodoo Tip 10.21 Summary of twenty ways to collect child support.

Voodoo Tip 10.22 Promptly notify the state child support enforcement office.

Voodoo Tip 10.23 When all else fails, consider relief pursuant to the Child Support Recovery Act of 1992.

Voodoo Tip 10.24 Report problems to the Federal Office of Child Support Enforcement.

Voodoo Tip 10.25 Call the state child support enforcement office.

Voodoo Tip 10.26 Locate deadbeats.

Voodoo Tip 10.27 Watch out for child support blackmail.

Voodoo Tip 10.28 Negotiate past due child support.

Voodoo Tip 10.29 Statute of Limitations.

Voodoo Tip 10.30 For further support contact a Parents Without Partners group.

Voodoo Tip 10.31 If no reciprocal agreement exists with your state and the foreign country, retain a foreign attorney.

Voodoo Tip 10.32 Contact the foreign-based employer.

Voodoo Tip 10.33 Collect support from a parent who is serving abroad in the United States military or who is a U.S. military retiree residing abroad.

Voodoo Tip 10.34 Locate military personnel.

VOODOO SPELL
TO GET CHILD SUPPORT

Fasten a dollar bill around a green candle. Light the candle. Place the following ingredients in your gris-gris bag: Alfalfa, Almond, Ash Tree Leaves, Basil, Buckwheat, Calendula, Cascara Sagrada, Catnip, Gravel Root, Lucky Hand Root, Marigold, Mint, Pine, and Trillium. Place a magnet in the gris-gris bag. Place the names of your children on a blank checking account deposit slip. Place your blank checking account deposit slip in a spider's web. Take the dollar bill that had been wrapped around the lit green candle and attach a feather to it.

VOODOO SPELL
TO GET AN INCREASE IN CHILD SUPPORT

Follow the same steps to get child support and bills regarding your children's care onto the voodoo doll.

VOODOO SPELL
TO GET A DECREASE IN CHILD SUPPORT

Light a green candle. Place a dollar bill around the candle. Get documents evidencing your children's expenses. Place them in a folder with a copy of your paycheck. Send the folder to your attorney.

VOODOO INGREDIENT NUMBER 11

Property Division

You have already taken advantage of the tips provided in the chapter encouraging you to "Get Possessed!"

To recap, get possession of the following:

1. Your children
2. Money
3. Your house or apartment
4. All important documents and
5. *Voodoo Divorce*

> **Real Life Experience:** *Clark J.*
> Age 46, Married, Three Children
> Restaurant Owner; Boca Raton, Florida
>
> *"I need to maintain control of my assets while I'm going through this process."*

Voodoo Tip 11.1

PROTECT YOUR PROPERTY

After you locate, inventory, and possess all documents, assets, and debts, you must continue to protect these items.

1. After speaking with your attorney, consider changing the locks to your dwelling
2. Get restraining orders against your spouse's use, disposal, or alienation of your marital property, separate, and/or personal

3. Having inventoried, photographed, and/or videotaped your belongings, if your furniture, tools, jewelry, or other items "mysteriously" disappear, then you have record and evidence of their existence
4. Give your attorney any documents that you fear will be lost or taken
5. Put all valuables in a secure location that your spouse cannot get to

Real Life Experience: *Caroline C.*
Age 33, Married, One Child
Housewife; Taos, New Mexico

"I married a man substantially older than me. He's very shrewd. He and his partner have done quite well. Before we got married, he treated me like a princess. Now he treats me like a possession. I've had enough. I hope he doesn't try to screw me like another one of his business deals."

Voodoo Tip 11.2

LOCATE HIDDEN ASSETS

Quite often, a spouse attempts to hide assets or income. Your attorney should know how to discover these deceptive practices. For example, a spouse who tries to hide income may have more expenses than the income that he is claiming. A review of these expenses may reveal to the court that your spouse has not been honest. You should assist your lawyer by suggesting the following events:

1. Look for assets in the names of others or fictitious names
2. Tell your lawyer of your spouse's prior and present attempts to hide property and/or cheat others
3. Through proper discovery practices such as issuing subpoenas and taking depositions, your attorney may find these hidden assets or income and
4. Have a discussion with your attorney about your concerns that your spouse has hidden assets or income

Voodoo Tip 11.3

DIVIDE ALL PROPERTY AND DEBTS INTO CATEGORIES

Your lawyer will be able to assist protecting and maximizing your property interests after you provide him with a comprehensive list which is divided into meaningful categories. When you list assets into categories, do not concern yourself with whether you think that the item is "separate," "community," or any other legal description. Leave that task to your competent attorney. At this time, do not concern yourself with whether or not your spouse is claiming property as being "separate," "marital," or "community." The most important task for you to accomplish is to divide the assets into the following categories:

1. Property owned by you prior to the marriage
2. Property owned by your spouse prior to the marriage
3. Property solely held in your name that was acquired after the marriage (but before the filing of the divorce petition/complaint)
4. Property solely held in your spouse's name that was acquired after the marriage (but before the filing of the divorce petition/complaint)
5. Property items held jointly by you and your spouse that were purchased after marriage (but before the filing of the divorce petition/complaint)
6. Property acquired by you after the filing of the divorce petition/complaint
7. Property acquired by your spouse after the filing of the divorce petition/complaint
8. Property acquired jointly by you and your spouse after the filing of the divorce petition/complaint
9. Contributions that you made to the acquisition or improvement of property owned in the name of your spouse
10. Contributions that you made to the acquisition or improvement of property owned in the name of both you and your spouse
11. Debt created by you prior to the marriage
12. Debt created by your spouse prior to the marriage
13. Debt that was incurred in your name alone that was created after the marriage
14. Debt that was incurred in your spouse's name alone that was created after the marriage
15. Debt created in your name as well as the name of your spouse that was created after the marriage
16. Debt created by you after the filing of the divorce petition/complaint
17. Debt created by your spouse after the filing of the divorce petition/complaint

18. Debt created by both you and your spouse after the filing of the divorce petition/complaint

Dividing assets and liabilities into the above categories is a painstaking and tedious task, yet your efforts will provide very helpful information for your attorney's use. Your efforts will be rewarded during the litigation in many ways, including but not limited to, lowering your attorney fees.

Don't forget to list anticipated tax refunds and previously paid utility deposits.

Voodoo Tip 11.4

PROVIDE VALUES FOR EACH PIECE OF PROPERTY

For each asset that you listed and categorized, provide your attorney the known cost of each asset, along with the date (approximate date) of purchase/acquisition. If you do not know the cost or value when acquired, simply indicate your lack of knowledge regarding that asset.

Additionally, provide your attorney with the fair market value of each item at the time of your marriage and/or at the present.

> **Real Life Experience:** *Gretchen O.*
> Age 35, Married, One Child
> Teacher; Kennebunkport, Maine
>
> *"Forrest and I have a very large stamp collection. How do I place a value on that?"*

Voodoo Tip 11.5

PROVIDE/SEEK APPRAISALS AND FINANCIAL STATEMENTS

Provide your attorney with a copy of any and all written valuations and/or appraisals of any asset. Your attorney may request further valuations/appraisals of certain items. Typical appraisals value the following:

1. Real Estate
2. Jewelry
3. Furniture
4. Artwork
5. Vehicles

For automobile valuations, refer to the Kelley Blue Book and the Kelley Blue Book Older Car Guides.

Also acquire statements from financial institutions which are valuable sources of information regarding the value of a stock and/or account at a particular point in time.

Naturally, each spouse will attempt to associate as little value as possible with each asset that he wishes to keep and will associate the highest value possible with each asset that he anticipates will be retained or attributed to the other spouse. The benefit of valuation lies in the art of finding the most favorable and persuasive appaiser(s). Speak to your attorney about his contacts and experiences with various appraisers.

When an appraisal is required and funds are tight, it may be beneficial to recommend that the parties split or pay a proportionate share for a single unbiased appraiser.

> **Real Life Experience:** *Amy M.*
> Age 21, Married, No Children
> Student; Cleveland, Ohio
>
> *"I have a shoe box full of unpaid bills."*

Voodoo Tip 11.6

PROVIDE VALUES FOR EACH DEBT

Provide a list of all debt, including the following:

1. The date the debt was created
2. The original amount of the debt
3. The amount/value of each debt at the date of marriage
4. The amount/value of each debt on the date of the filing of the divorce petition/complaint

Voodoo Tip 11.7

QUESTIONS THAT YOU SHOULD ANSWER REGARDLESS OF WHERE YOU LIVE OR WHERE THE PROPERTY IS LOCATED

1. Identify the asset/property
2. State the date acquired
3. State how it was acquired (e.g., gift, inheritance, purchase, etc.)
4. State who acquired it
5. State its value at the following times:
   a. On the date acquired
   b. On the date of your marriage

c. On the date sold
   d. On the date of the divorce
   e. On the date of trial
6. State whether there have been any enhancements or damage to item since acquisition
7. State the names of persons if the asset is registered, titled, or otherwise associated with a particular person
8. State whether the property is described as separate or otherwise based on a prenuptial or postnuptial agreement

> **Real Life Experience:** *Lindsay F.*
> *Age 64, Married, Two Adult Children*
> *Retired; Nashville, Tennessee*
>
> *"My husband and I have retired. That's our sole source of income. How can I insure that I get my fair share of the retirement plan?"*

Voodoo Tip 11.8

GET ALL RETIREMENT PLAN INFORMATION

In order to properly handle a property settlement or decree, your lawyer and the court need information about each spouse's retirement plans. According to the Employee Retirement Income Security Act (ERISA), information regarding pension plans and trusts should be made available to the plan participants and designated beneficiaries.

Various ERISA plans include defined benefit plans, defined contribution plans, profit sharing plans, stock bonus plans, stock option plans, Tax Reform Act stock plans, savings plans, incentive plans, thrift plans, and other plans. With this information, your attorney may negotiate a property settlement favorable to your needs.

Most plans have administrators who manage the retirement funds. The retirement plans of either spouse may have certain requirements necessary to alter the scheduled payments and/or recipients of the retirement funds. Your lawyer should seek an order, known as a qualified domestic relations order (QDRO), which is an order from the court instructing the retirement plan administrator to handle the plan in a particular manner. The QDRO should have the necessary language required by the retirement plan administrator.

> **Real Life Experience:** *John V.*
> Age 39, Married, Two Children
> Carpenter; Vicksburg, Mississippi
>
> *"I'm covered on my wife's HMO."*

Voodoo Tip 11.9

LOOK AT YOUR INSURANCE NEEDS BEFORE YOU DIVORCE

Upon a divorce decree, your medical insurance coverage may be affected.

Prior to the divorce, make arrangements to insure that you and your children shall remain covered. Generally, dependent children can remain on a policy after a divorce decree. Yet the non-employee spouse generally will be dropped from the policy unless other provisions are made.

Pursuant to federal law, a non-employee former spouse may remain on the employee spouse's medical insurance through the payment of additional premiums through COBRA. COBRA allows the non-employee former spouse to be maintained on the health insurance policy for up to three years after the divorce decree. Ask your attorney how to take advantage of the benefits provided by COBRA.

Additionally, a vindictive spouse may attempt to cancel the other spouse's medical and dental insurance coverage prior to the judgment of divorce. Ask your attorney to verify medical and dental insurance coverage and request that he file a restraining order that the insurance be maintained until the divorce is finalized.

Likewise, a spouse may attempt to change the life insurance beneficiaries prior to a divorce decree. Your attorney should request that the existing life insurance be maintained and the designated beneficiaries remain unchanged at the same coverage amount. Your attorney may request notification of any beneficiary change or failure to pay the premium.

Voodoo Tip 11.10

KNOW THE TAX CONSEQUENCES OF ANY TRANSACTION

There are many tax consequences associated with the transfer of property. Please refer to the Number 15 and consult a tax advisor regarding the ramifications of your divorce proceedings.

One notable present tax consequence is as follows:

If both spouses own a house titled in both of their names and one spouse transfers his interest in the house to the other spouse as part of a property settlement, then the spouse (recipient spouse) who receives the full title to the house and later sells the house, will have taxable capital gains in the amount of the difference of the original purchase price of the house and the ultimate sale price of the house. You may wish to have the potential capital gains tax taken into consideration in your negotiations associated with any property settlement.

> **Real Life Experience:** *Thomas C.*
> Age 37, Married, One Child
> Professional Photographer
> Laguna Beach, California
>
> *"She won't drop the bogus sexual abuse charges unless I give her the house free and clear."*

BLACKMAIL FOR GAIN OF PROPERTY RIGHTS

As with issues of child support and alimony, refrain from giving into a spouse's threats to challenge custody or other issues unless you concede your property rights. Report any such threats to your attorney. Any evidence of these threats should be tendered to your lawyer.

> **Real Life Experience:** *Vicki T.*
> Age 28, Married, One Child
> Retail Sales Associate; Tucson, Arizona
>
> *"I have no idea what property is considered 'community' and what is 'separate.'"*

Voodoo Tip 11.11

DON'T GET HUNG UP ON DEFINITIONS OF PROPERTY

Many books go into lengthy discussions of how you should legally define an asset or debt. These books often fail to emphasize the importance of data gathering and categorization as set forth above. Don't get caught up in the trap of trying to "define" whether certain property is "separate," "marital," or "community." After you have accomplished the above tasks, then you should have a discussion with your attorney as to the legal interpretation ("definition") of each asset and debt. Ultimately this is a job for your attorney; that's what you pay him for. Although there is a natural tendency for you to try to "define" each asset and debt, you have not been trained to interpret the legal description of assets. Let your lawyer do his job. Ask him to provide you with his interpretation of how each asset and debt likely will be categorized by the court as well as the ramifications of such interpretations.

WAYS TO DIVIDE PROPERTY

Each state has a slightly different way to divide property of a divorcing couple.

The three basic ways that states divide assets are as follows:

1. Equitable distribution
2. Community property
3. Common law

EQUITABLE DISTRIBUTION

Equitable distribution is the most common means of property division. Under the equitable distribution basis, property is divided and/or distributed based on concepts of fairness and equity. Many lawyers casually refer to spouses as if they were partners in a business endeavor.

EQUITABLE DISTRIBUTION STATES

Alabama	Maine	Oklahoma
Alaska	Maryland	Oregon
Arkansas	Massachusetts	Pennsylvania
Colorado	Michigan	Rhode Island
Connecticut	Minnesota	South Carolina
Delaware	Missouri	South Dakota
Florida	Montana	Tennessee
Georgia	Nebraska	Utah
Hawaii	New Hampshire	Vermont
Illinois	New Jersey	Virginia
Indiana	New York	Virgin Islands
Iowa	North Carolina	Washington D.C.
Kansas	North Dakota	West Virginia
Kentucky	Ohio	Wyoming

COMMUNITY PROPERTY STATES

Community property states acknowledge a general joint interest in property acquired during the marriage. Community property laws provide exceptions for property that was acquired with proceeds of separate property and as well as with property excluded by valid prenuptial or postnuptial agreements.

In general, separate property is defined as any property owned prior to the marriage, property acquired by inheritance, or by marital contract.

In evaluating which spouse gets certain marital property, courts may review the following:

1. The duration of the marriage
2. The respective age, health, skills, and abilities of each spouse
3. The standard of living of each party
4. The financial needs of each spouse
5. The financial resources of each spouse
6. The separate and postmarital property of each spouse
7. Each spouse's contribution to the acquisition and/or improvement of the marital or separate property
8. Each spouse's contribution to the education and/or increased earning capacity of the other spouse
9. Tax consequences for each party
10. The need of the custodial parent to remain in family home with minor children
11. Any award of alimony and/or child support
12. The liquidity of property
13. The ability of a spouse to operate a "family business"
14. The anticipated wasteful dissipation of property by a party
15. The potential loss or gain of inheritance and pension rights of a spouse upon divorce
16. Individual gifts/donations to a party
17. Other considerations deemed relevant by the court

COMMUNITY PROPERTY STATES

Arizona	Puerto Rico	Washington
California	Nevada	Wisconsin
Idaho	New Mexico	
Louisiana	Texas	

STATE THAT DISTRIBUTES BY TITLE ("COMMON LAW")

Mississippi

Mississippi is the sole state that distributes property on the basis of whose name is on the title or registration of an asset. The state does not formally recognize the property value associated with homemaking and contributions to increased earnings capacity associated with the obtainment of professional degrees. Only that property that is jointly owned by both spouses can be divided by the court.

> **Real Life Experience:** *Howard N.*
> Age 55, Married, Two Adult Children
> Mechanic; Pueblo, Colorado
>
> *"Evelyn insists on keeping our lawn furniture. There's no way I'm going to let her have it!"*

Voodoo Tip 11.12

DON'T FIGHT OVER THE "TOASTER"

(Do not pay your lawyer more than what it's worth!)

It is remarkable how many people will spend hundreds or thousands of dollars in legal fees to fight over items that have nominal or no financial value at all. Although it may be worth a fight over sentimental property, generally a cost benefit analysis should be made. Don't fight over that toaster!

> **Real Life Experience:** *Jeb L.*
> Age 26, Divorced, No Children
> Clothing Sales Associate
> Minneapolis, Minnesota
>
> *"We agreed that I would get the Grand Prix. It's presently titled in her name."*

Voodoo Tip 11.13

HAVE ALL ASSETS THAT ARE DECREED TO YOU BE PLACED IN YOUR NAME

Have your attorney file all necessary documents (certificates of title, etc.) into the proper county/parish registry.

Summary of Voodoo Tips from Number 11

PROPERTY DIVISION

Voodoo Tip 11.1   Protect your property.

Voodoo Tip 11.2   Locate hidden assets.

Voodoo Tip 11.3   Divide all property and debts into categories.

Voodoo Tip 11.4   Provide values for each piece of property.

Voodoo Tip 11.5   Provide/seek appraisals and financial statements.

Voodoo Tip 11.6   Provide values for each debt.

Voodoo Tip 11.7   Questions that you should answer regardless of where you live or where the property is located.

Voodoo Tip 11.8   Get all retirement plan information.

Voodoo Tip 11.9   Look at your insurance needs before you divorce.

Voodoo Tip 11.10   Know the tax consequences of any transaction.

Voodoo Tip 11.11   Don't get hung up on definitions of property.

Voodoo Tip 11.12   Don't fight over the "toaster." (Do not pay your lawyer more than what it's worth.)

Voodoo Tip 11.13   Have all assets that are decreed to you be placed in your name and possession.

VOODOO SPELL TO GET PROPERTY

Get your kids and pets. Go to your bank. Take money out of any joint bank accounts. Use your joint credit cards to your full advantage. Stay in house (unless abuse exists). Keep your Voodoo Divorce Book in a safe place. Inventory and safeguard your possessions. Ask your lawyer to file requests for protective orders. Provide your attorney with an inventory of your assets and liabilities.

Light a red candle. Put the following ingredients in your gris-gris bag: Aloe, Angelica, Blood Root, Boldo Leaves, Cinquefoil, Cinnamon, Cowslip, Cypress, Lavender, and Orris Root.

Place a picture of your spouse and black mustard seed under your front door mat. You will start to feel the security that comes from being "possessed."

VOODOO INGREDIENT NUMBER 12

Prenuptial and Postnuptial Agreements

> **Real Life Experience:** *Lauren F.*
> Age 43, Married, No Children
> Office Manager, Metairie, Louisiana
>
> *"My husband is a doctor. He said he wouldn't marry me unless I signed a prenuptial agreement. At first, I resisted, but I finally gave in. Although I understand why he asked me to sign one, somewhere deep in my psyche I feel cheated."*

WHAT IS A PRENUPTIAL AGREEMENT?

A prenuptial agreement is a contract entered by the future bride and groom prior to the marriage. The contracting parties attempt to bind various aspects regarding money and property in the event of a divorce. Remember that between forty three (43%) to fifty (50%) of all people who enter into a marriage get a divorce.

A major criticism about prenuptial agreements is that it sets up the marriage for failure and that it creates an expectation of divorce.

> **Real Life Experience:** *Jennifer T.*
> Age 32, Single
> Contemplating Marriage, No Children
> Advertising Agent; Boca Raton, Florida
>
> *"My fiancé gave me a prenuptial agreement to review and sign. I'm not going to sign it, but I made an appointment with an attorney so that I can tell my boyfriend that the lawyer recommended that I not sign it."*

Voodoo Tip 12.1

BLAME YOUR LAWYER

In order to defeat your honey bun's complaints about entering into a prenuptial agreement, be honest or blame it on your lawyer.

> **Real Life Experience:** *Tiffany L.*
> Age 38, Married
> One Child from Previous Marriage
> Housewife; Palm Springs, California
>
> "When I married my current husband, I signed a prenuptial agreement. Things aren't working out. He wants to control my every move. If I leave, I leave with nothing. Things would be different if I could challenge the prenuptial."

ARE PRENUPTIAL AGREEMENTS ENFORCEABLE?

Whether a prenuptial agreement is enforceable is the most common question asked about these agreements. The answer is . . . It depends!

1. Does the agreement violate the state law or public policy?
2. Did the parties in good faith enter into a fair agreement being fully informed and of their own free will?

> **Real Life Experience:** *Kyle S.*
> Age 53, Divorced Twice
> Contemplating Third Marriage
> Three Children From Prior Marriages
> Attorney; Boston, Massachusetts
>
> "I can't tell you how much trouble it was to divorce my former wives. It cost me a fortune. This past year, I've finally found someone special that I want to spend the rest of my life with. But being in love doesn't mean you have to be stupid. My attorney has drafted a prenuptial agreement. I sure wish I had one for each of my other marriages!"

Voodoo Tip 12.2

INCREASE YOUR CHANCES OF HAVING AN ENFORCABLE PRENUPTIAL AGREEMENT

In order to increase your chances that a court of law will enforce your prenuptial agreement, follow these steps:

1. The future bride and groom should have their own separate attorneys.

2. The prenuptial agreement should not be signed immediately prior to the wedding. A party might later claim that they signed under duress and coercion. Hence, both parties should sign the agreement as early as possible before the date of the wedding ceremony.
3. Fully disclose your wealth, including all assets and debts. It's best to list and specifically identify as many assets and liabilities as possible.
4. The prenuptial agreement should contain written language that the legal rights have been explained to both parties.
5. Videotape the ceremony of signing the prenuptial agreement which helps show that the other party entered the agreement without correction or duress.

> **Real Life Experience:** *Manny D.*
> Age 49, Divorced, Two Children
> Entrepreneur/Real Estate Developer
> Lake Tahoe, Nevada
>
> *"Shall I disclose the full extent of my wealth to my fiancé?"*

Voodoo Tip 12.3

OVERESTIMATE YOUR WORTH WHEN DISCLOSING YOUR WEALTH

> **Real Life Experience:** *Patrick S.*
> Age 35, Single, Contemplating Marriage
> Architect; New Haven, Connecticut
>
> *"I want to work with my attorney to design an agreement that works totally in my favor."*

Voodoo Tip 12.4

PRENUPTIAL CLAUSES THAT ARE FROWNED UPON

Here are some additional tips to keep in mind when creating a prenuptial agreement:

1. Don't add clauses that would clearly be unenforceable such as strict agreements on custody and/or child support. Judges are hesitant to enforce agreements that restrict children's rights.
2. Don't add clauses that would restrict the other spouse's right to defend himself. This might be construed as a clause that would encourage or facilitate divorce.

3. Be careful to add clauses that would provide for a gross inequity in the distribution of property.

Additionally, ask your attorney if any of the prenuptial agreement clauses may be construed as being against the state's public policy.

> **Real Life Experience:** *Deborah D.*
> Age 52, Married, One Adult Child
> Housewife; Manhattan, New York
>
> *"Can I beat this unfair prenuptial agreement?"*

Voodoo Tip 12.5

HOW TO DEFEAT A PRENUPTIAL AGREEMENT

In order to successfully argue to a judge that he should render the agreement unenforceable, attack the following potential flaws in the contract:

- Refer to state laws that the agreement violates
- Refer to public policy that the agreement violates (i.e., encouraging divorce)
- Refer to the unfair nature of the agreement
- Refer to the other party's lack of good faith
- Refer to any and all duress or coercion that you experienced before or at the time of signing
- Refer to any influences of alcohol or drugs that you may have been under the influence of at the time of signing
- Refer to any illnesses at the time of signing
- Refer to your tender age at the time of signing
- Refer to any mental illness that you experienced at the time of signing
- Refer to the fact that the agreement was signed immediately prior to the wedding ceremony
- Refer to the lack of witnesses to the signing of the contract
- Refer to the lack of full disclosure of assets, liabilities and wealth at the time of signing
- Refer to the fact that you did not create the document
- Refer to oral promises and/or comments made before or at the time of signing that are not reflected in the agreement

Consult your attorney for other defects in the creation or execution of the agreement that might make the agreement or a part thereof unenforceable.

> **Real Life Experience:** *Jason T.*
> Age 42, Married, Three Children
> Dentist; Shreveport, Louisiana
>
> *"My wife has created a severe debt problem. I wish I had entered into a prenuptial agreement before the marriage, but now it's too late. Can I enter into a similar type of agreement now?"*

WHAT ARE POSTNUPTIAL AGREEMENTS?

Postnuptial agreements are agreements that are similar to prenuptial agreements; however, they are executed some time after the marriage ceremony. In most states, in order to enter into a postnuptial agreement, a court must formally approve the agreement.

The enforceability and/or impeachability of the agreement are dependent upon similar inquiries as referred to for prenuptial agreements.

Voodoo Tip 12.6

BEFORE ENTERING INTO ANY PRENUPTIAL OR POST-NUPTIAL AGREEMENT, CONSULT A LAWYER WHO HAS EXTENSIVE EXPERIENCE IN DRAFTING AND/OR LITIGATING THE VALIDITY OF THESE AGREEMENTS

Summary of Voodoo Tips from Number 12

PRENUPTIAL AND POSTNUPTIAL AGREEMENTS

Voodoo Tip 12.1	Blame your lawyer.
Voodoo Tip 12.2	Increase your chances of having an enforceable. prenuptial agreement.
Voodoo Tip 12.3	Overestimate your worth when disclosing your wealth.
Voodoo Tip 12.4	Prenuptial clauses that are frowned upon.
Voodoo Tip 12.5	How to defeat a prenuptial agreement.
Voodoo Tip 12.6	Before entering into any prenuptial or postnuptial agreement, consult a lawyer who has extensive experience in drafting and/or litigating the validity of these agreements.

**VOODOO SPELL
TO GET YOUR FUTURE SPOUSE TO SIGN
A PRENUPTIAL AGREEMENT**

Light purple and yellow candles. With red paint, put your fiancee's name on a horseshoe. Place the horseshoe on the drafted agreement. Put the following ingredients in your red flannel gris-gris bag: Ague Root, Alfalfa, Allspice, Almond, Ash Tree Leaves, Aspen, Bayberry, Blood Root, Buckwheat, Catnip, Frankincense, Goat's Leaves, Irish Moss, Lucky Hand Root, Marigold, Mint, and Pine.

VOODOO INGREDIENT NUMBER 13

Don't Stand for Abuse or Being Falsely Accused of Abuse

> **Real Life Experience:** *Missy V.*
> Age 33, Deceased, Two Children
> Springfield, Illinois
>
> NO QUOTE—*She was killed by her husband.*

Quick Facts:

Experts estimate each year approximately 3 to 10 million children are impacted by domestic violence. (American Bar Association, Division of Media Relations and Public Affairs; Straus, M.A. *Children as Witnesses to Marital Violence: A Risk Factor for Lifelong Problems Nationally Representative Sample of American Men and Women*, Paper presented September 1991, Washington, D.C.); B.E. Carlson, *Children's Observations of Interparental Violence, in Battered Women and Their Families* 147–167 (A.R. Roberts ed., 1984).

Law enforcement officers spend approximately one-third of their time responding to domestic violence complaints. Annually, over one million women seek medical assistance as a result of injuries caused by domestic battery. (U.S. Department of Health and Human Services, 1991; Ohio Domestic Violence Network)

In 1996, of the 3.5 million cases of alleged child abuse reported to child protection agencies, investigators verified that 1,250,000 children had been neglected and/or abused. Approximately 16 out of every 1,000 children are verified victims of abuse. Of these abused children, 26 percent of the children were physically abused, 15 percent were sexually abused, 45 percent were neglected, and 3 percent endured emotional abuse. The remaining 12 percent of the abused children encountered other abuse or abandonment. Unfortunately, we have no idea how many cases of neglect and abuse go unreported. Most abuse occurs at home.[1]

The Child Protection Services Agencies have confirmed approximately 2,000 annual fatalities related to child abuse and neglect. In seems almost inconceivable that nearly five or six children perish each day from abuse or neglect.

Abuse can take three basic forms:

1. *Harassment*—This abuse takes the form of verbal and non-verbal acts that are intended to emotionally hurt, demean, and ridicule the other person;
2. *Physical Abuse*—This abuse involves acts of physical contact intended to create fear, pain and/or injury to the other person; and
3. *Sexual Abuse*—This abuse involves acts of unconsenting sexual behavior often accompanied by the threat of force or greater emotional pain. Sexual abuse also can take the form of sexual demands, violence, and fetishes.

The most common trait of someone who is being abused is that he mistakenly believes that the abuser will change and ultimately cease the abuse. Unfortunately, this is rarely the case without significant legal and mental health intervention. The abuser's primary goal is to control, manipulate, and have power over the victim.

Abuse is behavior used to control or dominate the other person by means of threats, manipulation, physical and/or sexual assaults. The abuser creates hurtful feelings of fear, insecurity, helplessness, guilt, paranoia, rejection, isolation, humiliation, ridicule, shame, denial, and/or depression. The abuse is often accompanied by chemical and/or financial dependency. A major hurdle that you must overcome is the fear of the abuser's retaliation.

---

1. American Bar Association, Division of Media Relations and Public Affairs; *Third National Incidence Study of Child Abuse and Neglect, Executive Summary*, U.S. Department of Health and Human Services, September 1996; and *Child Maltreatment 1994: Reports from the States to the National Center on Child Abuse and Neglect*, U.S. Department of Health and Human Services, 1996.

Quick Fact: According to the United States Department of Justice, although victims of abuse can be either men or women, approximately ninety-five (95%) percent of reported abuse victims are women. The pervasiveness of abuse in our society is appalling, with most cases remaining unreported. Refer to the Appendix (Voodoo Spice Number 25) for statistics regarding child abuse.

Real Life Experience: *Georgia C.*

Age 32, Married, Three Children
Housewife; Newport, Rhode Island

"I don't know what to do. I've never cared for the children all by myself. Jay has always been there to help. But now I'm afraid that the kids are in danger too."

The first rule to follow if you or your children are being abused is to apply the following tip:

Voodoo Tip 13.1

IMMEDIATELY PROTECT YOUR CHILDREN AND YOURSELF!

The safest way to protect your children and yourself is to flee to a safe location. If that is not possible, immediately call the police and/or your lawyer.

The safest action is to:

1. Flee with your children
2. Call the police
3. Call your attorney

Voodoo Tip 13.2

FLEE

To flee is not an act of cowardice; it is usually the most prudent thing for you to do. Be sure to keep your location a secret from your abusive spouse.

> **Real Life Experience:** *Sheila W.*
> Age 27, Married, No Children
> Unemployed; Salt Lake City, Utah
>
> *"If I leave the apartment, I have no place to live."*

Voodoo Tip 13.3

WHERE TO GO

A significant problem of most people being abused by their spouse is that they have no planned destination in the event that abuse or a threat of abuse occurs.

Consider temporary housing with the following:

1. Other family members
2. Friends
3. Shelters for Battered Women (or Men)
4. Hospitals
5. YMCA or YWCA
6. Hotels/Motels
7. New Apartments
8. Community Centers
9. Churches
10. Other Shelters and/or
11. Your own house or apartment after it is secured and/or restraining orders or peace bonds have been placed against the abuser

Voodoo Tip 13.4

GO TO A BATTERED WOMEN'S SHELTER OR A RAPE CRISIS CENTER

Use the local yellow pages to find the hospitals, clinics, and treatment programs that are available in your community. There are over one thousand battered women's shelters across the country. The yellow pages usually lists these services under the following categories:

"Social Services"
"Shelters"
"Crisis Intervention Services"
"Support Groups"
"Counseling"
"Women's Services"

Should you be unsuccessful in finding a battered women's shelter or rape crisis center through the telephone directory or directory assistance, then call the National Domestic Violence Hotline at the following number:

1-800-799-SAFE.

This Hotline is answered twenty-four hours a day, seven days a week, including holidays. They can refer you to shelters in your community. For additional information regarding protecting yourself and your family from abuse, call the National Coalition Against Domestic Violence at the following number:

(303) 839-1852.

Many of these shelters will allow you to stay there for up to one or two months.

If your child is being abused, telephone the National Child Abuse Hotline at the following number:

1-800-422-4453.

Voodoo Tip 13.5

REFER TO THE SHELTERS FOUND IN APPENDIX OF THIS BOOK

For a quick listing of some shelters in the country's major metropolitan areas, refer to the Appendix (Voodoo Spice Number 26: Directory of Violence and Abuse Support Groups).

Real Life Experience: *Susan E.*
Age 41, Married, One Child
Travel Agent; New Rochelle, New York

"Cindy told me that her daddy is playing with her 'pee-pee.' I confronted him with this and he angrily denied it. I'm taking her to her pediatrician tomorrow. I pray to God it's not true."

Voodoo Tip 13.6

IN CASES OF SEXUAL OR PHYSICAL ABUSE

Go to the hospital and/or rape crisis center. If you suspect that your children have been physically or sexually abused, call the child protection agency in your community.

> **Real Life Experience:** Rhonda R.
>
> Age 36, Married, Two Children
> Waitress; Philadelphia, Pennsylvania
>
> *"For the last few years, he's much more physically and sexually aggressive. When he thinks I'm not home, I catch him watching porn video tapes while he masturbates. He makes me do things that I don't want to do. If I don't, he hits me. He hurts me. He started sodomizing me a couple of months ago. If I don't do what he wants, he'll leave me. He's normally good to me, but I can't stand this."*

Voodoo Tip 13.7

SPOUSAL RAPE

The primeval notion that a husband, while married, cannot rape his own wife is coming to an end. Many states have implemented criminal laws that create crimes should one spouse force the other into non-consensual sexual acts. Should this occur, contact the police or a rape crisis center.

Voodoo Tip 13.8

LOVE AND RESPECT YOURSELF

A common trait of persons subjected to a long history of abuse is that they have learned to become helpless against the abuse. Continual degradation by the abuser creates learned helplessness and insecurity in the victim. The victim believes that she or he cannot predict the behavior of the abuser and the victim feels a huge sense of having no control. You must understand that all violence is unacceptable. You are not to blame for the abuse, you are valuable and deserve to love and respect yourself.

Voodoo Tip 13.9

LEAVE THE HOUSE OR GET A LAWYER TO KEEP SPOUSE OUT OF HOUSE

State laws have been created that legally will force an abuser out of the house or apartment in which you live. You should contact your lawyer about the details necessary to accomplish these goals.

Voodoo Tip 13.10

GET *EX PARTE* ORDERS AND/OR A PEACE BOND

Temporary court orders can assist you in most abusive situations. These orders can address the victim's safety at home, work, school, and/or any other location that the victim may be. Such orders may also prohibit telephone threats of intimidation.

A peace bond is a court order that requires the abuser to put up money that will be forfeited to the court if the abuser violates the order.

Although your spouse may not have harassed you during your marriage, it is remarkable the acts of harassment and abuse that occur after one files for a divorce. Like Dr. Jeckle and Mr. Hyde, your once passive spouse may become a dangerous monster when issues regarding custody and money are raised. When in doubt, get a protective order against such potential harassment, stalking, violence, and/or abuse.

Refer to Number 5 on *Ex Parte* Relief.

> **Real Life Experience:** *Mary A.*
> Age 32, Married, One Child
> Graphic Artist; Bethany Beach, Delaware
>
> *"My lawyer got a restraining order so that Bret can't come by the house or my work. I feel better, but a piece of paper won't stop him."*

Voodoo Tip 13.11

CHANGE LOCKS AND ALARM CODES

Should you get the sole possession of your residence, change the locks and alarm codes. If you don't have an alarm, consider getting one. Many alarm companies offer personal alarm devices that you can wear around your neck. Once you press the button, you can immediately summon the police.

Also consider adding dead bolts, garage door locks, as well as locks to your fuse box.

Voodoo Tip 13.12

GET EXTRA KEYS TO YOUR HOUSE AND CAR

As a measure of additional control, an abuser may take all of the keys to your house or car. In order to prevent the abuser's desired result, have additional copies of your keys made and put them in a secure location outside of the abuser's reach. Also consider keeping another set of keys in your wallet or purse.

> **Real Life Experience:**   *Nat L.*
> Age 44, Married, One Child
> Veterinarian; Chesapeake, Virginia
>
> *"When she pops her pills and drinks, she gets argumentative and violent. Last night, she didn't like what I brought to eat and she stabbed me with a fork."*

Voodoo Tip 13.13

CALL THE POLICE AND GET A POLICE REPORT

In many states, if you call the police as a result of your spouse striking you, the police officers shall have no alternative but to take your spouse to jail. Call 911 or your local police telephone number.

Voodoo Tip 13.14

GET EVIDENCE OF YOUR ABUSE

1. Get a police report or incident number:
   Don't forget to ask the police officer to write a police report. Get the incident number from the police officer, then later you or your attorney can get the police report. This can be a valuable tool in your divorce case.
2. Take photographs of any bruises, scratches, and cuts.
3. Go to a doctor and/or hospital.
   Ask for your medical, psychological, and/or psychiatric records.
4. Get audio or video tapes.
5. Collect all pieces of physical evidence of the abuse including broken dishes, torn articles of clothing, weapons, and the like.
6. Get witnesses' names, addresses and telephone numbers.

> **Real Life Experience:** *Francis G.*
> Age 25, Married, One Child
> Nurse's Aid; Jackson Hole, Wyoming
>
> *"I don't want him around my little girl when he drinks. His drinking has gotten so bad that he often passes out. He also drives drunk. I'm scared to death that he's going to put Beth in the car when he's been drinking."*

Voodoo Tip 13.15

REQUEST TERMINATED OR SUPERVISED VISITATION OF YOUR SPOUSE

Voodoo Tip 13.16

SAVE MONEY FOR EMERGENCY FUND

> **Real Life Experience:** *Beth T.*
> Age 38, Married, Three Children
> Paralegal; Montgomery, Alabama
>
> *"We left him a few days ago. I'm not going to let him hit me anymore."*

Voodoo Tip 13.17

TALK WITH YOUR CHILDREN

Children can be affected by the abuse of a parent from the time the child is a fetus until he or she dies of old age. If abuse occurs, tell the children that they are not to blame themselves for the abuse. Tell them that you will protect them and encourage them to talk about their concerns. The generation cycle of abuse must stop through your courage to end the abuse and seek appropriate counseling.

> **Real Life Experience:** *Helen F.*
> Age 31, Married, Two Children
> Housewife; Fort Worth, Texas
>
> *"When the children get out of line, Cory uses his belt. Sometimes the spankings cause welts."*

Voodoo Tip 13.18

PREVENT EXCESSIVE CORPOREAL PUNISHMENT BY YOUR SPOUSE

Many parents take the disciplining of a child to an extreme that borders on and/or crosses the line of abuse. Should your spouse use excessive force or extremely unorthodox measures to discipline the children, consider getting a court order against this excessive punishment. If the extreme corporeal punishment continues, consider the other measures discussed in this chapter.

Voodoo Tip 13.19

LIST EMERGENCY TELEPHONE NUMBERS AND ADDRESSES

Keep an list of telephone numbers to use in the case of an emergency. Keep the telephone numbers in a near and secure place.

> **Real Life Experience:** *Troy H.*
> Age 46, Divorced, No Children
> Optician; Cedar Springs, Iowa
>
> *"I divorced Vicky in December. She won't leave me alone. I constantly see her parked outside of the condo. She also leaves messages on my answering machine and leaves me notes saying that she will never let me go. Last month, I came home with a date and Vicky was sitting at my front door at one o'clock in the morning."*

Voodoo Tip 13.20

STOP THE STALKER

Stalking is an obsessive pattern of behavior, primarily motivated by passion, anger and/or rejection, intended to get the attention of and/or frighten the victim. Most states have implemented anti-stalking laws that provide potentially harsh criminal penalties against the stalker.

Unfortunately, laws, police and courts cannot guarantee protection against a stalker. Avoiding contact with the stalker is your safest plan of action. You also may take self-defense classes and/or learn to use defensive weapons such as mace, pepper spray, and/or a whistle.

Voodoo Tip 13.21

TAKE VALUABLES AND SENTIMENTAL ITEMS

Should you have the time to accumulate your valuable and sentimental items, do so. Once you leave or otherwise seek help, the abuser may hide, sell or destroy these items out of revenge and anger.

Voodoo Tip 13.22

TAKE YOUR IMPORTANT RECORDS

If you leave the abuser, take all the important records that you can find. A list of the types of documents to look for can be found Number 4 of this book.

> **Real Life Experience:** *Connie R.*
>
> Age 41, Married, One Child
> Sales Associate; Tulsa, Oklahoma
>
> *"If he hits me again, I'll kill the son of a bitch!"*

Voodoo Tip 13.23

DO NOT TAKE THE LAW INTO YOUR OWN HANDS

Do not shoot the abuser unless it is clearly in self defense and you are in legitimate and reasonable fear of severe bodily harm or death. The abuser is not worth going to prison over. Get the police involved and walk away.

> **Real Life Experience:** *Renée S.*
> Age 25, Married, Two Children
> Graduate Student; Baltimore, Maryland
>
> *"My attorney got restraining orders against Harris. He is not supposed to be around the kids."*

Voodoo Tip 13.24

ALERT WORK, SCHOOLS, AND DAY-CARE CENTERS

Your spouse may attempt to harass you at work. Alert your boss, the receptionist and the building security of any potential problems.

Your spouse also may attempt to take your children out of their school or day-care facility. Have your lawyer get an order prohibiting your spouse from contacting your children at school and from taking the children away from the school or day-care center. Once you have this order, provide the principal, pertinent teachers, and day-care providers with a certified copy of the order instructing them to call you and the police should your spouse attempt to violate the order.

> **Real Life Experience:** *Tony A.*
> Age 43, Divorced, Two Children
> Engineer; Dover, New Hampshire
>
> *"She called child protection claiming that my son was returned from visitation with bruises on his arms and back. This is absolutely absurd. My son gets scrapes and scratches just like any other active boy. She's trying to keep my children from me."*

Voodoo Tip 13.25

DEFENDING A FALSE ALLEGATION

A despicable act that is becoming more prevalent in divorce cases occurs when one spouse falsely accuses the other of verbal harassment or physical and/or sexual abuse to get the upper hand in a custody battle or to create leverage for a money or property settlement.

Since the courts have a paramount duty to protect your children, the mere allegation of child abuse can drastically affect custody. The accused is often presumed guilty until proven otherwise as the court will likely act to protect the children until such time, should it occur, that the truth is revealed. This often results in court orders giving temporary sole physical custody to the accuser, provisional termination of your custody rights, terminated visitation, or the implementation of supervised visitation. Child protection services, doctors, and/or other evaluators are usually called in for further in-depth evaluations. The district attorneys' office may also be called in for a criminal investigation regarding the allegations of abuse.

The accused parent will be forced to spend significant effort and money defending his innocence. Often it is extremely difficult to prove that something did not occur. Furthermore, should the accuser fail to prove that the alleged abuse occurred, many times it is difficult to prove that the accuser intentionally made false allegations of abuse.

If falsely accused of having sexually abused a child, immediately request the court to order medical examinations of the child and psychological evaluations of all parties. The best defense is a better offense.

Voodoo Tip 13.26

IF THE ALLEGATIONS ARE PROVEN TO BE FALSE, FIGHT BACK!

Should a court render the allegations of abuse to be false and that the accuser lied, you may ask for custody of the children, that the accuser be held in contempt of court, sanctioned, pay attorney fees, all costs associated with the defense of your case regarding the allegations of abuse, and even ask that the false accuser be incarcerated for her contemptuous lies. Most states also allow courts to impose further sanctions for frivolous motions. You should also consider filing a separate lawsuit against the accuser for malicious prosecution, intentional infliction of mental distress, defamation and/or other actions recommended by your attorney.

Summary of Voodoo Tips from Number 13

DON'T STAND FOR ABUSE OR BEING FALSELY ACCUSED OF ABUSE

Voodoo Tip 13.1	Immediately protect your children and yourself.
Voodoo Tip 13.2	Flee.
Voodoo Tip 13.3	Where to go?
Voodoo Tip 13.4	Go to a battered women's shelter or a rape crisis center.
Voodoo Tip 13.5	Refer to the shelters found in the Appendix.
Voodoo Tip 13.6	In cases of sexual or physical abuse.
Voodoo Tip 13.7	Spousal rape.
Voodoo Tip 13.8	Love and respect yourself.
Voodoo Tip 13.9	Leave the house or get a lawyer to keep spouse out of the house.
Voodoo Tip 13.10	Get *ex parte* orders and/or a peace bond.
Voodoo Tip 13.11	Change locks and alarm codes.
Voodoo Tip 13.12	Get extra keys to your house and car.
Voodoo Tip 13.13	Call the police and get a police report.
Voodoo Tip 13.14	Get evidence of your abuse.
Voodoo Tip 13.15	Request terminated or supervised visitation of your spouse.
Voodoo Tip 13.16	Save money for emergency fund.
Voodoo Tip 13.17	Talk with your children.

Voodoo Tip 13.18 Prevent excessive corporeal punishment by your spouse.

Voodoo Tip 13.19 List emergency telephone numbers and addresses.

Voodoo Tip 13.20 Stop the stalker.

Voodoo Tip 13.21 Take valuables and sentimental items.

Voodoo Tip 13.22 Take your important records.

Voodoo Tip 13.23 Do not take the law into your own hands.

Voodoo Tip 13.24 Alert work, schools, and day-care centers.

Voodoo Tip 13.25 Defend a false allegation.

Voodoo Tip 13.26 If the allegation are proven to be false, fight back!

**VOODOO SPELL
TO PREVENT ABUSE**

Contact your attorney and call the National Domestic Violence Hotline at the following number:

1-800-799-SAFE.

VOODOO INGREDIENT NUMBER 14

Prevent Parental Kidnapping and Prohibit Your Spouse from Taking Your Children Out of the State and Country

> **Real Life Experience:** *Elliot M.*
> Age 41, Divorced, Two Children
> Importer; Anchorage, Alaska
>
> *"My ex-wife continually threatens to take the kids to her native country of Costa Rica. She has a very large influential family there. If she takes my boys to Costa Rica, I don't think that I will be able to get them back."*

Although not likely to occur, it is wise to take serious any of your spouse's threats that he will take the children out of the state or country. By taking preventative measures and gathering information, you will be able to properly cope with these concerns.

Quick Facts:

In 1995, The FBI reported that 969,264 persons were reported missing and entered into the National Crime Information Computer. The FBI estimates that 85 to 90 percent of these missing persons are children (850,000 to 875,00 missing children). (Source: Child Find of America, Inc.). The number of parents who wrongfully take a child out of the state or country has been steadily growing. An estimated 354,100 children have been abducted by family members. Parents also are refusing to return children after scheduled visitation. The majority of these abducted children are less than ten years old. Approximately 90%

of the parental abductors are emotionally unstable and/or are substance abusers.

Family abductions occur in two basic ways (each occurs approximately 50 percent of the time):

1. The child is taken in violation of a custody order or agreement; or
2. The parent refuses to return the child according to a custody order or agreement.

Eighty one percent of family abductions occur by parents during a divorce proceeding or custody battle. Statistics indicate that parental abductions occur in a relatively equal number by men and women. (Sources: The National Incidence Studies of Missing, Abducted, Runaway, and Throwaway Children in America, 1988; The American Bar Association; Child Find of America).

Voodoo Tip 14.1

PROTECT YOUR CHILDREN FROM PARENTAL KIDNAPPING

If serious threats are made, take the following steps to lessen the chances of a parental kidnapping:

1. Inform your attorney of these threats and instruct him to file restraining orders against the other parent.
2. Without scaring your children, tell them your concerns and inform them what to do if the other parent tries to take them away.
   a. Speak with your children to set up a daily schedule (a ritual).
   b. Teach your children a "Mayday" password or phrase that your children can use if they are unable to normally communicate with you, their teachers, baby-sitters, etc.
   c. Teach your children to notice their whereabouts.
   d. Teach your children to memorize your address and telephone numbers.
3. Speak with your children's teachers, school principals, supervisors at day-care facilities, and baby-sitters about the threats of abduction. Provide each of these individuals with a certified copy of the restraining and/or custody order obtained by your attorney.
4. Take a color photograph of your child every six months.
5. Ask the court to require supervised visitation with specific instructions to the person supervising in the event that the parent attempts to remove the child.

6. Ask the court to require the other parent to post a hefty bond, that would be forfeited if there were any attempt to abduct.

> **Real Life Experience:** *Demetris G.*
> Age 34, Married, Three Children
> Pastry Chef; Brooklyn, New York
>
> *"I have temporary custody of my children. Andreas is furious. He will take the children to Greece before he will let me have them."*

Voodoo Tip 14.2

A PREREQUISITE TO ANY CLAIM THAT THE OTHER PARENT WRONGFULLY HAS YOUR CHILD IS TO OBTAIN A CERTIFIED COPY OF THE CUSTODY/VISITATION ORDER

Make sure you have several certified copies of the custody/visitation order.

> **Real Life Experience:** *Hailey H.*
> Age 26, Married, Two Children
> Medical Assistant; Wichita, Kansas
>
> *"He has taken the kids before. I didn't get to see them for over two weeks. I've been straight for several months now, but he won't forgive me. I don't want to lose my kids. If he takes them, I may never see them again."*

Voodoo Tip 14.3

KEEP FILE ON SPOUSE AND CHILDREN

By answering all of the information sought in the data sheets found in the Appendix (Voodoo Spice Number 1), you will have collected valuable information that can be used to help identify and locate the abducting parent.

Additional information and documents that will assist your search are as follows:

1. Photographs of spouse and children
2. Addresses of relatives, friends, employers, and business associates
3. Spouse's driver's license and social security numbers
4. Information of spouse's vehicle, including license plate numbers
5. Spouse's credit card numbers
6. List of all magazine subscriptions and club memberships

7. Your children's identification cards, including pictures, finger prints, and notices of birth marks and/or scars
8. Child's passport (Know passport number, date, and place of issuance)
9. List possible airlines or public transportation that spouse would likely use

VOODOO TIP 14.4

USE AND SAFEGUARD YOUR CHILD'S IDENTIFICATION RECORD (Appendix: Voodoo Spice Number 14)

Keep all of this information in a secure location.

THE LAW

The Uniform Child Custody Jurisdiction Act (UCCJA) provides that a state lacks jurisdiction over a custody dispute if a child has been wrongfully transported into the state. Unfortunately, the act also provides for an "Emergency" condition that allows emergency jurisdiction in cases where the child is in the state and there are allegations that the child is imminently in harm's way.

Federal law also provides that every state shall enforce and not modify any child support determination by a court of another state. (The Parental Kidnapping Prevention Act—28 U.S.C. 1738A) This federal law applies to all judgments, decrees, or other orders of a court providing for the custody or visitation of a child, including permanent and temporary orders.

What you should do if a parent wrongfully takes a child to another state and refuses to return the child

If your child is missing, immediately contact your attorney, the police, the National Center for Missing and Exploited Children, your local prosecutor's office, and the FBI (when applicable). In each case, provide your contact with a certified copy of your custody or visitation order that currently is in effect.

> **Real Life Experience:** Scott S.
> Age 39, Married, One Child
> Investment Broker; Meridian, Mississippi
>
> *"I came home on Friday and the house was empty. My wife took her clothes and all of the baby's things. Katelin and the baby have been gone for three days. She didn't leave a note. She still hasn't called me. I called her mother's and she claims that she's not there."*

Voodoo Tip 14.5

CALL THE POLICE

When you call the police, file a missing person report. Additionally, give them your spouse's car description and license plate number so that they can enter the information in the National Crime Information Center (NCIC) computer. Likewise, request the law enforcement agency to contact the Federal Parent Locator Service.

Voodoo Tip 14.6

CONTACT THE NATIONAL CENTER FOR MISSING AND EXPLOITED CHILDREN

The National Center for Missing and Exploited Children
2101 Wilson Boulevard
Suite 550
Arlington, VA 22201
Toll Free: 1-800-843-5678

> **Real Life Experience:** Bridgett F.
> Age 36, Married, One Child
> Owner of Tour Service
> Charleston, South Carolina
>
> *"That bastard took my son to Tennessee. He called and said that Kendall is all right. I have custody papers. I want my son back right now."*

Voodoo Tip 14.7

REPORT THE PARENTAL KIDNAPPING TO THE FBI

If the child is wrongfully taken across state lines, the FBI can be of assistance. The FBI will get involved if you have an order showing custody, a local felony warrant has been issued, and the local district attorney's office has sent a letter to the FBI requesting assistance. Speak to your local district attorney's office to expedite the process.

> **Real Life Experience:** Wayne K.
>
> Age 26, Married, One Child
> Asst. Manager of Lawn Maintenance Company
> Buena Vista, Virginia
>
> *"I bet that Melanie took Zachary to her momma's house."*

Voodoo Tip 14.8

CONTACT RELATIVES AND FRIENDS OF ABDUCTING PARENT

See if child is at the residence of the abductors' friends or family. Ask them to contact you if the abductor of child arrives.

PREVENT CHILD FROM LEAVING THE UNITED STATES

Quick Fact: Since the late 1970s, the United States Department of State has been contacted with over 11,000 inquiries for assistance in recovering children who were wrongfully taken outside the country by a parent.

Voodoo Tip 14.9

CONTACT THE STATE DEPARTMENT

There are 43 foreign countries that are participants to honor other countries' custody orders (Known as "the Hague Convention"). These countries are as follows:

Argentina, Australia, Austria, Bahamas, Belize, Bosnia & Herzegovina, Burkina Faso, Canada, Chile, Colombia, Croatia, Cyprus, Denmark, Ecuador, Finland, France, Germany, Greece, Honduras, Hong Kong, Hungary, Iceland, Ireland, Israel, Italy, Luxembourg, Former Yugoslav Republic of Macedonia, Mauritius, Mexico, Monaco, Netherlands, New Zealand, Norway, Panama, Poland, Portugal, Romania, Slovenia, South Africa, Spain, St. Kitts and Nevis, Sweden, Switzerland, United Kingdom, Venezuela, and Zimbabwe.

The State Department will work with one of the above countries in an attempt to have your child returned. You may contact the State Department at the following address and telephone number:

Office of Children's Issues
U.S. Department of State
Room 4811
Washington, D.C. 20520-4818
(202) 736-7000
Fax: (202) 647-2835

> **Real Life Experience:** *Robin H.*
> Age 36, Married, One Child
> Flight Attendant; Los Angeles, California
>
> *"How do I keep my husband from taking my daughter out of the country?"*

Voodoo Tip 14.10

KEEP CHILD'S PASSPORT AND/OR FLAG CHILD'S PASSPORT

If your child previously has been issued a passport, keep it. If your child has not been issued a passport, contact the Office of Passport Policy and Advisory Services and request that it flag your child's name. The office has a name check service. Give the office a certified copy of your custody/visitation order that shows that you have sole custody or that the other parent is prohibited from taking the child out of the country. Note that the State Department will not revoke a passport once it has been issued to a child.

Office of Passport Policy and Advisory Services
Passport Services
Suite 260
1111 19th Street, N.W.
Washington, D.C.
(202) 955-0377
Fax: (202) 955-0230

Summary of Voodoo Tips from Number 14

PREVENT PARENTAL KIDNAPPING AND PROHIBIT YOUR SPOUSE FROM TAKING YOUR CHILDREN OUT OF THE STATE AND COUNTRY

Voodoo Tip 14.1 Protect your children from parental kidnapping.

Voodoo Tip 14.2 A prerequisite to any claim that the other parent wrongfully has your child is to obtain a certified copy of the custody/visitation order.

Voodoo Tip 14.3 Keep file on spouse and children.

Voodoo Tip 14.4 Use and safeguard your child's identification record.

Voodoo Tip 14.5 Call the police.

Voodoo Tip 14.6 Contact the National Center for Missing and Exploited Children.

Voodoo Tip 14.7 Report the parental kidnapping to the FBI.

Voodoo Tip 14.8 Contact relatives and friends of abducting parent.

Voodoo Tip 14.9 Contact the State Department.

Voodoo Tip 14.10 Keep child's passport and/or flag child's passport.

**VOODOO SPELL
TO PREVENT PARENTAL KIDNAPPING**

Make sure you have several *certified* copies of the custody/visitation order.

Contact your attorney. Additionally, contact The National Center for Missing and Exploited Children (800) 843-5678, and the Office of Passport Policy and Advisory Services, Passport Services (202) 955-0377.

VOODOO INGREDIENT NUMBER 15

Taxes

> **Real Life Experience:** *Ruben F.*
> *Age 47, Married*
> *One Minor Child and One Adult Child*
> *Garment Wholesaler; Yonkers, New York*
>
> *"I consider myself a good businessman; however, I have to admit that I'm not sure how this divorce is going to affect my taxes."*

Divorced and separated individuals should be aware of the tax consequences of their changing marital status. The following discussions regarding tax are general principals that may be subject to modifications, exceptions and/or other requirements. To get a precise evaluation regarding your particular situation, you should always consult a tax advisor and/or the Internal Revenue Service. The following tax tips shall provide you with necessary information to plan a strategy to maximize your tax benefits and eliminate tax pitfalls—the bottom line—saving you money.

Voodoo Tip 15.1

INFORM THE IRS OF ANY CHANGE OF ADDRESS

If you have moved, contact the IRS and ask for Form 8822, *Change of Address*.

Properly filing this form will prevent your spouse from withholding your future forms and other vital communications from the IRS.

> **Real Life Experience:** Cassandra I.
> Age 29, Divorced, One Child
> Pet Groomer; Durango, Colorado
>
> *"I got divorced on November 23rd. What is my filing status for this past year?"*

Voodoo Tip 15.2

KNOW YOUR FILING STATUS

Your tax status establishes your tax filing requirements as well as determines eligibility to claim various deductions and credits. The primary factor in establishing your filing status is to determine your marital status on December 31st of the taxable year.

Filing status is divided into the following categories:

1. Unmarried/single
2. Married

Voodoo Tip 15.3

DOES THE IRS CONSIDER YOU SINGLE?

You may have an unmarried filing status for the entire tax year if one of the following events occurs:

A. You have obtained a divorce or separation decree by the last day of your tax year. (However, you must file under a married status if you get a divorce decree in one year in order to obtain an unmarried tax status, and intend to remarry the following year—"Fat chance of that happening!")

B. You have obtained a decree of annulment.

Voodoo Tip 15.4

THE IRS MAY CONSIDER YOU MARRIED AFTER YOUR DIVORCE

Even if you get divorced on January 1, you will have a "married" filing status for the entire tax year. The IRS considers you married for the whole year until the year after you obtain a divorce or separation decree. (However, if you live apart from your spouse, under certain exceptions, you may be able to file as the "Head of Household"—see below.)

> **Real Life Experience:** *Donald J.*
> Age 34, Divorced, No Children
> Landscape Architect; Raleigh, North Carolina
>
> *"During our marriage, I was the only one who worked. We were divorced in May. Do I file a joint return this year?"*

Voodoo Tip 15.5

KNOW THE FACTS ABOUT FILING A JOINT TAX RETURN

You may file a joint return under the requirements noted above. If you qualify under those circumstances, you may file a single joint return including the income, exemptions, deductions, and credits applicable for both spouses. A joint return may be filed in cases where both spouses receive income or where only one spouse has income or deductions.

To file a joint return, at least one spouse must be a United States citizen or legal resident during the tax year.

Voodoo Tip 15.6

A JOINT RETURN REQUIRES BOTH SIGNATURES

In order for a tax return to be considered as "joint," both spouses must sign it.

> **Real Life Experience:** *Regan F.*
> Age 46, Divorced, One Adult Child
> Marine Biologist; San Diego, California
>
> *"My ex-husband always had our joint returns prepared. He simply gave the papers to me for my signature. The IRS has contacted me indicating that he did not pay his share of the taxes for our last year of marriage. Now, they want me to pay."*

Voodoo Tip 15.7

YOU ARE LIABLE FOR TAXES, INTEREST AND PENALTIES ASSOCIATED WITH A JOINT RETURN

Regardless of whether your spouse had earned all of the income, both spouses are legally responsible for all taxes, interest, and penalties due pursuant to the joint tax return. This means the IRS can come after either spouse it desires. Think twice before signing a joint return if you have concerns about your spouse's desire, intent, and/or ability to contribute to paying the joint tax debt. If you believe that these concerns are legitimate, consult a tax expert.

Even if you are divorced during a tax year, you remain jointly liable for the taxes, interest, and penalties of a joint return *regardless if you have entered into an agreement or divorce decree that attempts to allocate the tax debt to a particular spouse.*

HERE'S SOME GOOD NEWS

If you are an "innocent spouse," under non-community property rules, you may not be responsible for the further tax debt associated with an understatement of more than $500 on the joint return if your spouse either omitted income or claimed an improper deduction and/or credit. To be an "innocent spouse," you must prove that you were not aware of the tax understatement and that it would be "unfair" for you to be levied with the additional tax debt.

> **Real Life Experience:** Arthur C.
> Age 61, Divorced, Three Adult Children
> Mechanical Engineer; Fairfax, Virginia
>
> *"I've consulted with my CPA who indicates that I should file a separate tax return."*

Voodoo Tip 15.8

KNOW THE FACTS ABOUT FILING SEPARATE RETURNS

If you are eligible to file a separate return, you should only report your income, exemptions, deductions, and credits.

If both you and your spouse file separate returns, you shall only be responsible for the tax debt associated with *your* return.

Voodoo Tip 15.9

FIGURE YOUR TAXES UNDER JOINT AND SEPARATE RETURNS

The IRS suggests that if both spouses earn income, you should calculate your taxes under both a joint return as well as with separate returns in order to determine which means of filing gives you the lowest tax (Internal Revenue Service, Publication 504, 1997).

After considering the above facts, it is important to know that generally the combined federal tax debt of both spouses will be higher if you file separate returns instead of filing a joint return because the tax rate is higher for people filing married and separate returns.

WHO IS THE "HEAD OF HOUSEHOLD"?

The IRS may consider you the "Head of Household" if you are unmarried at the end of the tax year and have paid for more than half of the household upkeep costs for more than half of the year. Household upkeep costs include mortgage payments (including interest, taxes and home insurance), rent, utilities, repairs and maintenance, and food consumed at home.

If you qualify as the "Head of Household," you can claim the following tax benefits:

1. Regardless of whether your spouse itemizes deductions on a married filing separate return, you may qualify for the standard deduction.
2. You will qualify for a higher standard deduction than would be otherwise allowed by filing a separate single or married return.
3. You may be entitled to additional credits.
4. Your tax rate may be lower than would be otherwise allowed by filing a separate single or married return.

> **Real Life Experience:** *Sally H.*
> Age 30, Divorced, One Child
> Florist; Cincinnati, Ohio
>
> *"Now that I'm divorced, how many exemptions can I claim?"*

Voodoo Tip 15.10

KNOW YOUR EXEMPTIONS

Under current tax law, you are permitted a deduction of $2,650 per exemption that you are entitled to claim (special phase-out rules apply for individuals who make higher incomes). Consult your tax advisor.

You are entitled to your own exemption unless someone else is claiming you as a dependent. If you are filing a joint return, you and your spouse may claim an exemption for each person. If you filed a separate return, you may claim your spouse only if your spouse makes no income and is not a claimed dependent of someone else. Furthermore, in the year that you paid alimony to your spouse, you cannot take an exemption for that spouse.

Voodoo Tip 15.11

YOU LOSE THE EXEMPTION OF YOUR FORMER SPOUSE

For the tax year that you obtained a divorce decree, you are not able to take an exemption for that former spouse.

Voodoo Tip 15.12

TAKE EXEMPTIONS FOR DEPENDENTS

You may take an exemption for each person who qualifies as a "dependent." To be a "dependent," the person must satisfy the following requirements:

1. The dependent must be "related"* to you or have lived in your household for an entire year (exceptions apply).
2. The dependent has not filed a joint tax return for the taxable year.
3. The dependent must be a United States citizen or resident, or a resident of either Canada or Mexico during some part of the year.
4. The dependent cannot receive more than $2,650.
5. The dependent must have received at least fifty percent of his support for the year from you.

(*) To be considered "related" to you, the person must be one of the following:

Child	Half-brother	Son-in-law
Stepchild	Half-sister	Daughter-in-law
Mother	Stepbrother	
Father	Stepsister	*If related by blood:*
Grandparent	Stepmother	Uncle
Great-grandparent, etc.	Stepfather	Aunt
Brother	Mother-in-law	Nephew
Sister	Father-in-law	Niece
Grandchild	Brother-in-law	
Great-grandchild, etc.	Sister-in-law	

(Source: Department of Treasury, Internal Revenue Service)

> **Real Life Experience:** Natasha Z.
> Age 28, Divorced, Two Children
> Sociologist; Oklahoma City, Oklahoma
>
> *"Randy and I have shared custody of our children on a roughly fifty-fifty basis. We never got an order regarding custody because we have very strong beliefs that both of us should be integrally involved in our children's lives."*

Voodoo Tip 15.13

WHO IS THE PRIMARY CUSTODIAL PARENT?

Generally, the primary custodial parent who has custody of a child for the greater portion of the year is entitled to claim the dependency exemption as long as the other dependency requirements have been met. The IRS will look at the most recent applicable custody decree (or custody agreement in the absence of a custody decree).

In cases where no custody decree or agreement exists, or where a split custody decree or agreement is implemented, the parent who had physical custody for the majority of the time will be entitled to claim the dependency exemption.

> **Real Life Experience:** Emily F.
> Age 33, Divorced, Two Children
> Physician; Savannah, Georgia
>
> *"Steven and I came to the agreement that he could have the dependency exemptions in exchange for some concessions in our division of property and retirement benefits."*

Voodoo Tip 15.14

THE NONCUSTODIAL PARENT MAY GET THE DEPENDENCY EXEMPTION

A noncustodial parent who does not have physical custody of a child for the majority of time may be able to claim the child as a dependent if the other parent signs IRS FORM 8332 (Appendix: Voodoo Spice Number 29). IRS Form 8332, *Release of Claim to Exemption for Child of Divorced or Separated Parents*, provides that the custodial parent agrees not to take the dependency exemption. The noncustodial parent must attach the signed form to his federal tax return.

Additionally, a noncustodial parent may use the dependency exemption if a *pre-1985* decree or custody agreement provides that the noncustodial parent provides at least $600 of support for the child during the tax year and is entitled to the dependency exemption.

If a modification is made after 1984, which states that the provision does not apply, then the regular dependency rules apply.

> **Real Life Experience:** Terri T.
> Age 29, Divorced, One Child
> Dietitian; Providence, Rhode, Island
>
> *"My daughter has battled asthma for years. Can I claim a deduction for my out-of-pocket medical expenses?"*

Voodoo Tip 15.15

MEDICAL EXPENSE DEDUCTION

The divorced or separated parent who incurs medical expenses for his dependent child may deduct these expenses regardless of which parent claims the child as a dependent for exemption purposes.

> **Real Life Experience:** Wade N.
> Age 47, Divorced, One Child
> Lab Technician; Marina del Rey, California
>
> *"Can I deduct my alimony payments to my ex-wife?"*

Voodoo Tip 15.16

KNOW THE TAX CONSEQUENCES AND REQUIREMENTS OF ALIMONY

Alimony creates a tax deduction for the payer in the year paid and is taxable as income to the recipient in the year received. The Internal Revenue Service treats alimony completely different than its treatment of child support. The payment of child support is neither deductible nor treated as income to either the payer or the recipient.

For spousal support to meet the requirements to be considered deductible alimony for tax purposes (for divorce/separation agreements executed after 1985), all of the following requirements must be met:

1. *Cash*

    The spousal support payments must be paid in cash, which includes checks and money orders [see I.R.C. 71 (b)(1)]. The cash can be paid directly to the other spouse, or can be paid indirectly on the spouse's behalf under the terms of an agreement or decree to pay for expenses such as rent, mortgage payments, spouse tuition, health insurance, medical and/or dental payments [see I.R.C.71(b)(1)(A)].

The payment of spousal support with property or services does not satisfy the requirements of the Internal Revenue Service. Property settlements, whether lump sum or installments, are not considered as alimony for tax purposes.

2. *Order or Agreement*

   A court order (decree) or written agreement is required in which the payments are designated as alimony and are not designated for another purpose. Any payment to a spouse that is made without a decree or written agreement shall not be considered alimony for tax purposes [see I.R.C. 71 (b)(2)].

3. *Not Members of Same Household*

   After the divorce or during the separation, you and your spouse cannot be living in the same household when the payment is made [see I.R.C. 71(b)(1)(C)].

4. *Alimony Has No Life after Death*

   The obligation to pay alimony must not exist beyond the death of the recipient spouse [see I.R.C. 71(b)(1)(D)]. The decree or written agreement must have provisions that the alimony ends upon the death of the spouse, if not before. Alimony does not have to continue until one's death in order to be deductible; however, it cannot outlive its recipient.

5. *Alimony Is Not Intended as Child Support or a Property Division*

   The alimony payment cannot be treated as child support. [see I.R.C. 71(1)(c)and(f)]. If there is a decree of both alimony and child support, and the payer pays less than the total required by both alimony and child support orders, then the first payments made shall be treated by the IRS as child support payments until such time that the entire current child support obligation is satisfied. The surplus payments, above and beyond the child support obligation, may be considered as alimony.

   Caution: In order for the alimony payment to be deductible, it cannot be linked to any consideration regarding your children. Although the written agreement may call a payment "alimony," if the payment is connected to a contingent event related to your child, then it will not be considered deductible alimony by the IRS. (e.g., A provision in a written agreement or decree that provides for payments called "alimony" that call for a change in the amount of the payments upon the child's eighteenth birthday or upon the child's graduation from high school, will not be considered deductible alimony).

Also note that it is unwise to have an agreement with provisions of alimony and child support that do not distinguish between the specific amount to be paid for alimony and the specific amount to be paid in child support.

Voodoo Tip 15.17

AN AGREEMENT TO TAKE OR RECEIVE ALIMONY INSTEAD OF CHILD SUPPORT CAN HAVE TAX BENEFITS OR CONSEQUENCES THAT SHOULD BE WEIGHED THOROUGHLY

Speak to your attorney and/or tax advisor before entering into any agreement regarding alimony and/or child support.

Caution: As an additional consideration, no one can claim the tax benefits of alimony in any year that the spouses file a joint tax return.

Voodoo Tip 15.18

BE AWARE OF THE "RECAPTURE" RULES

Congress enacted laws that discourage attempts to characterize property distributions as alimony. The "Recapture" rules apply to "alimony" that is "front-loaded" (having excessive payments in the first three years of the alimony agreement). If the alimony payments decrease or cease during the first three years, then the payer spouse must "recapture" the funds and include them in his or her taxable gross income. Whether an alimony payment is excessive depends on the calculation of front-loading rules followed by the federal government. Consult your attorney and tax advisor as to whether these rules may apply to you.

> **Real Life Experience:** *Mitch E.*
>
> Age 62, Divorced, One Adult Child
> Insurance Adjuster; Omaha, Nebraska
>
> *"Harriet and I may have to live off the retirement money. How does all of this work since we got divorced?"*

Voodoo Tip 15.19

KNOW HOW A QUALIFIED DOMESTIC RELATIONS ORDER (QDRO) AFFECTS YOU

A qualified domestic relations order, known as a QDRO, is a court's decree which may relate to allocation of benefits to the spouses in a qualified retirement plan and/or a tax sheltered annuity; the payment of child support and alimony; and the division of marital property.

Under a QDRO, benefits paid to the child or dependent or the retirement plan's participant, are treated for tax purposes as though they were paid directly to the plan's participant. Yet, benefits allocated to a spouse or former spouse made pursuant to a QDRO are included in the recipient spouse's income for tax purposes.

Generally, retirement plan benefits that are allocated to the spouse of a retirement plan participant can be "rolled over" tax free into the recipient spouse's new or existing individual retirement arrangement (IRA) or other qualified retirement plan as long as the transfer occurs within 60 days. Special rules apply, so contact your tax specialist or the Internal Revenue Service for more details.

Voodoo Tip 15.20

INDIVIDUAL RETIREMENT ARRANGEMENTS (IRAs)

As stated above, a transfer to a spouse of all or a portion of funds in an IRA can be accomplished tax free as long as the transfer is made pursuant to a court order or written agreement formally associated with the court order. From the date of the official transfer of funds, the interest accruing on the transferred IRA funds shall be considered as the interest of the recipient spouse.

> **Real Life Experience:** *Alicia A.*
> Age 48, Divorced, Two Adult Children
> Interior Designer; Albuquerque, New Mexico
>
> "We are in the process of working out a property agreement. I want to keep the house in exchange for my share of Ramon's retirement."

Voodoo Tip 15.21

PROPERTY SETTLEMENTS

The IRS does not consider a transfer of property between spouses as a taxable gain or loss. However, for a transfer of property to a former spouse to have no taxable gain or loss, then the transfer must occur incident to the divorce.

If the marital property is sold to a third party while it is still owned by both spouses then each spouse must report as a gain or loss the proceeds or loss attributed to each spouse by virtue of property settlement.

Voodoo Tip 15.22

WATCH OUT FOR TRANSFER OF PROPERTY TO THIRD PARTIES

Although a transfer between spouses is generally considered a tax free event, a subsequent transfer to a third party is a taxable event to the spouse who became the recipient owner of the property. Pursuant to Internal Revenue Code Section 1041, the owner former spouse who shall be subject to tax consideration based on any capital gain or loss. The IRS has special methods to calculate the capital gain or loss. Consult your tax advisor for the precise tax ramifications that may affect you.

Voodoo Tip 15.23

REMEMBER TO CONSULT YOUR TAX ADVISOR PRIOR TO ENTERING INTO ANY PROPERTY AGREEMENT OR TRANSFER

The most important message that you should take from this chapter is to use a tax expert to advise you on any agreement or property transfer. The cost of the advisor's services should be worth the advice as the tax ramifications of an agreement or transfer can be significant.

Summary of Voodoo Tips from Number 15

TAXES

Voodoo Tip 15.1	Inform the IRS of any change of address.
Voodoo Tip 15.2	Know your filing status.
Voodoo Tip 15.3	Does the IRS consider you single?
Voodoo Tip 15.4	The IRS may consider you married after your divorce.
Voodoo Tip 15.5	Know the facts about filing a joint tax return.
Voodoo Tip 15.6	A joint return requires both signatures.
Voodoo Tip 15.7	You are liable for taxes, interest, and penalties associated with joint returns (look at "innocent spouse" exception).
Voodoo Tip 15.8	Know the facts about filing separate returns.
Voodoo Tip 15.9	Figure your taxes under joint and separate returns.
Voodoo Tip 15.10	Know your exemptions.
Voodoo Tip 15.11	You lose the exemptions of your former spouse.

Voodoo Tip 15.12 Take exemptions for dependents.

Voodoo Tip 15.13 Who is the primary custodial parent?

Voodoo Tip 15.14 The non-custodial parent may get the dependency exemption (use IRS Form 8332, Appendix: Voodoo Spice Number 29).

Voodoo Tip 15.15 Medical Expense deduction.

Voodoo Tip 15.16 Know the tax consequences and requirements of alimony.

Voodoo Tip 15.17 An agreement to take or receive alimony instead of child support can have tax benefits or consequences that should be weighed thoroughly.

Voodoo Tip 15.18 Be aware of the "Recapture" rules.

Voodoo Tip 15.19 Know how a qualified domestic relations order (QDRO) affects you.

Voodoo Tip 15.20 Individual Retirement Arrangements (IRAs).

Voodoo Tip 15.21 Property settlements.

Voodoo Tip 15.22 Watch out for transfers of property to third parties.

Voodoo Tip 15.23 Remember to consult your tax advisor prior to entering into any property agreement or transfer.

VOODOO SPELL TO PAY LESS TAXES

Fasten a copy of your blank tax return around a green candle. Light the candle. Place the following ingredients in your gris-gris bag: Alfalfa, Almond, Ash Tree Leaves, Basil, Buckwheat, Calendula, Cascara Sagrada, Catnip, Gravel Root, Lucky Hand Root, Marigold, Mint, Pine, and Trillium. Place a magnet in the gris-gris bag. Take the blank tax return off of the green candle and give it to a certified public accountant. Ask your accountant to contact your attorney.

VOODOO INGREDIENT NUMBER 16

Credit Concerns and Bankruptcy

> **Real Life Experience:** *Chris P.*
>
> Age 42, Divorced, Three Children
> Building Contractor
> Greenwood, Arkansas
>
> *"I worked my whole life to live the 'American Dream.' It's now become a nightmare. I have to pay my subcontractors and other bills, but the money is not coming in. I'm also several months behind in my child support payments. Bankruptcy is now a real option."*

Quick Facts: American families have an average credit card debt balance of $4,000.00. In 1996, national credit card debt reached approximately 400 billion dollars (nearly forty percent of the one trillion dollar national consumer debt).

Personal bankruptcies have steadily increased throughout the past decade. In 1996, personal bankruptcies reached an all time high of over one million filings. For a summary of the past United States bankruptcy filings since 1980, refer to the Appendix.

"Financial problems" is one of the most cited reasons why people file for divorce. When the stress of financial concerns is compounded by the seemingly insurmountable anxiety associated with a divorce, many people feel overwhelmed, throw up their hands, give up, and file for bankruptcy protection.

Even when you have no intent to file bankruptcy, you may continue to have legitimate concerns about how a bankruptcy could affect you if your spouse files or threatens to file for bankruptcy protection.

Voodoo Tip 16.1

GAIN CONTROL BY KNOWING THE RAMIFICATIONS OF BANKRUPTCY THAT MAY BE APPLICABLE TO YOU

Many people file for bankruptcy protection in order to gain control of their finances and the associated stress. Before you take this leap that could affect you for at least ten years, first consider the potential negative stigma and other ramifications of a potential bankruptcy.

The most common type of bankruptcy is a Chapter 7 bankruptcy. Chapter 7 allows for a liquidation and complete discharge on non-exempt debts. Individuals, partnerships, and corporations may file a Chapter 7 bankruptcy. Others bankruptcies are available under Chapters 11, 12, and 13 which allow for rehabilitation through an extended time to pay the debts. Then a bankruptcy trustee is appointed to supervise the assets and devise a plan to ultimately pay off creditors. Consult a qualified bankruptcy attorney to see what type of bankruptcy, if any, would be appropriate for you.

Additionally, you should examine how bankruptcy affects your rights associated with the following issues:

1. Child support
2. Alimony/spousal maintenance
3. Property division
4. Other considerations

Real Life Experience: *Diana V.*

Age 34, Divorced, Two Children
Cellular/Digital Telephone Sales Associate
San Francisco, California

"My ex has threatened to file bankruptcy if I take him to court to get the child support arrearages."

Voodoo Tip 16.2

CHILD SUPPORT IS NOT DISCHARGABLE IN BANKRUPTCY

When a debt is considered "discharged" in a bankruptcy proceeding, the creditor cannot collect the debt from the debtor. The "discharged" debt is forgiven for the person who filed for federal bankruptcy protection.

The obligation of child support is not dischargeable in bankruptcy. The person that has past due and/or present child support obligations will continue to have the same child support debt regardless of the bankruptcy proceeding.

Once a spouse who owes child support files bankruptcy, the family court will be able to enforce child support orders during the pendency of the bankruptcy proceeding; however, the family court cannot rule on a modification of child support until the bankruptcy proceeding is over. Under a Chapter 13 bankruptcy, a payment plan may be approved by the bankruptcy court to allow past due child support to be paid in full within three to five years.

> **Real Life Experience:** *Robert C.*
> Age 61, Divorced, Three Adult Children
> Office Administrator; New Orleans, Louisiana
>
> *"I owe my ex-wife around twenty thousand dollars in alimony. She has hired a high-powered lawyer to get it. I'll file bankruptcy before I'll pay."*

Voodoo Tip 16.3

ALIMONY/SPOUSAL MAINTENANCE IS NOT DISCHARGEABLE IN BANKRUPTCY

Similar to child support payments, alimony is not dischargeable in a bankruptcy proceeding.

Under a Chapter 13 bankruptcy, a payment plan may be approved by the bankruptcy court to allow past due alimony to be paid in full within three to five years.

Voodoo Tip 16.4

SOME ATTORNEY FEES ARE NOT DISCHARGEABLE

A bankruptcy will not relieve a debtor spouse from being required to pay court ordered attorney's fees to the other spouse's attorney.

Voodoo Tip 16.5

A PROPERTY DEBT MAY BE DISCHARGEABLE

Generally, the debt of a spouse created and/or recognized by a family court associated with a property settlement may be dischargeable in bankruptcy. There are exceptions to this general rule, so consult a qualified bankruptcy attorney with your concerns.

If you enter into a property settlement in which your former spouse will owe you property or will agree to pay a debt in which both of you are responsible, you may be devastated if that spouse files for bankruptcy and has his obligation discharged. In other words, you may lose your ability to collect a debt from your spouse and remain responsible to the creditors for debts that you and your spouse were jointly legally responsible. This creates an opportunity for the spouse considering or threatening bankruptcy to intimidate the other spouse.

Voodoo Tip 16.6

A BANKRUPTCY MAY AFFECT YOUR ABILITY TO GET A JOB

Employers are able to obtain your credit report in order to evaluate your job qualifications. Since October of 1997, employers require your consent to investigate your credit history for employment-related purposes.

> **Real Life Experience:** *Tanisha B.*
> Age 35, Divorced, Two Children
> Physical Therapist; Detroit, Michigan
>
> *"I'm not going to be intimidated by his threats of bankruptcy."*

Voodoo Tip 16.7

BEWARE OF "BANKRUPTCY BLACKMAIL"

Many spouses may threaten to file bankruptcy to gain advantage during a divorce or property division proceeding. Now you are equipped with the knowledge that child support and alimony obligations are not dischargeable. You also are aware of the potential detrimental results that can occur if your spouse owes you other debts or property. Now, you are able to work with your attorney to devise a property agreement that will take into consideration the risks of your spouse filing for bankruptcy protection. As with other acts of intimidation, relate all such threats to your attorney.

Voodoo Tip 16.8

GET A LIEN OR MORTGAGE

If you are concerned that your spouse may file for bankruptcy that would detrimentally affect your property rights, insist that your attorney seek a lien or mortgage on your spouse's property that would be owed to you in a property settlement. If you have a properly recorded lien or mortgage on a property that your spouse is attempting to get discharged, then your attorney can attempt to seize the property pursuant to the lien or mortgage.

Voodoo Tip 16.9

SOME DEBTS ARE NOT DISCHARGEABLE IN BANKRUPTCY

The following debts are not forgiven in a bankruptcy proceeding:
1. Child support
2. Alimony/spousal maintenance
3. Some property settlement obligations (see your bankruptcy attorney)
4. Certain tax debts
5. Debts created by fraudulent or unlawful acts
6. Some student loans
7. Certain fines, restitution, or penalties ordered by criminal courts
8. Other specific debts associated with federal depository institutions
9. Other items to be identified by your bankruptcy attorney

Voodoo Tip 16.10

CONSIDER BANKRUPTCY FROM AN INFORMED STANDPOINT

After reviewing the above information and consulting a qualified bankruptcy attorney, you may continue to consider taking that large step and decide to file for bankruptcy protection. If you have made an informed decision to file for bankruptcy, know that you are not alone. The number of personal non-business bankruptcies has steadily increased over the last few decades.

Voodoo Tip 16.11

REVIEW YOUR CREDIT REPORT

Your credit history is kept on your credit report which is maintained by consumer reporting agencies/credit bureaus. The Fair Credit Reporting Act was created to insure that accurate information is maintained on your credit report.

Accurate information on your credit report cannot be removed for seven years. If you file for bankruptcy, information regarding your bankruptcy shall remain on your report for ten years.

In order to get a copy of your credit report, you should send a letter to one of the following agencies requesting the report that includes the following information:

1. Your full name (including maiden name)
2. Your current address
3. Any prior addresses if your are requesting a five year credit history
4. Your date of birth
5. Your social security number and
6. Your signature

The three major national consumer reporting agencies/credit bureaus are the following:

Equifax
P.O. Box 740241
Atlanta, GA 30374-0241
(800) 685-1111

Experian (Formerly TRW)
P.O. Box 949
Allen, TX 75013
(800) 682-7654

Trans Union
760 West Sproul Road
P.O. Box 390
Springfield, PA 19064-0390
(800) 916-8800

Real Life Experience: *Roy M.*

Age 29, Divorced, One Child
Medical Student; Houston, Texas

"My credit report incorrectly shows that I owe past due child support."

Voodoo Tip 16.12

KNOW YOUR RIGHTS PURSUANT TO THE FAIR CREDIT REPORTING ACT

Under the Fair Credit Reporting Act, you have the following rights:
1. You have a right to receive your credit report.
2. You have the right for the credit report to disclose the identities of those entities that made inquiries about your credit within the last year.
3. You have the right for the credit report to disclose the identities of those entities that made inquiries for employment purposes within the last two years.
4. You have the right to receive a free copy of your credit report after being denied credit. You have sixty days to request the free copy.
5. You may dispute the accuracy of any entry on your report. The consumer reporting agency/credit bureau must investigate the disputed credit entry.
6. You have the right to submit a written explanation or comment to be supplemented to your record regarding the discrepancy in a disputed credit entry. Other than stated above, a consumer reporting agency may charge up to eight dollars for a copy of your credit report.

Real Life Experience: *Mark B.*

Age 49, Divorced, No Children
Owner of Dry Cleaner; Little Rock, Arkansas

"My finances are a wreck. Now that I understand that my arrearages in child support cannot be discharged in bankruptcy, what can I do to get my financial situation under control?"

Voodoo Tip 16.13

**PRIOR TO FILING BANKRUPTCY,
CONSIDER CONSUMER CREDIT COUNSELING SERVICE**

Consumer Credit Counseling Service is a national non-profit organization sponsored by business interests. This organization will help you work with your creditors to get your financial status under control. Consumer Credit Counseling Service has made remarkable strides in their ability to get creditors to work with you and provide concessions regarding the terms of payment, interest owed, and the extent of the debt. This service assists with budget counseling, debt management, and correcting incorrect negative information on credit reports. You can find a local office of Consumer Credit Counseling Service in your yellow pages telephone directory.

Consumer Credit Counseling Service can advise you on how to control your spending.

> **Real Life Experience:** *Angie A.*
> Age 37, Married, One Child
> Unemployed; Evanston, Illinois
>
> *"Everyday I get harassing phone calls from creditors. Since I filed for divorce, my husband has not paid a single bill."*

Voodoo Tip 16.14

TAKE ADVANTAGE OF THE FAIR DEBT COLLECTION PRACTICES ACT

The last thing you need during your divorce, custody battle, or property dispute is to deal with harassing telephone calls and intimidating letters from creditors and collection agencies. The federal government has provided you with some relief from improper collection tactics. Pursuant to the Fair Debt Collection Practices Act (15 United States Code 1692), you can severely restrict the ways that a creditor can communicate with you.

Send the creditor and/or collection agency a letter notifying them that you are aware of the alleged debt and inform them that you are asserting your rights pursuant to the Fair Debt Collection Practices Act. Request that they cease further communications with you except at the specific times and places designated by you and for the specific reasons set forth in the federal law. Upon your written request, debt collectors must stop contacting you.

If desired, you may designate a certain telephone number and a specific time period in which you may be contacted (i.e., between 6:00 and 8:00 p.m.).

Regardless of whether you send a letter to a debt collector, the Fair Debt Collection Practices Act provides your with the following rights:

1. Debt collectors may not harass you
2. Debt collectors may not use obscene or profane language
3. Debt collectors may not advertise your debt
4. Debt collectors may not misrepresent the amount of your debt
5. Debt collectors may not state that you will be arrested if you do not pay your debt

6. Debt collectors must properly identify themselves on all telephone calls
7. Debt collectors must not falsely imply that you have committed a crime
8. Debt collectors may not contact you at work after they become aware of your employer's disapproval of such communications[89]
9. Debt collectors can only contact you between the hours of 8:00 a.m. to 9:00 p.m., unless you agree otherwise

If you have a debt collector who is violating any of these rights, immediately inform your attorney, your state attorney general's office, and/or the Federal Trade Commission.

Voodoo Tip 16.15

CLOSE JOINT CREDIT ACCOUNTS

A creditor cannot close a joint credit account merely because you and your spouse are divorced or have filed for a divorce. However, upon the request of either spouse, the account can be closed.

A creditor is not under any obligation to change a joint account into an individual account. You may have to individually reapply for credit once the account is closed. It may be difficult to get individual credit if you do not have sufficient income potential and/or a favorable personal credit history.

Keep in mind that in community property states (Arizona, California, Idaho, Louisiana, Nevada, New Mexico, Texas, Washington, and Wisconsin), you may still be liable for debts incurred during the marriage on individual credit accounts of your spouse. Contact each credit company and inquire how you can terminate any further responsibility associated with your spouse's future use on his individual credit accounts. Speak to your attorney about other actions that can protect your interests.

> **Real Life Experience:**   *Max Z.*
> Age 44, Divorced, One Child
> Orthodontist; Portland, Maine
>
> *"I promised her that she could have the house when we got divorced."*

Voodoo Tip 16.16

**GET YOUR NAME OFF THE HOUSE MORTGAGE
IF YOU ARE NOT KEEPING THE HOUSE**

The only way to get your name off the house mortgage is to sell the house or get refinancing purely in the name of the spouse that is retaining the house. It is highly unlikely, that a lender would allow your name to be removed from the mortgage without a sale or refinancing. If your name remains on the mortgage note, then your ability to obtain future credit may be detrimentally affected.

Summary of Voodoo Tips from Number 16

CREDIT CONCERNS AND BANKRUPTCY

Voodoo Tip 16.1	Gain control by knowing the ramifications of bankruptcy that may be applicable to you.
Voodoo Tip 16.2	Child support is not dischargeable in bankruptcy.
Voodoo Tip 16.3	Alimony/spousal maintenance is not dischargeable in bankruptcy.
Voodoo Tip 16.4	Some attorney fees are not dischargeable.
Voodoo Tip 16.5	A property debt may be dischargeable.
Voodoo Tip 16.6	A bankruptcy may affect your ability to get a job.
Voodoo Tip 16.7	Beware of "bankruptcy blackmail."
Voodoo Tip 16.8	Get a lien or mortgage.
Voodoo Tip 16.9	Some debts are not dischargeable in bankruptcy.
Voodoo Tip 16.10	Consider bankruptcy from an informed standpoint.
Voodoo Tip 16.11	Review your credit report.
Voodoo Tip 16.12	Know your rights pursuant to the Fair Credit Reporting Act.
Voodoo Tip 16.13	Prior to filing bankruptcy, consider a consumer credit counseling service.
Voodoo Tip 16.14	Take advantage of the Fair Debt Collection Practices Act.
Voodoo Tip 16.15	Close joint credit accounts.
Voodoo Tip 16.16	Get your name off the house mortgage if you are not keeping the house.

VOODOO SPELL TO PROTECT YOUR CREDIT

Light white, green, red, and purple candles. Place the following ingredients in your gris-gris bag: Alfalfa, Almond, Ash Tree Leaves, Basil, Buckwheat, Calendula, Cascara Sagrada, Catnip, Gravel Root, Lucky Hand Root, Marigold, Mint, Pine, and Trillium. Place a magnet in the gris-gris bag.

VOODOO INGREDIENT NUMBER 17

Discovery Pleadings

Discovery pleadings help your attorney receive information to aid in the litigation of your domestic issues. These pleadings are essential building blocks in your case. You may be shocked by the information that you discover through your spouse's answers to the discovery pleadings. Discovery also includes other procedures such as blood tests and psychological evaluations. The goal is to seek the true financial picture and the factual merits of one's quest for custody, visitation, alimony, child support, property division, and the like.

Typical discovery methods include the following:
1. Interrogatories
2. Requests for Production of Documents and Things
3. Depositions
4. Requests for Admissions of Facts
5. Physical and/or Psychological Evaluations/Tests
6. Inspections

INTERROGATORIES

"Interrogatories" are written questions prepared by your attorney for which the other party must provide written answers under oath. Most states limit the amount of interrogatories that are propounded to the other party to twenty five to thirty five questions (including sub-parts). Your lawyer can file a motion requesting that he propound in excess of the amount of interrogatories allowed without further court approval.

Sample interrogatories are found in the Appendix (see Voodoo Spice Number 31).

REQUESTS FOR PRODUCTION OF DOCUMENTS AND THINGS

"Requests for production of documents and things" are formal requests to a party to produce or allow available for inspection, documents and things that are relevant to your litigation. Requests for productions or documents and things often are tendered to the other party, along with interrogatories. It is wise to use the "requests for production of documents and things" for documentary and/or other tangible evidence that support answers to specific interrogatory inquiries.

Sample requests for production of documents and things are found in the Appendix (see Voodoo Spice Number 32).

DEPOSITIONS

A "deposition" is the sworn oral questioning of a party. The oral answers are provided under oath. The deposition can be taken with a stenographer and/or by videotape.

Before you are deposed, speak with your attorney and go over the anticipated questioning. Be honest, yet answer only what has been asked of you. If you don't know the answer to a question, it's all right to indicate that you "don't know" or "don't recall."

An opposing attorney may attempt to take your deposition at a very inconvenient time. Inform your lawyer of the dates and times of your availability. If your deposition is set at a bad time, don't hesitate to ask your attorney to move the deposition time or date.

(The same is true regarding a court date. If the date is inconvenient or you are otherwise unable to attend on that date, inform your attorney immediately.)

Real Life Experience: *Virginia F.*

Age 26, Married, One Child
Receptionist; Atlantic City, New Jersey

"Tomorrow, I'm being deposed by my husband's attorney. I'm somewhat nervous about the deposition. I'm worried that I'm going to make some mistake."

Voodoo Tip 17.1

IF YOU ARE BEING DEPOSED, FOLLOW THESE TIPS:

1. Always tell the truth
2. If you do not know the answer to the question, do not speculate
3. Answer only the question asked and do not volunteer additional information

REQUESTS FOR ADMISSIONS OF FACTS

"Requests for admissions" are written statements that are sent to the other party that require the party to admit, deny, or object to the statement. These "requests for admissions" assist in narrowing the issues in dispute before the court.

PHYSICAL AND/OR PSYCHOLOGICAL EVALUATIONS/TESTS

In domestic disputes, physical and/or mental well-being becomes an important inquiry in custody and visitation battles. Physicians, psychiatrists, sociologists, and social workers are called on to assist the court in determining what custody and/or visitation arrangement is in the "best interest" of the children. Drug/alcohol tests assist the court in custody evaluations. Additionally, blood/DNA testing is used to establish paternity.

INSPECTIONS

Your lawyer can make inspections of various locations and things.

Voodoo Tip 17.2

USE AN ACCOUNTANT/CPA AND A CERTIFIED FINANCIAL PLANNER

An accountant who is trained in inspecting business and marital assets can greatly assist your attorney in the discovery of hidden assets and undisclosed income.

Spouses attempt to hide assets and income in the following illustrative ways:

1. Property is hidden at remote locations, safety deposit boxes, and safes
2. Title to property is placed in another person's name

3. An arrangement is made with spouse's employer to defer income
4. Money is taken out of the bank and/or credit card advance and the cash disappears
5. Spouse lies on tax returns
6. Spouse opens a secret checking account at another bank
7. Wages are paid to third party for work performed by spouse
8. Spouse forms corporations or partnerships that assists in sheltering funds
9. Spouse is not paid in cash for work performed (barter)

Your attorney's discovery pleadings, along with inspections by other experts, can assist you in locating and evaluating hidden assets and income.

Other discovery techniques are also available.

Summary of Voodoo Tips from Number 17

DISCOVERY

Voodoo Tip 17.1   If you are being deposed, follow the tips found in this chapter.

Voodoo Tip 17.2   Use an accountant/CPA and a Certified Financial Planner.

VOODOO INGREDIENT NUMBER 18

Mediation and Arbitration

> **Real Life Experience:** *Kay B.*
> *Age 32, Married, Two Children*
> *Pharmaceutical Sales Representative*
> *Asheville, North Carolina*
>
> *"Michael and I probably can work out our differences regarding custody and visitation if we just sit down and honestly look at what is best for the kids."*

Mediation and arbitration are two alternatives to allowing a judge to try and resolve your case. They are intended to reduce the time, cost, and pain of litigation.

MEDIATION

Mediation is the process whereby a third person assists both spouses in attempting to resolve disputes regarding child support, alimony, property distribution, and other divorce-related issues.

Mediation is a growing means to resolve many issues in the divorce proceeding. In mediation, you and your spouse attempt to settle as many disputes as possible with the assistance of a impartial mediator. Mediation allows you to explore various options to resolve your dispute. Usually, lawyers are not allowed to attend the meetings; however, it is very common for your attorney to review and seek to revise any proposed agreement.

In order for mediation to be meaningful, effective, and fair, the following should occur:

1. Both spouses have relatively equal "bargaining power." Neither party is domineering nor controlling.

2. Both spouses are operating in "good faith."
3. Both spouses are mentally and physically able to participate. If either party is too emotional, angry, intimidated, or fearful, then mediation is not appropriate.
4. Both spouses are willing and able to openly communicate.
5. Both spouses have been fully informed about the existence and value of all relevant issues (i.e., assets and liabilities). All relevant information should be disclosed. Mediation should not be used as a "fishing expedition" to discover the other side's strengths and weaknesses. Furthermore, in custody and visitation disputes, both parents have fully evaluated each other's abilities and weaknesses as well as what is in the "best interest" of the children.
6. The mediator should be neutral, fair, and impartial. The mediator is not your advocate.
7. The mediator knows the divorce laws of your state.
8. The mediator should be aware of the tax consequences of all proposed resolutions.

Mediation may be less expensive than using your attorney to negotiate, yet it can be costly if the mediation is unsuccessful and/or if you have a duplication of costs as your attorney should review any proposed written agreements.

> **Real Life Experience:** *Dean E.*
> Age 38, Married, One Child
> Speech Therapist; St. Louis, Missouri
>
> *"My wife and I met with a court appointed mediator on four separate occasions. The mediator drafted an agreement that was derived from these meetings. I am relatively comfortable with the provisions, but I want to make sure that I am not giving up other rights that I haven't thought of."*

Voodoo Tip 18.1

HAVE ANY WRITTEN AGREEMENT REVIEWED BY PROFESSIONALS

It is prudent to have any proposed mediated written agreement reviewed by your attorney and/or tax advisor prior to signing.

> **Real Life Experience:** *April V.*
> Age 41, Married, One Child
> Pet Groomer; Washington, D.C.
>
> *"As soon as I walked into the mediation session, I could tell that I wasn't going to like the results. The mediator seemed awfully chummy with Todd. After the first thirty minutes, it was obvious that the mediator was agreeing with everything that Todd was saying. Quite frankly, I don't think that the mediator knew what she was doing.*
>
> *It was also obvious that Todd was lying to the mediator, he was never active in our child's life. Now he pretends to be the father of the year."*

Voodoo Tip 18.2

DON'T BE AFRAID TO WALK AWAY

If the mediation process is not working out, or if you feel that one or more of the above factors for fair mediation is being violated, then you should not hesitate to end the session and walk away. You can resume the mediation process if any unfair advantage is removed; otherwise, your attorney is ready and willing to assist you with further litigation.

In the following states, courts can order parents to participate in mediation prior to bringing a custody and/or visitation matter to court:

Alabama, Alaska, Arizona, California, Colorado, Connecticut, Delaware, Florida, Idaho, Illinois, Indiana, Iowa, Kansas, Kentucky, Louisiana, Maine, Maryland, Michigan, Minnesota, Mississippi, Missouri, Montana, Nevada, New Jersey, New Mexico, North Carolina, North Dakota, Ohio, Oregon, Pennsylvania, Rhode Island, South Carolina, South Dakota, Texas, Utah, Virginia, Washington, West Virginia, and Wisconsin.

Mediation can be quite useful; however, it is not a panacea to every case. Review the above considerations, and see whether mediation is right for you. Mediation resources are provided in Appendix: Voodoo Spice Number 33.

> **Real Life Experience:** *Keith M.*
> Age 45, Divorced, Two Children
> Carpenter; Spokane, Washington
>
> *"My ex has proposed that we go to arbitration, instead of having our property division heard before the court. Is this a good idea?"*

ARBITRATION

Arbitration is different from mediation as a panel of arbitrators become the decision makers. Most arbitration decisions are enforceable in courts of law. Although your attorney is generally present during the process, the decision is non-appealable. Thus arbitration is a less formal and flexible process than mediation. It can save cost and time in an otherwise bogged down court system.

Summary of Voodoo Tips from Number 18

MEDIATION AND ARBITRATION

Voodoo Tip 18.1 Have any written agreement reviewed by professionals.

Voodoo Tip 18.2 Don't be afraid to walk away.

**VOODOO SPELL
TO WIN IN MEDIATION OR ARBITRATION**

Light a brown candle. Place the following ingredients in your gris-gris bag: Adam and Eve Root, Ague Root, Althea, Broom Tops, Calendula, Cascara Sagrada, Cedar, Corn Flower, Elder Bark, Gardenia, Gilead Buds, Goat's Leaves, Irish Moss, Lilac, Magnolia, Marigold, Rose Petals, and Violet.

VOODOO INGREDIENT NUMBER 19

Be Prepared for Trial

> **Real Life Experience:** *Jeannie S.*
> Age 39, Married, Two Children
> Teacher; Atlanta, Georgia
>
> *"I'm very pleased with my lawyer's performance. So far, he has kept my husband at bay. I think that the interrogatories and other discovery pleadings intimidated my husband. Last week's deposition was very emotional, but quite worth it. I'm looking forward to getting this over with. I feel good about our chances."*

Your trial date has arrived. With the help of this book, you are prepared because you have accomplished the following goals:

1. You have chosen the right attorney.
2. You made the appropriate fee arrangements with your attorney so that he had enough financial resources to do his job.
3. Your attorney has propounded discovery pleadings and appropriate responses have been given.
4. You have sufficiently tabled your emotions to be as persuasive as possible.
5. You have taken possession of your children, the house, the available money, other valuable documents, and other evidence.
6. Your lawyer has been successful in getting the judge to sign the appropriate restraining orders.
7. You have either attempted mediation or decided that it is not appropriate for your case.

8. You have weighed any settlement proposals that have been discussed between the parties.
9. In custody and visitation disputes, you have consciously weighed what is in the "best interests" of your children.
10. You are ready to fight for your rights and the rights of your children.

If you have read this book in the middle of your domestic litigation, you may not have accomplished all of the goals set forth above. However, your chances of realistically achieving many of these goals is significantly enhanced by your application of the tips found in this book.

Knowing that you have become empowered through your preparation and knowledge, you should attempt to calm your concerns. Understand that it is natural to be nervous. Rest assured, your spouse should be nervous as well. Staying focused on your goals for the trial or hearing should channel the nervous energy into pure motivation to get the results that you want with your case.

> **Real Life Experience:** Brian H.
> Age 34, Married, One Child
> Paramedic; Erie, Pennsylvania
>
> *"I want to see how fair our judge is. I've heard the judge is ornery and short tempered."*

Voodoo Tip 19.1

BEFORE YOUR COURT DATE, GO AND WATCH YOUR JUDGE CONDUCT A TRIAL

As your trial approaches, pick a day to go to court when your judge is presiding over a domestic matter. This will give you a good idea of what you may expect on your trial date. Hopefully, this will alleviate some of your possible courtroom jitters. If you find that being a spectator in the courtroom has caused you more concerns, discuss your concerns with your attorney. Remember, knowledge is power.

Voodoo Tip 19.2

SEVERAL DAYS BEFORE TRIAL, SCHEDULE AN OFFICE MEETING WITH YOUR ATTORNEY TO GO OVER YOUR CASE AND TO ASK ANY REMAINING QUESTIONS THAT YOU MAY HAVE

SETTLEMENT DISCUSSIONS

> **Real Life Experience:** *Loren A.*
> Age 62, Married, Two Adult Children
> Retired; Fort Lauderdale, Florida
>
> *"I would like to settle this without having to go to court."*

IT IS ALWAYS BETTER TO NEGOTIATE FROM A POSITION OF STRENGTH AND NOT WEAKNESS!

The information that you have gained and the preparation that you have made with your attorney should place you in a position of strength.

Voodoo Tip 19.3

WHEN APPROPRIATE, ENTERTAIN SETTLEMENT DISCUSSIONS

A judge does not like to hear that you have not had settlement discussions with your spouse. It may be advantageous for your attorney to tell the judge that you tried to resolve the matter and the other party would not cooperate. On the other hand, if there is no room for negotiations, any attempt to settle could be a sign of weakness and vulnerability. Discuss these thoughts with your attorney.

It may be possible for you to resolve some of the issues before the court. You are ready for trial after the settlement discussions have rendered only partial or no results.

> **Real Life Experience:** *Susan P.*
> Age 25, Married, Two Children
> Receptionist; Greenville, South Carolina
>
> *"Bill keeps on calling me, proposing settlement."*

Voodoo Tip 19.4

**ALL SETTLEMENT NEGOTIATIONS
SHOULD BE HANDLED THROUGH YOUR ATTORNEY**

By allowing your attorney to "relay" settlement proposals and responses to offers, you are lessening the chances for negotiations to break down because of the fragile emotional state of one or more of the parties.

Voodoo Tip 19.5

ALWAYS NEGOTIATE LESS CONTROVERSIAL ISSUES FIRST

By negotiating less heated issues first, you are able to eliminate many issues that otherwise would be caught up in the emotional quagmire associated with other more volatile points of dispute (i.e., agree on who gets the use of which cars, and save the heated dispute on who gets custody of the children for last).

Voodoo Tip 19.6

HAVE A PLAN AND KNOW YOUR "BOTTOM LINE"

It is wise to anticipate any settlement proposals that your spouse may make prior to going to trial. Many opponents strategically wait until trial begins to throw out a proposal that you would not remotely consider except while under the stress of the moment. By knowing your "bottom line," you can undermine these efforts and focus on the trail at hand. By preplanning a negotiation strategy, you have eliminated a potential plan of attack for a manipulative opponent.

Don't be swayed by emotions; and follow your intuition.

IT'S TIME FOR TRIAL!

Evidence can be elicited in three general ways:
1. By stipulation
2. By testimony
3. By exhibits

Stipulations occur when both parties agree that:
1. Certain "facts" be admitted into evidence as being true

2. Certain "agreements of the parties" have been made that become a judgment of the court and/or
3. Certain "documents and/or things" are admitted into evidence

WHO WILL TESTIFY?

Once the trial begins, witnesses will be called to testify under oath. Depending on the issues litigated, the witnesses called may include various people that have been discussed throughout the book.

"Lay" witnesses are witnesses who are not "experts" in a field that they are testifying in. They testify to facts as known through their own personal knowledge. These individuals could include persons such as the following:

Each parent, teachers, day-care providers, baby-sitters, nannies, coaches, doctors, dentists, priests, rabbis, neighbors, the children (if deemed mature enough), the children's friends (if deemed mature enough), boy scout leaders, girl scout leaders, school principals, Sunday school teachers, guidance counselors, police officers, housekeepers, private investigators, etc.

Usually, the court will limit the number of witnesses that are anticipated to testify in similar fashion.

"Expert" witnesses are persons that have an expertise recognized by the court. These persons are able to provide "expert opinions" based on information and/or hypothetical situations that are posed to them. Typically, expert witnesses include persons such as the following:

Psychiatrists, sociologists, other physicians, social workers, vocational rehabilitation experts, accountants, handwriting specialists, real estate appraisers, etc.

WHEN IT'S YOUR TURN TO TESTIFY:

Here are some general tips to allow you to maximize your courtroom presentation:

Attire:
- Dress neatly (don't dress in "extremes"—either too causal or too formal)
- Do not wear a hat in court
- Do not chew gum
- Do not smoke
- Do not wear expensive jewelry

Listen, wait, think, then answer:
- Be truthful (you have not withheld information from your attorney)
- Be courteous and polite
- Listen to each question
- Pause and think of your answer before you respond to each question
- If you do not understand the question, tell the questioning attorney that you do not understand the question and to restate or rephrase it
- If you do not know or recall the answer, say so
- Answer only the question asked

Maintain self-control:
- Have good eye contact with the judge (and jury, if one exists)
- Do not swear or make obscene gestures
- Do not call your spouse bad names (i.e., "that despicable maggot in the blue shirt")
- Do not speak to your spouse in the courtroom
- Do not let the opposing attorney get you angry and emotional
- Do not bring your children to court unless and until you have a prior discussion with your attorney
- Be a gracious winner

Voodoo Tip 19.7

ALWAYS MAINTAIN GOOD EYE CONTACT WITH THE JUDGE/JURY

When answering questions asked by either attorney, address your answers to the judge, while you maintain good eye contact with him. Good body language and eye contact will reinforce the truthfulness and rightfulness of your position. You want to maintain "good" eye contact. Don't "stare down" the judge or jury!

Voodoo Tip 19.8

BRING ALL NEEDED DOCUMENTS AND THINGS TO COURT

You should have previously provided your attorney with all of the documents and things that he or the opposing attorney have requested. As a precaution, bring all of the relevant documents and things in your possession, and tell your lawyer what you have brought.

> **Real Life Experience:** *Mary R.*
> Age 32, Married, Two Children
> Office Manager; Brentwood, California
>
> *"I've prayed that the children will be properly provided for. I deeply want what's best for my kids."*

Voodoo Tip 19.10

DO WHAT IS BEST FOR YOUR CHILDREN,
THEN DO WHAT IS BEST FOR YOU. HOPEFULLY THEY ARE THE SAME.

Summary of Voodoo Tips from Number 19

BE PREPARED FOR TRIAL

Voodoo Tip 19.1	Before your court date, go and watch your judge conduct a trial.
Voodoo Tip 19.2	Several days before trial, schedule an office meeting with your attorney to go over your case and ask any remaining questions that you may have.
Voodoo Tip 19.3	When appropriate, entertain settlement discussions.
Voodoo Tip 19.4	Any settlement negotiations should be handled through your attorney.
Voodoo Tip 19.5	Always negotiate less controversial issues first.
Voodoo Tip 19.6	Have a plan and know your "bottom line."
Voodoo Tip 19.7	Always maintain good eye contact with the judge/jury.
Voodoo Tip 19.8	Bring all needed documents and things to court.
Voodoo Tip 19.9	Do what is best for your children, then do what is best for you. Hopefully, they are the same.

**VOODOO SPELL
TO BE PREPARED FOR TRIAL**

Light a brown candle. Place the following ingredients in your red flannel gris-gris bag: Allspice, Aloe, Basil, Broom Tops, Dill, Honeysuckle, marigold, Pine, Shark Cartilage, and Yarrow.

The night before trial, buy Cow Tongue and eat it for dinner. Write your attorney's name on a dollar bill and pin it to the voodoo dolls's left hand. Write your name on a twenty dollar bill and pin it to the voodoo doll's right hand.

Write your spouse's name on a piece of scrap paper. Tear it up and flush it down the commode.

Collect all of the information and documents gathered through the tips found in *Voodoo Divorce*. As you leave your house, casually step on the front doormat that hides your spouse's picture.

Smile. You're ready for court.

VOODOO INGREDIENT NUMBER 20

Conclusion

Now that you have reviewed all of the insights found here, you have the significant advantage of being informed and prepared. You are equipped with the ability to work with your attorney to reach the most advantageous outcome. You have the ability to control your emotions and financial security. You have minimized the chance that your spouse can take advantage of you. One of the most dramatic messages found here is that you are not alone. In the time that it took you to read this book, thousands more have divorced. The great distinction between you and the literal millions who have ventured these perilous times is that you are prepared for the test. Additionally, if you desire further assistance, the author is available for your inquiries. Discovering the voodoo ingredients is empowering. The potion created by your recipe for success is complete. The greatest "Hex on Your Ex" is conjured by the creation of your emotional and financial well-being. The best result from your Voodoo Divorce spell is to find your own *happiness*.

THE ULITMATE VOODOO DIVORCE SPELL

Become prepared and knowledgeable.

Appendices

Voodoo Spice Number 1

VOODOO DIVORCE CHECKLIST

YOUR PERSONAL PROFILE

Your name: _____

Your address: _____

_____

_____

Your home telephone number: _____

Your work telephone number: _____

Your pager number: _____

Can your attorney mail you or call you at all of the above addresses and telephone numbers? If not, please explain, and state how you can be contacted: _____

_____

_____

Your social security number: _____

Your driver's license number (also indicate state): _____

Your date of birth: _____

Your place of birth: _____

Your religious affiliation: _____

Your passport number: _____

Name of person that your attorney can contact in the case of an emergency or if your attorney cannot locate you: _____

Address and telephone number of contact person: _____

What is your relationship with this contact person (i.e., mother, employer, friend): _____

Name of prior spouse(s) (if any): _____

Date of divorce, annulment, or death of former spouse: _____

MARRIAGE INFORMATION

Date of marriage: _____

City and state of marriage: _____

Date of separation from your spouse: _____

Date of divorce, if any: _____

Your spouse's full name (including maiden name): _____

Your spouse's current address: _____

Your spouse's current residential telephone number: _____

Your spouse's current work telephone number: _____

Your spouse's social security number: _____

Your spouse's driver's license number (also include state): _____

Your spouse's date of birth: _____

Your spouse's place of birth: _____

Your spouse's religious affiliation: _____

Your spouse's passport number: _____

Has your spouse been previously married? If so, state to who, identify when divorce or widowed, and date and place of divorce, if any: _____
_____

Does your spouse have any children from another relationship? _____

MINOR CHILDREN

Minor children of the marriage or union *between you and your spouse* **(other parent).**

Name of child (1): _____

Date of birth of child (1): _____

Place of birth of child (1): _____

Person with physical custody of child (1): _____

Name of child (2): _____

Date of birth of child (2): _____

Place of birth of child (2): _____

Person with physical custody of child (2): _____

Name of child (3): _____

Date of birth of child (3): _____

Place of birth of child (3): _____

Person with physical custody of child (3): _____

Name of child (4): _____
Date of birth of child (4): _____
Place of birth of child (4): _____
Person with physical custody of child (4): _____

Your minor children *not* born of the marriage or union between you and your spouse (other parent).

Name of child (N-1): _____
Date of birth of child (N-1): _____
Place of birth of child (N-1): _____
Parent of child (N-1): _____

Name of child (N-2): _____
Date of birth of child (N-2): _____
Place of birth of child (N-2): _____
Parent of child (N-2): _____

Name of child (N-3): _____
Date of birth of child (N-3): _____
Place of birth of child (N-3): _____
Parent of child (N-3): _____

Name of child (N-4): _____
Date of birth of child (N-4): _____
Place of birth of child (N-4): _____
Parent of child (N-4): _____

Adopted Children

Your minor children *adopted* by you and/or your spouse.

Name of adopted child (A-1): _____
Date of birth of adopted child (A-1): _____
Place of birth of adopted child (A-1): _____
Date of adoption (A-1): _____
Place of adoption (A-1): _____
Person with physical custody of adopted child (A-1): _____

Name of adopted child (A-2): _____
Date of birth of adopted child (A-2): _____
Place of birth of adopted child (A-2): _____
Date of adoption (A-2): _____
Place of adoption (A-2): _____
Person with physical custody of adopted child (A-2): _____

Adult Children

Name of adult child (Ad-1): _____
Date of birth of adult child (Ad-2): _____
Name of adult child (Ad-2): _____
Date of birth of adult child (Ad-2): _____

YOUR PARENTS' INFORMATION

Father's name: _____
Father's address: _____
Father's telephone numbers: _____
Is father living? _____
Father's date of birth: _____
Is your father a favorable witness for you? _____

*****

Mother's name: _____
Mother's address: _____
Mother's telephone numbers: _____
Is mother living? _____
Mother's date of birth: _____
Is your mother a favorable witness for you? _____

SIBLING INFORMATION

Your brother/sister's (1) name: _____
Your brother/sister's (1) address: _____
Your brother/sister's (1) residential telephone number: _____
Your brother/sister's (1) work telephone number: _____
Is brother/sister (1) living? _____
Brother/sister's (1) date of birth: _____
Is your brother/sister (1) a favorable witness for you?

*****

Your brother/sister's (2) name: _____
Your brother/sister's (2) address: _____
Your brother/sister's (2) residential telephone number: _____
Your brother/sister's (2) work telephone number: _____
Is brother/sister (2) living? _____
Brother/sister's (2) date of birth: _____
Is your brother/sister (2) a favorable witness for you? _____

*****

Your brother/sister's (3) name: _____
Your brother/sister's (3) address: _____
Your brother/sister's (3) residential telephone number: _____
Your brother/sister's (3) work telephone number: _____
Is brother/sister (3) living? _____
Brother/sister's (3) date of birth: _____
Is your brother/sister (3) a favorable witness for you? _____

*****

Your brother/sister's (4) name: _____
Your brother/sister's (4) address: _____
Your brother/sister's (4) residential telephone number: _____
Your brother/sister's (4) work telephone number: _____
Is brother/sister (4) living? _____
Brother/sister's (4) date of birth: _____
Is your brother/sister (4) a favorable witness for you? _____

Add additional information for additional siblings on a separate and attached sheet of paper.

Voodoo Spice Number 2

FINANCIAL INFORMATION

YOUR MONTHLY INCOME/DEDUCTIONS AND EMPLOYMENT INFORMATION

EARNINGS: (circle one for each category)

INCOME:

DEDUCTIONS:
    Minus the following deductions:
    Federal income tax/FICA withheld:
    State income tax deduction:
    Insurance premium deductions:
    Any child support garnishments:
    Other garnishments/deductions:

NET EARNIINGS:
    Net monthly wages (after deductions) $

EMPLOYER:

Name of your employer: _____

Address of your employer: _____

_____

_____

Your employer's telephone number: _____

YOUR SPOUSE'S (OTHER PARENT'S) MONTHLY INCOME/ DEDUCTIONS AND EMPLOYMENT INFORMATION

EARNINGS:

Spouse's gross salary (before deductions): _____
$_____ per (month /year/not applicable)

Spouse's overtime: _____

Spouse's commissions: _____

Spouse's bonus(es): _____

Spouse's interest income: _____

Spouse's trust income: _____

Spouse's dividend income: _____

Spouse's spousal support: _____

Spouse's social security benefits: _____

Spouse's retirement benefits: _____

Spouse's worker's compensation benefits: _____

Spouse's Income/Earning From Any Other Source: _____

DEDUCTIONS:

Minus the following deductions: _____

Federal income tax/FICA withheld: _____

State income tax deduction: _____

Insurance premium deductions: _____

Any child support garnishments: _____

Other garnishments/deductions: _____

NET EARNINGS:

Net monthly wages (after deductions) $ _____

EMPLOYER:

Name of spouse's employer: _____

Address of spouse's employer: _____

Spouse's employer's telephone number: _____

Name of spouse's employer: _____

Address of spouse's employer: _____

_____

Spouse's work telephone number: _____

Voodoo Spice Number 3

YOUR EXPENSES

(Note—your children's expenses shall be listed separately)

HOUSING EXPENSES:
- Housing (rent or mortgage note payment): _____
- Property insurance and taxes: _____
- Premises/yard maintenance and repair: _____
- Condominium assessments: _____
- Furniture payments: _____
- Household supplies: _____

UTILITIES:
- Electricity:
- Gas: _____
- Heating oil: _____
- Water/sewerage: _____
- Garbage collection/recycling service: _____
- Telephone: _____
- Long distance telephone: _____
- Cable: _____

HOUSING MAINTENANCE:
- Maid expense: _____
- Household cleaning supplies: _____
- Lawn and garden maintenance: _____
- Exterminator expense: _____
- Plumbing expense/repair: _____
- Major appliance expense/contract/repair: _____
- Electrical expense/repair: _____
- Painting: _____
- Firewood: _____
- Snow removal: _____
- Miscellaneous housing maintenance: _____

HOUSEHOLD ACCOMMODATIONS:
   Furniture purchase/rental expense: _____
   Appliance purchase/rental expense: _____
   Other household purchases/rental expenses: _____

FOOD:
   Groceries: _____
   Meals eating out/incl. work/school lunches: _____
   Liquor/cordials: _____
   Catered special events: _____

CLOTHING AND PERSONAL GROOMING:
   Your clothing: _____
   Dry cleaning/laundry: _____
   Alteration/tailor expense: _____
   Shoe repair: _____
   Special equipment: _____
   Fur storage: _____
   Miscellaneous clothing expense: _____
   Haircut/styling/coloring: _____
   Manicures/pedicures: _____
   Facials/waxing/massages: _____
   Health club/spas: _____

MEDICAL (Not Covered by Insurance):
   Medical expenses: _____
   Dental expenses: _____
   Orthodontic expenses: _____
   Chiropractic expenses: _____
   Prescriptions: _____
   Non-prescription medication: _____
   Co-payments/deductibles: _____
   Eye examination/glasses/contacts: _____
   Contraceptives: _____
   Physical therapy: _____
   Other miscellaneous medical expenses: _____
   Childrens' medical expenses: _____

TRANSPORTATION:
    Car note/lease: _____
    Gasoline: _____
    Car maintenance: _____
    Parking: _____
    Toll: _____
    Taxi/bus/train/ferry: _____
    Oil change: _____
    Tires: _____
    Repair: _____
    Registration/inspection fees: _____
    Car rental: _____
    Auto club expense: _____
    Towing: _____
    Other transportation expenses: _____

INSURANCE:
    Health/medical: _____
    Automobile: _____
    Life: _____
    Disability: _____
    Funeral/burial: _____
    Homeowners/renters: _____
    Fire: _____
    Flood: _____
    Theft: _____
    Travel: _____
    Other insurance: _____

EDUCATION (For Yourself):
    School/lessons/tutoring/fees: _____
    School loans: _____
    Books/supplies: _____
    Extracurricular/military uniforms: _____
    Miscellaneous education expenses: _____

ENTERTAINMENT/RECREATION:

    Restaurants (not listed in food category): _____

    Theater/opera/symphony/movie/movie rental/concert: _____

    Sporting events: _____

    Vacation expense: _____

    Club dues: _____

    Hobby expense: _____

    Other entertainment expense: _____

CHILD CARE /CHILD SCHOOL EXPENSES:

    Tuition/school/education: _____

    Uniforms: _____

    School lunches: _____

    Day care/before and after school care/baby sitting: _____

    Tutoring: _____

    Children's clothing: _____

    Children's allowances: _____

    Children's books and supplies: _____

    Children's room and board expense: _____

    Children's travel expense: _____

    Lessons: _____

    Camp: _____

    Extracurricular/military/sports uniforms and equipment: _____

    Child's transportation expenses
        (not previously listed in transportation category): _____

    Miscellaneous child related expenses: _____

OTHER LEGAL OBLIGATIONS:

    Child support for other children: _____

    Spousal support to a former spouse: _____

    Taxes (federal and state)
        (not previously listed in housing category): _____

    Other taxes: _____

LEGAL EXPENSES:

    Attorney fees: _____

Court costs: _____

Legal expenses: _____

Expert witness fees: _____

Other legal expenses: _____

MISCELLANEOUS EXPENSES:

Pet/pet supplies: _____

Nursing home care: _____

Professional licenses and dues: _____

Union dues: _____

Religious tithes: _____

Gifts and donations (incl. holidays): _____

Children's gifts to others: _____

Other debts: _____

    Specify creditor: _____

    Specify creditor: _____

    Specify creditor: _____

    Specify creditor: _____

FINANCE/INVESTMENT CHARGES:

Accounting fees: _____

Brokerage fees: _____

Bank finance charges: _____

Credit card interest charges: _____

Tax preparation services: _____

FUTURE KNOWN EXPENSES NOT LISTED ABOVE: (Specify)

_____

_____

CHILDREN'S MEDICAL EXPENSE: _____

_____

*****

TOTAL MONTHLY EXPENSES: _____

Voodoo Spice Number 4

SUMMARY OF YOUR INCOME AND EXPENSES

Total Gross Monthly Income $ _____

    Minus (–)

Total Monthly Expenses $ _____

    Equals (=)

YOUR NET MONTHLY INCOME $ _____

SUMMARY OF YOUR SPOUSE'S (OTHER PARENT'S) INCOME AND EXPENSES

Total Gross Monthly Income $ _____

    Minus (–)

Total Monthly Expenses $ _____

    Equals (=)

Other Spouse's/Parent's
NET MONTHLY INCOME $ _____

YOUR ANNUAL GROSS INCOME (for last five years)

    This year's year-to-date gross income: _____

    Last year's gross income: _____

    Your gross income two years ago (199__/200__): _____

    Your gross income three years ago (199__/200__): _____

    Your gross income four years ago (199__/200__): _____

    Your gross income five years ago (199__/200__): _____

Information Regarding Your Spouse

YOUR SPOUSE'S ANNUAL GROSS INCOME (for last five years)

This year's year-to-date gross income: _____

Last year's gross income: _____

Spouse's gross income two years ago (199__/200__): _____

Spouse's gross income three years ago (199__/200__): _____

Spouse's gross income four years ago (199__/200__): _____

Spouse's gross income five years ago (199__/200__): _____

BANK ACCOUNTS

Name of banking/savings and loan: _____

Address of bank/savings and loan: _____

Type of account (checking/savings/certificate of deposit)

Account number: _____

Name or names in which the account is/was listed: _____

Amount in the account as of (date): _____

* * *

Name of banking/savings and loan: _____

Address of bank/savings and loan: _____

Type of account (checking/savings/certificate of deposit):

Account number: _____

Name or names in which the account is/was listed: _____

Amount in the account as of (date): _____

* * *

Name of banking/savings and loan: _____

Address of bank/savings and loan: _____

Type of account (checking/savings/certificate of deposit):

Account number: _____

Name or names in which the account is/was listed: _____

Amount in the account as of (date): _____

Voodoo Spice Number 5

YOUR OWNERSHIP INTEREST IN A BUSINESS

Name of business: _____

Address of business: _____

Telephone number of business: _____

Type of business: _____

Form of business: _____
(sole proprietorship, corporation, joint venture, partnership, etc.)

Position held (if any): _____

Voodoo Spice Number 6

REAL ESTATE

PRESENTLY OWNED:
Address/location: _____
Date acquired: _____
Purchase price: _____
Down payment: _____
Equity: _____
Debt still owed: _____
First mortgage holder and amount: _____
Second mortgage holder and amount: _____
Other mortgages: _____
Liens: _____
Persons/entities named as owners on the act of sale or donation: _____
: _____

PREVIOUSLY OWNED WITHIN LAST THREE YEARS:
Address/location: _____
Date acquired: _____
Date sold by you/your spouse: _____
Purchase price: _____
Purchase down payment: _____
Price sold: _____
Any owner financing, if so amount and terms: _____
Persons/entities named as owners on the act of sale or donation: _____
_____

Voodoo Spice Number 7

STATE BAR ASSOCIATIONS

Alabama State Bar Association
415 Dexter Avenue
P.O. Box 671
Montgomery, AL 36101
(334) 269-1515

Alaska State Bar Association
P.O. Box 100279
Anchorage, AK 99510
(907) 272-7469

State Bar of Arizona
111 W. Monroe, Suite 1800
Phoenix, AZ 85003
(520) 340-7200

Arkansas State Bar Association
400 W. Markham
Little Rock, AR 72201
(501) 375-4606

State Bar of California
555 Franklin Street
San Francisco, CA 94102

Colorado Bar Association
1900 Grant Street, Suite 950
Denver, CO 80203
(303) 860-1115

Connecticut Bar Association
101 Corporate Place
Rocky Hill, CT 06067
(860) 721-0025

District of Columbia Bar Association
1250 H Street, 6th Floor
Washington, D.C. 20005
(202) 737-4700

Bar Association of the District of Columbia
1819 H Street, N.W., 12th Floor
Washington, D.C. 20006
(202) 223-6600

Delaware State Bar Association
1201 Orange Street
Wilmington, DE 19801
(302) 658-5279

Florida Bar Association
650 Apalachee Parkway
Tallahassee, FL 32399
(904) 561-5600

State Bar of Georgia
800 The Hut Building
50 Hurt Plaza
Atlanta, GA 30303
(800) 334-6865

Hawaii State Bar Association
Penthouse 1
1136 Union Mall
Honolulu, HI 96813
(808) 537-1868

Idaho State Bar Association
525 W. Jefferson Street
P.O. Box 895
Boise, ID 83701
(208) 334-4500

Illinois State Bar Association
424 S. Second Street
Springfield, IL 52701
(217) 525-1760

Indiana State Bar Association
230 E. Ohio Street, 4th Floor
Indianapolis, IN 46204
(317) 639-5465

Iowa State Bar Association
521 E. Locust
Des Moines, IA 50309
(515) 243-3179

Kansas Bar Association
1200 Harrison Street
P.O. Box 1037
Topeka, KS 66601
(913) 234-5696

Kentucky Bar Association
514 W. Main Street
Frankfort, KY 40601
(502) 564-3795

Louisiana State Bar Association
601 St. Charles Avenue
New Orleans, LA 70130
(504) 566-1600

Maine State Bar Association
124 State Street
P.O. Box 788
Augusta, ME 04332
(207) 622-7523

Maryland State Bar Association
520 W. Fayette Street
Baltimore, MD 21201
(410) 685-7878

Massachusetts Bar Association
20 West Street
Boston, MA 02111
(617) 542-3602

State Bar of Michigan
306 Townsend Street
Lansing, MI 48933
(517) 346-6331

Minnesota State Bar Association
514 Nicollet Mall, #300
Minneapolis, MN 55402
(612) 333-1183

Mississippi Bar Association
643 N. State Street
P.O. Box 2168
Jackson, MS 39225
(601) 948-4471

Missouri Bar Association
326 Monroe
P.O. Box 119
Jefferson City, MO 65101
(314) 635-4128

State Bar of Montana
46 N. Last Chance Gulch, Suite 2A
P.O. Box 577
Helena, MT 59624
(406) 442-7660

Nebraska State Bar Association
635 S. 14th Street, 2nd Floor
P.O. Box 81809
Lincoln, NE 68508
(402) 475-7091

State Bar of Nevada
201 Las Vegas Blvd. S, Suite 200
Las Vegas, NV 89101
(702) 382-2200

New Hampshire Bar Association
112 Pleasant Street
Concord, NH 03301
(603) 224-6942

New Jersey State Bar Association
New Jersey Law Center
One Constitution square
New Brunswick, NJ 08901
(908) 249-5000

State Bar of New Mexico
5121 Masthead NE
Albuquerque, NM 87109
(505) 797-6000

New York State Bar Association
One Elk Street
Albany, NY 12207
(518) 487-5557

North Carolina State Bar
208 Fayetteville Street Mall
P.O. Box 25908
Raleigh, NC 27611

North Carolina Bar Association
P.O. Box 3688
Cary, NC 27519
(919) 677-0561

State Bar Association of North Dakota
515 1/2 E. Broadway, Suite 101
P.O. Box 2136
Bismark, ND 58502
(701) 255-1404

Ohio State Bar Association
1700 Lake Shore Drive
P.O. Box 16562
Columbus, OH 43216
(614) 487-2050

Oklahoma Bar Association
1901 N. Lincoln
P.O. Box 53036
Oklahoma City, OK 73152
(405) 524-2365

Oregon State Bar Association
5200 SW Meadows Road
P.O. Box 1689
Lake Oswego, OR 97035
(503) 620-0222

Pennsylvania Bar Association
100 South Street
P.O. Box 186
Harrisburg, PA 17108
(717) 238-6715

Puerto Rico Bar Association
P.O. Box 1900
San Juan, PR 00902
(809) 721-3358

Rhode Island Bar Association
115 Cedar Street
Providence, RI 02903
(401) 421-5740

South Carolina Bar Association
950 Taylor Street
P.O. Box 608
Columbia, SC 29202
(803) 799-6653

State Bar Association of South Dakota
222 E. Capitol Avenue
Pierre, SD 57501
(605) 224-7554

Tennessee Bar Association
3622 W. End Avenue
Nashville, TN 37205
(615) 383-7421

State Bar of Texas
1414 Colorado
P.O. Box 12487
Austin, TX 78711
(512) 463-1463

Utah State Bar Association
Utah Law and Justice Center
645 S. 200 E. #310
Salt Lake City, UT 84111
(801) 531-9077

Vermont Bar Association
P.O. Box 100
35-37 Court Street
Montpelier, VT 05601
(802) 223-2020

Virgin Islands Bar Association
P.O. Box 4108
Christiansted, VI 00822
(809) 778-7497

Virginia State Bar
707 E. Main Street, suite 1500
Richmond, VA 23219
(804) 775-0551

Virginia Bar Association
701 E. Franklin Street, Suite 1120
Richmond, VA 23219
(804) 644-0041

Washington State Bar Association
2101 Fourth Avenue, Fourth Floor
Seattle, WA 98121
(206) 727-8200

West Virginia State Bar Association
2006 Kanawha Blvd. E
Charleston, WV 25311
(304) 558-7993

State Bar of Wisconsin
402 W. Wilson
P.O. Box 7158
Madison, WI 53707
(608) 257-3838

Wyoming State Bar Association
500 Randall Avenue
P.O. Box 109
Cheyenne, WY 82003
(307) 632-9061

Voodoo Spice Number 8

DIVORCE STATISTICS

ANNUAL NATIONAL DIVORCE AND ANNULMENT RATE

Year	Number of Divorces & Annulments	Rate per 1,000 People	Year	Number of Divorces & Annulments	Rate per 1,000 People
1940	264,000	2.0	1968	584,000	2.9
1941	293,000	2.2	1969	639,000	3.2
1942	321,000	2.4	1970	708,000	3.5
1943	359,000	2.6	1971	773,000	3.7
1944	400,000	2.9	1972	845,000	4.0
1945	485,000	3.5	1973	915,000	4.3
1946	610,000	4.3	1974	977,000	4.6
1947	483,000	3.4	1975	1,036,000	4.4
1948	408,000	2.8	1976	1,083,000	5.0
1949	397,000	2.7	1977	1,091,000	5.0
1950	385,000	2.6	1978	1,130,000	5.1
1951	381,000	2.5	1979	1,181,000	5.3
1952	392,000	2.5	1980	1,189,000	5.2
1953	390,000	2.5	1981	1,213,000	5.3
1954	379,000	2.4	1982	1,170,000	5.1
1955	377,000	2.3	1983	1,158,000	5.0
1956	382,000	2.3	1984	1,168,000	5.0
1957	381,000	2.2	1985	1,190,000	5.0
1958	368,000	2.1	1986	1,178,000	4.9
1959	395,000	2.2	1987	1,166,000	4.8
1960	393,000	2.2	1988	1,167,000	4.8
1961	414,000	2.3	1989	1,157,000	4.7
1962	413,000	2.2	1990	1,182,000	4.7
1963	428,000	2.3	1991	1,189,000	4.7
1964	450,000	2.4	1992	1,215,000	4.8
1965	479,000	2.5	1993	1,187,000	4.6
1966	499,000	2.5	1994	1,191,000	4.6
1967	523,000	2.6	1995 *	1,169,000	4.4

SOURCE: U.S. Center for Health Statistics, *Vital Statistics of the United States,* annual; *Monthly Vital Statistics Report*; and other unreported data.

* Provisional data.

Voodoo Spice Number 9

STATE BY STATE DIVORCE STATISTICS

Ranking by State	Number of Divorces	Rate per Thousand
Nevada	13,061	9.0
Arkansas	17,458	7.1
Oklahoma	21,855	6.7
Tennessee	34,167	6.6
Wyoming	3,071	6.5
Indiana	*	6.5
Alabama	26,116	6.2
Idaho	7,075	6.2
New Mexico	9,882	6.0
Florida	82,963	5.9
Arizona	23,725	5.8
Kentucky	22,211	5.8
Mississippi	15,212	5.7
Washington	29,976	5.6
Alaska	3,354	5.5
Texas	99,073	5.4
Oregon	16,307	5.3
Georgia	37,001	5.2
Colorado	18,795	5.1
North Carolina	36,292	5.1
West Virginia	9,179	5.0
Missouri	26,324	5.0
Montana	4,153	4.9
Delaware	3,385	4.8
Utah	8,999	4.7
Kansas	12,093	4.7
Virginia	30,016	4.6
Ohio	49,968	4.5
New Hampshire	5,041	4.4
Maine	5,433	4.4
California	*	4.3
Hawaii	4,979	4.2
South Carolina	15,301	4.2
South Dakota	3,022	4.2
Michigan	38,727	4.1
Vermont	2,316	4.0
Nebraska	6,547	4.0
Iowa	10,930	3.9
Washington D.C.	2,244	3.9
Illinois	43,398	3.7
Louisiana	*	3.6

Ranking by State	Number of Divorces	Rate per Thousand
Minnesota	16,217	3.6
Maryland	17,439	3.6
North Dakota	2,201	3.4
Wisconsin	17,478	3.4
Pennsylvania	40,040	3.3
New York	59,195	3.3
Rhode Island	3,231	3.2
New Jersey	23,899	3.0
Connecticut	9,095	2.8
Massachusetts	14,530	2.4

SOURCE: *1994 Statistics from Monthly Vital Statistics*, Vol 43, No. 13, October 23, 1995, Centers for Disease Control and Prevention/National Health Statistics. All data is for 1994 with the exception of California (1987), Indiana (1987), and Louisiana (1983).

Voodoo Spice Number 10

DIVORCE STATISTICS

RATE OF DIVORCES AND ANNULMENTS
BY AGE AND GENDER AT THE TIME OF THE DECREE

WOMEN

Under 20 years	48.6 %
20–24 years	46.0
25–29 years	36.6
30–34 years	27.9
35–39 years	23.1
40–44 years	19.3
45–49 years	13.8
50–54 years	8.2
55–59 years	4.8
60–64 years	2.9
65 years and older	1.4

MEN

Under 20 years	32.8 %
20–24 years	50.2
25–29 years	39.3
30–34 years	31.9
35–39 years	25.9
40–44 years	21.9
45–49 years	17.3
50–54 years	12.0
55–59 years	7.8
60–64 years	4.7
65 years and older	2.1

SOURCE: *Advance Report of Final Divorce Statistics, 1989 and 1990. Monthly Vital Statistics Report*; Vol. 43 no.8, Supp. Hyattsville, Maryland; National Center for Health Statistics, 1995.

Voodoo Spice Number 11

DIVORCE STATISTICS

PERCENT DISTRIBUTION OF DIVORCES AND ANNULMENTS BY AGE OF WIFE AND HUSBAND AT THE TIME OF THIS MARRIAGE

WIFE

Under 20 years	27.6 %
20–24 years	36.6
25–29 years	16.4
30–34 years	8.5
35–39 years	5.1
40–44 years	2.7
45 years and over	3.0

HUSBAND

Under 20 years	11.7 %
20–24 years	38.8
25–29 years	22.3
30–34 years	11.6
35–39 years	6.5
40–44 years	3.9
45 years and over	5.2

SOURCE: *Advance Report of Final Divorce Statistics, 1989 and 1990. Monthly Vital Statistics Report*; Vol. 43 no.8, Supp. Hyattsville, Maryland; National Center for Health Statistics, 1995.

Voodoo Spice Number 12

MY NOVEL TO MY ATTORNEY

CONFIDENTIAL/ATTORNEY-CLIENT WORK PRODUCT

Use your novel to evaluate the attributes and shortcomings of youself and your spouse. Freely write down everything that comes to your mind. Pour your thoughts onto paper.

Let's begin!

The following are my ATTRIBUTES as a "person":
(*Put responses on separate sheet*)

The following are my SHORTCOMINGS as a "person":
(*Put responses on separate sheet*)

The following are my spouse's ATTRIBUTES as a "person":
(*Put responses on separate sheet*)

The following are my spouse's SHORTCOMINGS as a "person":
(*Put responses on separate sheet*)

Now answer similar questions about you and your spouse as a PARENT.

The following are my ATTRIBUTES as a "parent":
(*Put responses on separate sheet*)

The following are my SHORTCOMINGS as a "parent":
(*Put responses on separate sheet*)

The following are my spouse's ATTRIBUTES as a "parent":
(*Put responses on separate sheet*)

The following are my spouse's SHORTCOMINGS as a "parent":
(*Put responses on separate sheet*)

Voodoo Spice Number 13

CUSTODY/VISITATION RESOURCE WORKSHEET

CHILD'S NAME:

Names, addresses and telephone numbers of the following persons:

Teacher: _____
Day-care providers: _____
Coach: _____
Doctor: _____
Dentist: _____
Priest/pastor/rabbi/spiritual leader: _____
Neighbors: _____
Child's best friends: _____
Boy scout/cub scout/girl scout/brownie leaders: _____
School principal: _____
PTA members: _____
Baby sitters: _____
Sunday school teacher: _____
Guidance counselor: _____
Relatives actively involved in child's life: _____
Other persons actively involved in child's life: _____
_____
_____

Police officer summoned to any domestic dispute: _____
Nanny: _____
Housekeeper: _____
Psychiatrist/sociologist/social worker: _____
School nurse: _____
Instructor of extracurricular activity: _____

Voodoo Spice Number 14

YOUR CHILD'S IDENTIFICATION RECORD

*Complete one for each child.
Update the photograph and signature every few years.*

Child's full name: _____

Child's current address: _____

Child's current telephone number: _____

Child's date of birth: _____

Child's place of birth: _____

Child's social security number: _____

Child's blood type and other special medical needs: _____
_____

All identifying marks, scars, birthmarks or other identifying characteristics: _____
_____

Child's passport number (if applicable): _____

Finger print each hand (all fingers and thumb).

LEFT HAND:

| Thumb | Finger | Finger | Finger | Finger |

RIGHT HAND:

| Thumb | Finger | Finger | Finger | Finger |

Date of signature: _____

Your child's signature: _____

Please Attach Recent Color Photograph of Child!

Voodoo Spice Number 15

VOODOO DIVORCE TELEPHONE LOG

Date of Call	Time/Begin	Time/End	Total Time	Issues Discussed

Voodoo Spice Number 16

Date:

To: _____, Attorney at Law
_____
_____

Check one or both:

_____ Via Facsimile Number:

_____ Via U. S. Mail, Certified Number:

Client Name:

Client Telephone Number:

Please note that I have telephoned your office on several occasions and you have not returned my telephone calls. I have telephoned you on the following date(s): _____
_____

Please provide me with your professional courtesy by immediately returning my telephone call(s). In so doing, please respond to the following inquiry or statement.

INQUIRY/STATEMENT:
_____
_____
_____
_____
_____
_____
_____

Thank you for your prompt attention to this matter.

                              With best regards, I remain
                              Very truly yours,

                              _____

Voodoo Spice Number 17

States that exclude the issue of fault in the determination of alimony:

Alaska, Arizona, Arkansas, California, Colorado, Delaware, Hawaii, Illinois, Indiana, Iowa, Kansas, Maine, Maryland, Massachusetts, Minnesota, Mississippi, Montana, Nebraska, Nevada, New Jersey, New Mexico, New York, Ohio, Oklahoma, Oregon, Vermont, Washington, Wisconsin, and Wyoming.

States that examine the issue of fault as to a bar to an award of alimony:

Alabama, Georgia, Louisiana, North Carolina, South Carolina, Virginia, and West Virginia.

Voodoo Spice Number 18

YOUR STATE'S TIME LIMIT TO ESTABLISH PATERNITY

State time limits to establish paternity by a parent:

No Time Limit:
Arkansas, Georgia, Massachusetts, Oregon, Rhode Island, South Dakota, and Virgin Islands.

The State's "Age of Majority":
Alabama, Alaska, Arizona, California (by IV-D), Colorado, Connecticut, Delaware, District of Columbia, Kansas, Kentucky, Louisiana, Maine, Minnesota, Missouri, Montana, New York, North Carolina, Oklahoma, Pennsylvania, South Carolina, Utah, Virginia, Washington, West Virginia.

Age 18:
Mississippi for OCSE

Age 19:
Alabama

Age 19: Age of majority plus one year:
Iowa and Tennessee

Age 19:
New Hampshire and Wisconsin

Age 20: Two years after child's 18th birthday:
Texas

Age 21:
Vermont and Wyoming

Age 21: Three years beyond the child's 18th birthday:
Hawaii, Nevada, New Mexico, and North Dakota,

Age 22: Four years after the child's 18th birthday:
Florida

Age 23:
Ohio

Five years beyond child's 18th birthday:
New Jersey

Four years after child's birth if brought by mother or alleged father;
18 years after child's birth if brought by guardian or next-friend of child:
Nebraska
Puerto Rico: During lives of presumptive parents and one year beyond their deaths except in following instances: (1) if father or mother died during minority of child in which case child may bring action before first 4 years of his having attained his majority shall have lapsed; (2) if after death of father or mother there shall appear a written statement or document, of which no notice was recognized, in this case action shall be established within next 6 months after document has been discovered.
Indiana
Michigan

Voodoo Spice Number 19

THRESHOLDS FOR GENETIC TEST RESULTS

(creating a rebuttable presumption if probability of paternity is equal to or greater than _____%)

95%:
Alaska, Arkansas, Arizona, Florida, Iowa, Montana, New York, North Dakota, Ohio, Oklahoma (Conclusive if 98%), and Puerto Rico (Conclusive 98%)

97%:
Alabama, Colorado, Georgia, Kansas, Massachusetts, Maine, New Hampshire, North Carolina, Rhode Island, South Carolina, and Wyoming

98%:
Missouri, Vermont, Virginia, Washington, and West Virginia

99%:
Connecticut, Delaware, District of Columbia, Hawaii, Indiana, Kentucky, Michigan, Minnesota (Temporary Orders With 92%), Mississippi, Nebraska, Nevada, New Jersey, New Mexico, Oregon, Pennsylvania, South Dakota, Tennessee, Texas, Utah, and Wisconsin

99.9%:
Louisiana
California—Paternity index of 100 or greater per California Family Code Section 7555(b)(2).

Voodoo Spice Number 20

SUPPORT GROUPS

American Divorce Association for Men
1008 White Oak street
Arlington Heights, IL 60005
(312) 870-1040

**America's Society of Separated
and Divorced Men**
575 Keep Street
Elgin, IL 60120
(847) 695-2200

Children's Defense Fund
122 C Street N.W., Suite 400
Washington, D.C. 20001

The Children's Foundation
725 15th St. N.W., Suite 505
Washington, D.C. 20005
(202) 347-3300
Fax: (202) 347-3382
cfwashdc@aol.com

Divorce Aid, Inc.
9109 Pelican Avenue
Fountain Valley, CA 92708
(714) 968-2973

Equal Rights for Fathers
P.O. Box 6327
Albany, CA 94706
(415) 848-2323

Family Law Action Council
P.O. Box 201
Fullerton, CA 92623

Family Law Council
U.S. Reform, Inc. (N.J.)
P.O. Box 217
Fair Lawn, NJ 07410
(201) 696-5156

**Family Law Reform &
Justice Council of Alaska**
P.O. Box 897
Ward Cove, AL 99928
(907) 225-6808

**Family Law Reform and
Justice Council of Pennsylvania**
P.O. Box 60
Broomail, PA 19008

Fathers Are Forever
P.O. Box 4804
Panorama City, CA 91412
(818) 846-2219

Fathers for Equal Rights, Inc.
3623 Douglas Avenue
Des Moines, Iowa 50310
(515) 277-8789

Fathers for Equal Rights, Inc.
P.O. Box 010847, Flagler Station
Miami, FL 33101
(305) 895-6351
(305) 895-7461
(305) 234-4156
http://netrunner.net/-fathers/

Fathers United for Equal Rights
P.O. Box 1224
Arlington, VA 22210
(703) 471-5535

Fathers United for Equal Rights, N.J. Inc.
P.O. Box 900
Maywood, NJ 07607
(201) 843-8156

**Fathers United for Equal Rights and
The Second Wives Coalition**
P.O. Box 7585
Baltimore, MD 21207
(301) 664-5819

**Fathers United for Equal Rights Foundation
of Montgomery County Maryland, Inc.**
P. O. Box 3308
Silver Spring, MD 20901

Florida Fathers for Equal Rights
1302 North East 118th Street
North Miami, FL 33161
(305) 893-9709

Grandparents Anonymous
1924 Beverly
Sylvan Lake, MI 48053

Grandparents'/Children's Rights
5728 Bayonne Avenue
Haslett, MI 48840
(517) 339-8663

Institute of Legal Research and Education, Inc.
P.O. Box 31813
Dallas, TX 75231
(214) 692-1492

Joint Custody Association
10606 Wilkins Avenue
Los Angeles, CA 90024
(213) 475-5352

Men's Defense Association
1785 Lyons Street
Forest Lake, MN 55025-8107
(612) 464-7887
Fax: (612) 464-7135
www.mensdefense.org
mensdefens@aol.com

Men's Rights Association
17854 Lyons
P.O. Box 189
Forest Lake , MN 55025
(612) 464-7887

National Center on Women and Family Law
799 Broadway, Room 402
New York, New York 10003

National Council on Family Law
P.O. Box 104
Foley, MS 63347

National Organization for Men
381 Park Avenue South
New York, NY 10016
(212) 766-4030

The National Organization for Women (NOW)
1401 New York Avenue N.W., Suite 800
Washington, D.C. 20005

National Women's Law Center
1616 P Street, N.W.
Washington, D.C. 20036

Parents Without Partners
401 N. Michigan Avenue
Chicago, IL 60611
(312) 644-6610
(800) 637-7974
http//:www.parentswithoutpartners.org

Parents Without Partners
7910 Woodmont Ave. Suite 1000
Bethesda, MD 20814
(Single Parent issues; newsletter and magazine)

Sisterhood of Black Single Mothers
1360 Fulton Street
Brooklyn, NY 11216
(718) 638-0413

The Stepfamily Association of America
602 East Joppa Road
Baltimore, MD 21204

Stepfamily Foundation
333 West End Avenue
New York, NY 10023
(212) 877-3244
Info (212) 799 STEP
Fax: (212) 362-7030
stepfamily@aol.com
www.stepfamily.org

Texas Fathers for Equal Rights
2514 West Mulberry
San Antonio, TX 78228
(512) 735-7461

Toughlove International
P.O. Box 1069
Doylestown, PA 18901
(215) 348-7090

United Parents of Absconded Children
Wolf Run Road, Box 127-A
Cuba, NY 14727
(716) 372-3416

United States Divorce Reform, Inc.
Box 243
Kenwood, CA 95452
(707) 833-2550

United States Divorce Reform Inc. of Minnesota
1031 Pleasant Avenue
St. Paul, MN 55102
(612) 224-6298

Washington Chapter United States Divorce Reform
P.O. Box 11
Auburn, WA 98002
(206) 863-5788

Women's Legal Defense Fund
2000 P Street N.W., Suite 400
Washington, D.C. 20036

Voodoo Spice Number 21

REGIONAL OFFICES OF CHILD SUPPORT ENFORCEMENT

REGION I
Connecticut, Maine, Massachusetts,
New Hampshire, Rhode Island, and Vermont

OCSE Regional Office
Administration for Children and Families
John F. Kennedy Federal Building
Room 2000
Boston, MA 02203
(617) 565-2478

REGION II
New York, New Jersey, Puerto Rico,
and Virgin Islands

OCSE Regional Office
Administration for children and Families
Federal Building, Room 4048
26 Federal Plaza
New York, NY 10278
(212) 264-2890

REGION III
Delaware, Maryland, Pennsylvania,
Washington D.C., and West Virginia

OCSE Regional Office
Administration for Children and Families
P.O. Box 8436
Philadelphia, PA 19104
(215) 596-4370

REGION IV
Alabama, Florida, Georgia, Kentucky,
Mississippi, North Carolina, South Carolina,
and Tennessee

OCSE Regional Office
Administration for Children and Families
101 Marietta Tower, Suite 821
Atlanta, GA 30323
(404) 331-2180

REGION V
Illinois, Indiana, Michigan, Minnesota, Ohio,
and Wisconsin

OCSE Regional Office
Administration for Children and Families
105 West Adams Street, 20th Floor
Chicago, IL 60603
(312) 353-4237

REGION VI
Arkansas, Louisiana, New Mexico, Oklahoma,
and Texas

OCSE Regional Office
Administration for Children and Families
1301 Young Street, Suite 945 (ACF-3)
Dallas, TX 75202
(214) 767-3749

REGION VII
Iowa, Kansas, Missouri, and Nebraska

OCSE Regional Office
Administration for Children and Families
601 East 12th Street, Suite 276
Kansas City, MO 64106
(816) 426-3584

REGION VIII
Colorado, Montana, North Dakota,
South Dakota, Utah, and Wyoming

OCSE Regional Office
Administration for Children and Families
Federal Office Bldg., Suite 325
1961 Stout Street
Denver, CO 80294-3538
(303) 844-3100

REGION IX
Arizona, California, Hawaii, Nevada, and
Guam

OCSE Regional Office
Administration for Children and Families
50 United Nations Plaza, Room 450
San Francisco, CA 94102
(415) 437-8459

REGION X
Alaska, Idaho, Oregon, and Washington

OCSE Regional Office
Administration for Children and Families
2201 Sixth Street, Mail Stop RX-70
Seattle, WA 98121
(206) 615-2547

Voodoo Spice Number 22

STATE CHILD SUPPORT ENFORCEMENT AGENCIES AND ENFORCEMENT SUPPORT GROUPS

ALABAMA

Alabama OCSE Agency and URESA Information Agent
Mr. Paul Vincent, Director
Bureau of Child Support
Dept. of Pensions & Security
64 North Union Street
Montgomery, Al 36130
Telephone: (205) 261-2872

Parents' Support Enforcement Group
Kids in Need Deserve Equal Rights (KINDER)
337 East Haven Dr.
Birmingham, Al 35215
Contact: Judy Jennings
(205) 251-2223 (day)

ALASKA

Alaska OCSE Agency
Mr. Dan Copeland, Director
Child Support Enforcement Agency
Department of Revenue
201 E. 9th Ave. #202
Anchorage, AK 99501
Telephone: (907) 276-3441

Alaska URESA Information Agent
Fred D. Smith,
Chief Enforcement Officer
Child Support Enforcement Agency
Department of Revenue
201 E. 9th Avenue, #202, MS 01
Anchorage, AK 99501
Telephone: (907) 276-3441, Ext. 266

ARIZONA

ARIZONA OCSE Agency and ERISA Interstate Inquiries and Complaints
Mr. John Ahl, Program Administrator
Child Support
Enforcement Administration
Dept. of Economic Security
P.O. Box 6123, Site Code 966C
Phoenix, AZ 85005
Telephone: (602) 255-3465

Arizona URESA Information Agent
Mr. Robert Corbin
Arizona Attorney General
P.O. Box 6123, Site Code 775 C
Phoenix, AZ 85005
Telephone: (602) 255-5556

Parents' Support Enforcement Group
Organization for Protection
of America's Children (OPAC)
P.O. Box 1907
Scottsdale, AZ 85252
Contact: Terry Raetz (602) 949-9803 (eve.)
Kathy Browne (602) 938-7206 (eve.)

ARKANSAS

Arkansas OCSE Agency
Mr. Ed Baskin, Director
Office of Child Support Enforcement
Arkansas Social Services Division
P.O. Box 3358
Little Rock, AR 72203
Telephone: (501) 371-2464

URESA Interstate Inquiries and Complaints
Mr. Ivan H. Smith
Director of Legal Services
Arkansas Social Services Division
P.O. Box 1437
Little Rock, Arkansas 72203
Telephone: (501) 371-1981

CALIFORNIA

California OCSE Agency
Mr. Robert A. Barton, Chief
Child Support Program
Management Branch
Department of Social Services
744 P Street
Sacramento, CA 95814
Telephone: (916) 323-8994

URESA Information Agent/Interstate Inquiries and Complaints
Ms. Gloria F. Dehart
Deputy Attorney General
Office of the Attorney General
6000 State Building
San Francisco, CA 94102
Telephone: (415) 557-0799

Parents' Support Enforcement Groups
Parents Organization for Support Enforcement (POSE)
5212 Fairfax Rd.
Bakersfield, CA 93306
Contact: Charlie Wells (805) 872-2985 (eve.)

Single Parent Action Network
10560 Colona Road
Rancho Cordova, CA 95670
Contact: Mary Drummond
(916) 635-9176 (eve.)

Single Parents United 'N' Kids (SPUNK)
P.O. Box 2161
Palm Springs, CA 92263
Contact: Teddy Kieley (619) 323-1559

COLORADO

Colorado OCSE Agency and URESA Interstate Inquiries and Complaints
Mr. James Galeotti, Chief
Child Support Enforcement Section
Dept. of Social Services
1575 Sherman St., Room 423
Denver, CO 80203
Telephone: (303) 866-2422

URESA Information Agent
Kenneth A. Switzer
Child Support Enforcement Section
Dept. of Social Services
1575 Sherman St.
Denver, CO 80203
Telephone: (303) 866-2422

Parents' Support Enforcement Group
Kids in Need Deserve Equal Rights (KINDER)
5420 Wild Lane
Loveland, CO 80537
Contact: Mary Alice Chaffin
(303) 663-0949 (eve.)

CONNECTICUT

Connecticut OCSE Agency
Mr. Anthony DiNallo, Chief
Div. of Child Support Enforcement
Dept. of Human Resources
110 Bartholomew Ave.
Hartford, CT 06115
Telephone: (203) 566-3053

URESA Information Agent and Interstate Inquiries and Complaints
Mr. A. J. Salius, Director
Superior Court, Family Division
28 Grand St.
Hartford, CT 06106
Telephone: (203) 566-8187

Parents' Support Enforcement Groups
Parents Enforcing Court Ordered Support (PECOS)
25 Indian Run
Enfield, CT 06082
Contact: Patricia Caputo (203) 749-0894

DELAWARE

Delaware OCSE Agency
Mr. Frank F. Hindman, Acting Chief
Bur. of Child Support Enforcement
Dept. of Health & Social Svcs.
P.O. Box 904
New Castle, DE 19720
Telephone: (302) 571-3620

URESA Information Agent and Interstate Inquiries and Complaints
Ms. Susan F. Paikin
Director of Support
Family Court of Delaware
900 King St., P.O. Box 2359
Wilmington, DE 19899
Telephone: (302) 571-3867

DISTRICT OF COLUMBIA

District of Columbia OCSE Agency
Mr. Luis Rumbaut, Acting Chief
Bureau of Paternity/
Child Support Enforcement
Dept. of Human Services
435 Eye St., N.W.
Washington, DC 20001
Telephone: (202) 727-8820

URESA Information Agent
Mr. Hugh O. Stevenson
Assistant Corporation Counsel
D.C. Office of Corporation Counsel
500 Indiana Ave. N.W., Rm. 4450
Washington, D.C. 20001
Telephone: (202) 727-3839

URESA Interstate Inquiries and Complaints
Ms. Annette Simpson, URESA Coordinator
Bureau of Paternity/
Child Sup. Enforcement
Dept. of Human Services
435 Eye St. N.W.
Washington, D.C. 20001
Telephone: (202) 727-5058

FLORIDA

Florida OCSE Agency, URESA Information Agent and URESA Interstate Inquiries and Complaints
Mr. Samuel G. Ashdown, Jr., Director
Child Support Enforcement
Dept. of Health & Rehabilitation Services
1317 Winewood Blvd.
Tallahassee, FL 32301
Telephone: (904) 488-9900

Parents' Support Enforcement Groups
Children Against Deadbeat Dads (CADD)
P.O. Box 2010 E.V.
Ormand Beach, FL 32074
Contact: Marj Van Brackle
(904) 672-3499 (eve.)

GEORGIA

Georgia OCSE Agency and URESA Interstate Inquiries and Complaints
Mr. Jerry Townsend, Director
Office of Child Support Recovery
Dept. of Human Resources
878 Peachtree St., N.E.,
P.O. Box 80000
Atlanta, GA 30357
Telephone: (404) 894-5087

URESA Information Agent
Mr. Spencer Lawton, Sr., Manager
Office of Child Support Recovery
Dept. of Human Resources
878 Peachtree St. NE,
P.O. Box 80000
Atlanta, GA 30357
Telephone: (404) 894-5933

Parents' Support Enforcement Groups
Coalition to Help Enforce Child Support
437 The North Chase
Atlanta, GA 30328
Contact: Arlene Gelbert (mail only)

GUAM

Guam OCSE Agency
Ms. Julia Perez, Program Coordinator IV
Child Support Enforcement Office
Dept. of Public Health and Social Services
P.O. Box 2816
Agana, GU 96910
Telephone: (671) 734-2947

Guam URESA Information Agent
Office of Attorney General
Department of Law
PDN Building, Suite 701
238 O'Hara St.
Agana, GU 96910
Telephone: (671) 462-6841

HAWAII

Hawaii OCSE Agency
Mr. James O'Brien, Director
Child Support Enforcement Agency
770 Kapiolani, Suite 606
Honolulu, HI 96813
Telephone: (808) 548-5779

Hawaii URESA Information Agent
Mr. James O'Brien, Director
Child Support Enforcement Agency
770 Kapiolani, Suite 606
Honolulu, HI 96813
Telephone: (808) 548-5779

**Hawaii URESA Interstate
Inquiries and Complaints**
Ms. Catherine J. Carman
Child Support Enforcement Specialist V
Child Support Enforcement Agency
770 Kapiolani Blvd., Suite 606
Honolulu, HI 96813
Telephone: (808) 548-6723

IDAHO

Idaho OCSE Agency
Ms. Patricia Barrell, Chief
Bureau of Support Enforcement
Dept. of Health & Welfare
Statehouse Mail
Boise, ID 83720
Telephone: (208) 334-4422

**Idaho URESA Information Agent and
Interstate Inquiries and Complaints**
Ms. Susan Peterson
Bureau of Support Enforcement
Dept. of Health & Welfare
Statehouse Mail
Boise, ID 83720
Telephone: (208) 334-4418

ILLINOIS

**Illinois OCSE Agency,
URESA Information Agent**
Mr. Gerald D. Slavens, Chief
Bureau of Child Support
Dept. of Public Aid
316 S. 2nd St.
Springfield, IL 62762
Telephone: (217) 782-1366

**Illinois URESA Interstate
Inquiries and Complaints**
Bureau of Child Support
Reciprocal Unit
225 S. 4th St.
P.O. Box 2127
Springfield, IL 62705
Telephone: (217) 782-1388

INDIANA

**Indiana OCSE Agency, URESA Information
Agent, and URESA Interstate
Inquiries and Complaints**
Ms. Paula Eggermann, Acting Director
Child Support Enf. Division
Dept. of Public Welfare
141 S. Meridian St., 4th Flr.
Indianapolis, IN 46225
Telephone: (317) 232-4885

Parents' Support Enforcement Group
Equal Rights for Children
181 Neringa Lane
Hobart, IN 46342
Contact: Cynthia Robbins
(219) 942-9973 (eve.)

IOWA

**Iowa OCSE Agency, URESA Information
Agent, and URESA Interstate
Inquiries and Complaints**
Ms. Christy Ill, Director
Child Support Recovery Unit
Dept. of Social Services
Hoover Building
Des Moines, IA 50319
Telephone: (515) 281-5580

KANSAS

Kansas OCSE Agency
Mr. Donald L. Bears, Administrator
Child Support Enforcement Program
Dept. of Social & Rehabilitation Services
Perry Building, 2700 W. 6th St.
Topeka, KS 66606
Telephone: (913) 296-3237

Kansas URESA Information Agent
Senior Legal counsel
Child Support Enforcement Program
Dept. of Social & Rehabilitation Services
Perry Building, 2700 W. 6th St.
Topeka, KS 66606
Telephone: (913) 296-3237

KENTUCKY

Kentucky OCSE Agency
Mr. Hanson Williams, Director
Div. for Child Support Enforcement
Cabinet for Human Resources
275 E. Main St., 6 Flr. E.
Frankfort, KY 40621
Telephone: (502) 564-2285

Kentucky URESA Information Agent
Mr. David E. Cathers, Staff Attorney
Office of the Counsel
Cabinet for Human Resources
275 E. Main St., 4 Flr. W.
Frankfort, KY 40621
Telephone: (502) 564-7900

Kentucky URESA Interstate Inquiries and Complaints
Mr. Steven P. Veno
Contracts Operation Section Spvsr.
Cabinet for Human Resources
275 E. Main St., 6 Flr. W.
Frankfort, KY 40621
Telephone: (502) 564-2285

Parents' Support Enforcement Group
Mothers for Child Support
Rte. 1 Box 358
Rineyville, KY 40162
Contact: Vicki Gaddie (502) 765-5733

LOUISIANA

Louisiana OCSE Agency, URESA Information Agent, URESA Interstate Inquiries and Complaints
Ms. Marjorie T. Stewart, Asst. Sec.
Support Enforcement Services
Dept. of Health & Human Resources
P.O. Box 44276
Baton Rouge, LA 70804
Attn: P. M. Blakney (OCSE)
Attn: Perry MacPee
(URESA Information Agent)
Telephone: (504) 342-4780

Parents' Support Enforcement Groups
Kids in Need Deserve Equal Rights
(KINDER)
P.O. Box 6225
Shreveport, LA 71136
Contact: Deborah Dean
(318) 747-0346 (eve.)

Support Your Children
P.O. Box 80836
Baton Rouge, LA 70898
Contact: Jane Crawford
(504) 388-6624 (day)

MAINE

**Maine OCSE Agency,
URESA Information Agent**
Mr. Colburn W. Jackson, Director
Support Enforcement Program
Department of Human Services
State House, Station 11
Augusta, ME 04333
Telephone: (207) 289-2886

MARYLAND

Maryland OCSE Agency
Ms. Ann C. Helton, Executive Director
Child Support Enforcement Admin.
Dept. of Human Resources
300 W. Preston St., 5th Flr.
Baltimore, MD 21201
Telephone: (301) 576-5388

Maryland URESA Information Agent and URESA Interstate Inquiries and Complaints
Mr. John M. Williams
Maryland Information Agent
DHR/Child Support Enf. Admin.
300 W. Preston St., Rm. 502
Baltimore, MD 21201
Telephone: (301) 576-5498

Parents' Support Enforcement Groups
Mothers United for Support Enforcement
3711 37th Avenue
Cottage City, MD 20722
Contact: Anna Angolia (301) 779-3999 (eve.)
Rosalind Johnson (301) 773-0976 (eve.)

Organization for the Enforcement of Child Support (OECS)
119 Nicodemus Road
Reistertown, MD 21136
Contact: Elaine and William Fromm
(301) 833-2458 (eve.)

MASSACHUSETTS

Massachusetts OCSE Agency and URESA Information Agent
Mr. Fred Brown, Director
Child Support Enforcement Unit
Department of Public Welfare
600 Washington St.
Boston, MA 02111
Telephone: (617) 727-7820

Child Support Enforcement Unit
Massachusetts Department of Revenue
215 First Street
Cambridge, MA 02142
(617) 621-4750

Parents' Support Enforcement Groups
Massachusetts Child Support Payment Friends
P.O. Box 142
Charlton Depot, MA 01509
Contact: Donna Bigelow
(617) 248-5271 (eve.)

Mothers United to Save the Children Through Legislative Efforts
(MUSCLE)
P.O. Box 176
Williamsburg, MA 01096
Contact: Cindy Foster
(413) 268-7028 (eve.)

MICHIGAN

Michigan OCSE Agency, URESA Information Agent, and URESA Interstate Inquiries and Complaints
Mr. Jerrold H. Brockmyre, Director
Office of Child Support
Department of Social Services
300 S. Capitol Ave., Box 30037
Lansing, MI 48909
Telephone: (517) 373-7570

MINNESOTA

Minnesota OCSE Agency and URESA Information Agent
Ms. Bonnie L. Becker, Director
Office of Child Support Enforcement
Department of Public Welfare
Space Center Building
444 Lafayette Rd.
St. Paul, MN 55101
Telephone: (612) 296-2499

Minnesota URESA Interstate Inquiries and Complaints
Ms. Mary L. Anderson, Program Adviser
Office of Child Support Enforcement
Department of Public Welfare
Space Center Bldg., 2nd Flr.
444 Lafayette Road
St. Paul, MN 55101
(612) 296-2555

MISSISSIPPI

Mississippi OCSE Agency
Mr. Monte L. Barton, Director
Child Support Division
Dept. of Public Welfare
515 E. Amite St., Box 352
Jackson, MS 39205
Telephone: (601) 354-0341, Ext. 503

Mississippi URESA Information Agent
Mr. Oscar Mackey
Assistant Attorney General
Mississippi Attorney General
P.O. Box 220
Jackson, MS 39205
Telephone: (601) 354-7130

Mississippi URESA Interstate Inquiries and Complaints
Director, Child Support Dept.
Dept. of Public Welfare
P.O. Box 352
Jackson, MS 39205
Telephone: (601) 354-0341, Ext. 502

MISSOURI

Missouri OCSE Agency, URESA Information Agent, and URESA Interstate Inquiries and Complaints
Mr. Paul R. Nelson, Administrator
Child Support Enforcement Unit
Division of Family Service
911 Missouri Blvd., Box 88
Jefferson, City, MO 65103
Telephone: (314) 751-4301

Parents' Support Enforcement Groups Organization for Child Support Action (OCSA)
P.O. Box 188
High Ridge, MO 63049
Contact: Beverly Bohmie
(314) 677-8911

Parents United for Lawful Support Enforcement (PULSE)
12 Parkview Dr.
St. Peters, MO 63376
Contact: Betty Murphy
(314) 279-1441 (eve.)

MONTANA

Montana OCSE Agency, URESA Information Agent
Mr. William Harrington, Chief
Inves. and Enforcement Bureau
Department of Revenue
P.O. Box 5955
Helena, MT 59604
Telephone: (406) 449-4614

Montana URESA Interstate Inquiries and Complaints
Ms. Dennis Shober, Program Manager
Child Support Enforcement Program
Department of Revenue
1410 1.2 8th Ave.
Helena, MT 59620
Telephone: (406) 444-3347

NEBRASKA

Nebraska OCSE Agency
Mr. Robert Houston, Administrator
Child Support Enforcement Office
Department of Social Services
301 Centennial Mall S., 5 Flr.
Box 95026
Lincoln, NE 68509

Nebraska URESA Information Agent and URESA Interstate Inquiries and Complaints
Ms. Gina C. Dunning, Director
Department of Social Services
301 Centennial Mall S., 5 Flr.
Box 95026
Lincoln, NE 68509
Telephone: (402) 471-3121

Parents' Support Enforcement Group Child Support Task Force
1514 N. 76th St.
Omaha, NE 68114
Contact: Kathy Schultz
Telephone: (402) 397-3284 (eve.)

NEVADA

Nevada OCSE Agency and URESA Interstate Inquiries and Complaints
Mr. William F. Furlong
Child Support Enforcement
Nevada State Welfare Division
251 Jeanell Drive
Carson City, NV 89710
Telephone: (702) 885-4744

Nevada URESA Information Agent
Mr. Brian McKay, Attorney General
Office of Attorney General
Hero's Memorial Building
Capitol Complex
Carson City, NV 89710
Telephone: (702) 885-4170

NEW HAMPSHIRE

New Hampshire OCSE Agency and URESA Information Agent
Mr. Arthur A. Stukas, Administrator
Office of Child Support
Enforcement Services
Division of Welfare
Health & Welfare Building, Hazen Dr.
Concord, NH 03301
Telephone: (603) 271-4426

NEW JERSEY

New Jersey OCSE Agency and URESA Interstate Inquiries and Complaints
Mr. Harry W. Wiggins, Chief
Bureau of Child Support &
Paternity Programs
Department of Human Services
C.N. 716
Trenton, NJ 08625
Telephone: (609) 633-6268

New Jersey URESA Information Agent
Mr. Robert D. Lipscher,
Administrative Office
Administrative Office of the Courts
C.N. 037
Trenton, NJ 08625
Telephone: (609) 292-1087

Parents' Support Enforcement Groups
Organization for Child Support Action
P.O. Box 1401
Burlington, NJ 08016
Contact: Judi Richter
(609) 386-6211 (eve.)

Organization for the Enforcement of Child Support (OECS)
P.O. Box 5227
Parsippany, NJ 07054
Contact: Janet Saulter-Hemmer
(201) 334-0281 (eve.)

NEW MEXICO

New Mexico OCSE Agency
Mr. Ben Silva, Chief
Child Support Enforcement Bureau
Department of Human Services
P.O. Box 2348, PERA Bldg.
Santa, Fe, NM 87503
Telephone: (505) 827-5591

New Mexico URESA Information Agent
Carliss Thalley
Legal Services Bureau
Department of Human Services
P.O. Box 2348
Santa Fe, NM 87503
Telephone: (505) 827-2305

NEW YORK

New York OCSE Agency
Mr. Meldon F. Kelsey, Director
Office of Child Support Enforcement
P.O. Box 14
One Commerce Plaza
Albany, NY 12260
Telephone: (518) 474-9081

New York URESA Information Agent and URESA Interstate Inquiries and Complaints
Mr. Joseph E. Bissell
Interstate Legal Unit
Office of Child Support Enforcement
P.O. Box 14, One Commerce Plaza
Albany, NY 12260
Telephone: (518) 473-0929

**Parents' Support Enforcement Groups
For Our Children and Us (FOCUS)**
550 Old Country Road
Hicksville, NY 11801
Contact: Fran Mattera (516) 433-6633

Separated Persons Living in Transition (SPLIT)
1805 Fifth Avenue
North Bay Shore, NY 11706
Contact: Virginia Engle (516) 435-0740

NORTH CAROLINA

North Carolina OCSE Agency
Ms. Susan C. Smith, Chief
Child Support Enforcement Section
Division of Social Services
Department of Human Resources
443 N. Harrington St.
Raleigh, NC 27603-1393
Telephone: (919) 733-4120

North Carolina URESA Information Agent
Mr. John Syria, Director
Division of Social Services
Department of Human Resources
443 N. Harrington St.
Raleigh, NC 27603-1393
Attn: Ms. Kathy Futrell
Telephone: (919) 733-4120

North Carolina URESA Interstate Inquiries and Complaints
Ms. Kathy L. Futrell
Interstate/URESA Coordinator
Child Support Enforcement Section
441-443 N. Harrington St.
Raleigh, NC 27603
Telephone: (919) 733-4120

NORTH DAKOTA

North Dakota OCSE Agency, URESA Information Agent, and URESA Interstate Inquiries and Complaints
Mr. Marcellus Hartze, Administrator
Child Support Enforcement Agency
Social Service Board of North Dakota
State Capital
Bismarck, ND 58505
Telephone: (701) 224-3582

OHIO

Ohio OCSE Agency
Chief
Bureau of Child Support
Department of Public Welfare
State Office Tower
30 Broad Street East, 31st Floor
Columbus, OH 43215
Telephone: (614) 466-3233

Ohio URESA Information Agent
Chief, State Departments Section
Office of Attorney General
State Office Tower
30 Broad Street East, 16th Floor
Columbus, OH 43215
Telephone: (614) 466-8600

Parents' Support Enforcement Groups
Association for Children for Enforcement of Support (ACES)
1018 Jefferson Avenue #204
Toledo, OH 43624
Contact: Geraldine Jensen
(419) 242-6129 (eve.)

Legal Advocacy for Women (LAW)
410 Bennett Street
Bridgeport, OH 43912
Contact: Pat Wilson (614) 676-2042

Non-Support, Inc.
544 Milan
Canal Fulton, OH 44614
Contact: Sandie Sterns (216) 644-0061

OKLAHOMA

Oklahoma OCSE Agency, URESA Information Agent
Wesley Rucker, IV-D Administrator
Attn: Division of Child Support
Department of Human Services
P.O. Box 25352
Oklahoma City, OK 73125
Telephone: (405) 424-5871

Oklahoma URESA Interstate Inquiries and Complaints
Mr. Robert Fulton, Director
Department of Human Services
P.O. Box 25352
Oklahoma City, OK 73125
Attn: Programs Administrator
Child Support Enf. Unit
Telephone: (405) 424-5871 Ext. 2642

Parents' Support Enforcement Groups
Support Our Children
P.O. Box 30888
Midwest City, OK 73140
Contact: Paula Brooks (405) 391-4027 (day)

OREGON

Oregon OCSE Agency
Mr. Leonard T. System, Manager
DHR/AFS Recovery Services Section
502 Public Service Building
P.O. Box 14506 (Zip 97309)
Salem, OR 97310
(503) 378-6093

Oregon URESA Information Agency and URESA Interstate Inquiries and Complaints
Mr. Jim Hunter, Administrator
Support Enforcement Division
Department of Justice
Justice Building
Salem, OR 97310
Telephone: (503) 378-4879

PENNSYLVANIA

Pennsylvania OCSE Agency, URESA Information Agent
Mr. John F. Stuff, Director
Child Support Programs
Dept. Of Public Welfare
P.O. Box 8018
Harrisburg, PA 17105
Telephone: (717) 783-1779

Pennsylvania URESA Interstate Inquiries and Complaints
Mr. Robert Barton, Manager
Parent Locator Services
Child Support Programs
P.O. Box 8018
Harrisburg, PA 17105

Parents' Support Enforcement Groups
Legal Advocacy for Women (LAW)
429 Forbes Avenue
Pittsburgh, PA 15219
Contact: Rosemary Palmer
(412) 255-6708 (day)
Monaca chapter: Melanie Summerville
(412) 728-0681 (eve.)
Somerset chapter: Phyllis Mitchell
(814) 443-2532
(814) 536-5115

Support for Dependent Children
318 Garber St.
Holidaysburg, PA 16648
Contact: Millie McClain (814) 695-5336

Women's Network
905 Atwood Road
Philadelphia, PA 19118
Contact: Leigh Fraser (215) 646-1363

PUERTO RICO

Puerto Rico OCSE Agency
Mr. Miguel A. Verdiales, Director
Child Support Enforcement Program
Department of Social Services
P.O. Box 11398
Fernandez Juncos Station
Santurce, PR 00910
Telephone: (809) 722-4731

Puerto Rico URESA Information Agent
Ms. Ada E. Rivera-Sepulveda, Chief
Reciprocal Support Division
Office of Court Administration
Hato Rey Station, Call Box 22A
Hato Rey, PR 00919
Telephone: (809) 764-7145

RHODE ISLAND

Rhode Island OCSE Agency and URESA Information Agent
Mr. George A. Moriarty
Chief Supervisor
Bureau of Family Support
77 Dorrance St.
Providence, RI 02903
Telephone: (401) 277-2409

Rhode Island URESA Interstate Inquiries and Complaints
Mr. Paul Palmera
Bureau of Family Support
77 Dorrance St.
Providence, RI 02903
Telephone: (401) 277-6933

SOUTH CAROLINA

South Carolina OCSE Agency
Mr. Paul W. Chavious, Director
Division of Child Support
Department of Social Services
P.O. Box 1520
Columbia, SC 29202
Telephone: (803) 758-3151

South Carolina URESA Information Agent
Division of Child Support
Department of Social Services
P.O. Box 1520
Columbia, SC 29202
Telephone: (803) 758-8860

Parents' Support Enforcement Group
Organization for Child Support Action
(OCSA)
Route 9, Box 272
Wyatt Drive #10
Spartanburg, SC 29301
Contact: Felicia Richards (803) 574-6347

SOUTH DAKOTA

South Dakota OCSE Agency
Terry Walter, Program Administrator
Office of Child Support Enforcement
700 N. Illinois St.
Pierre, SD 57501
Telephone: (605) 773-3641

South Dakota URESA Information Agent
Ms. Janice Godtland
Assistant Attorney General
Attorney General's Office
700 N. Illinois St.
Pierre, SD 57501
Telephone: (605) 773-3305

TENNESSEE

Tennessee OCSE Agency
Ms. Joyce D. McClaran, Director
Office of Child Support Services
Department of Human Services
111-19 7th Avenue N., 5 Flr.
Nashville, TN 37203
Telephone: (615) 741-1820

Tennessee URESA Information Agent
Department of Human Services
111-19 7th Avenue N., 5 Flr.
Nashville, TN 37203
Telephone: (615) 741-1939
Attn: Ms. Sue Ellis, Internal Coordinator
Office of Child Support Services

Tennessee URESA Interstate
Inquiries and Complaints
Ms. Sue Ellis, Interstate Coordinator
Department of Human Services
111-19 7th Avenue N., 5 Flr.
Nashville, TN 37203
Telephone: (615) 741-1939

TEXAS

Texas OCSE Agency
Mr. Lewis J. Zegub,
Assistant Commissioner
Child Support Enforcement Branch
Department of Human Resources
P.O. Box 2960
Austin, TX 78769
Telephone: (512) 835-0440

Texas URESA Information Agent
Child Support Enforcement Program
Office of the Attorney General
P.O. Box 12548
Austin, TX 78711-2548
Telephone: (512) 475-0990

Parents' Support Enforcement Groups
Parents for Child Support Enforcement
2930 Healey
Dallas, TX 75228
Contact: Doraldine Barrera
(214) 824-1620 (day)
(214) 270-6058 (eve.)

Parents for Kids
6913 Bal Lake Dr.
Fort Worth, TX 76116
Contact: Charlotte Boeker
(817) 451-0482 (eve.)
Stella Cable (817) 737-4115 (eve.)

UTAH

Utah OCSE Agency
Mr. John P. Abbott, Director
Office of Recovery Services
Bureau of Child Support Enforcement
3195 S. Main St., Box 15400
Salt Lake City, UT 84115
(801) 241-2868

Utah URESA Information Agent and URESA Interstate Inquiries and Complaints
Mr. Bruce Black, Manager
URESA Coordination
3195 S. Main St., Box 15400
Salt Lake City, UT 84115
Telephone: (801) 483-6274

VERMONT

Vermont OCSE Agency
Mr. William D. Kirby, Director
Child Support Division
Department of Social Welfare
103 S. Main St.
Waterbury, VT 05676
Telephone: (802) 241-2868

Vermont URESA Information Agent and URESA Interstate Inquiries and Complaints
Ms. Joan B. Kilton
Child Support Division
Department of Social Welfare
103 S. Main St.
Waterbury, VT 05676
Telephone: (802) 241-2846

VIRGIN ISLANDS

Virgin Islands OCSE Agency
Alden Martinez, Director
Paternity & Child Support Unit
Department of Law
P.O. Box 1074
Christiansted, St. Croix, VI 00820
Telephone: (809) 773-8240

Virgin Islands URESA Information Agent
Attorney General
Department of Law
P.O. Box 280, Charlotte Amalie
St. Thomas, VI 00801
Attn: URESA
Telephone: (809) 774-5666

VIRGINIA

Virginia OCSE Agency, URESA Information Agent, and URESA Interstate Inquiries and Complaints
Jean M. White, Director
Div. of Support Enforcement
Department of Social Services
8007 Discovery Drive
Richmond, VA 23288
Telephone: (804) 281-9154

Parents' Support Enforcement Groups
For Our Children's Unpaid Support (FOCUS)
P.O. Box 2183
Vienna, VA 22180
Contact: Bettianne Welsh (703) 860-1123

Virginians Organized in the Interest of Children's Entitlement to Support (VOICES)
P.O. Box 12060
Arlington, VA 22209
Contact: Linda Whittington
(703) 765-0492 (eve.)
Northern Virginia: Lori Morelock
(703) 281-3614 (eve.)
Richmond: Celia McGucklan
(804) 320-1871 (eve.)

WASHINGTON

Washington OCSE Agency
Jon Conine, Acting Director
Office of Support Enforcement
Dept. of Social & Health Services
P.O. Box 9162-MS PY-11
Olympia, WA 98504
Telephone: (206) 459-6481

Washington URESA Information Agent
Mr. David R. Minikel
Assistant Attorney General
Dept. of Social & Health SErvices
Attorney General Division
PY-13
Olympia, WA 98504
Telephone: (206) 459-6574

Parent Location Service
Ms. Carol Cole, SEO I
Locate Section
Office of Support Enforcement
Dept. of Social & Health Services
P.O. Box 9162-MS FU-11

Parents' Support Enforcement Group
Need for Support Enforcement
12638 SE 7th Place
Bellevue, WA 98005
Contact: Bea Kriloff (206) 453-1941

WEST VIRGINIA

West Virginia OCSE
Department of Human Services
1900 Washington Street, East
Charleston, WV 25305
(305) 348-3780

WISCONSIN

Wisconsin OCSE Agency
Department of Health and Human Services
Division of Community Services
1 West Wilson Street
P.O. Box 7851
Madison, WI 53707
(608) 266-9909

WYOMING

Wyoming OCSE Agency
Division of Public Assistance
and Social Services
Wyoming Department of Health
and Human Resources
Hathaway Building
Cheyenne, WY 82002
(307) 777-6083

Voodoo Spice Number 23

COLLECTING CHILD SUPPORT FROM THE MILITARY

AIR FORCE

Commander
Air Force Accounting and Finance Center
Attention: JA
Denver, CO 80279

ARMY

Commander
U.S. Army Finance and Accounting Center
Attention: FINCL-G
Indianapolis, IN 46249

MARINES

Commanding Officer (Code AA)
Marine Corps Finance Center
Kansas City, MO 64197

NAVY

Commanding Officer
Navy Family Allowance Activity
Department of the Navy
Cleveland, OH 44199

Voodoo Spice Number 24

CHILD SUPPORT CONTACTS FOR COUNTRIES WITH RECIPROCAL AGREEMENTS

AUSTRALIA
Attorney General's Department
International Civil and Privacy Branch
National Circuit
Canberra, ACT 2600
Australia
Telephone: 011-61-6-250-6211
Fax: 011-61-6-250-5939

AUSTRIA
Federal Ministry of Justice
P.O. Box 63, A-1016
Vienna, Austria

BERMUDA
The Family and Child Support Officer
Magistrates' Court
23 Parliament Street
Hamilton, HM 12
Bermuda

CANADA
Please see the following Canadian Provinces and Territories with reciprocal agreements:

Alberta
Alberta Justice
Maintenance Enforcement
P.O. Box 2404
Edmonton, Alberta,
Canada T5J 3Z7
Telephone: 1-403-422-5554
Fax: 1- 403-422-1215

British Columbia
Family Justice Programs Division
Reciprocal Program
304-1175 Cook Street
Victoria, British Columbia
Canada V8V 4A1
Telephone: 1-604-356-1555; x1560; x1563
Fax: 1-604-356-8902

Manitoba
Manitoba Justice
Maintenance Enforcement Program
Woodworth Building
Second Floor
405 Broadway
Winnipeg, Manitoba
Canada R3C 3L6
Telephone: 1-204-945-7133
Fax: 1-204-945-5449

New Brunswick
Registrar's Office
Court of Queen's Bench
Justice Bldg.
Room 201
P.O. Box 6000
Fredericton, New Brunswick
Canada E3B 5H1
Telephone: 1-506-453-2452
Fax: 1-506-453-7921

New Foundland/Labrador:
Director of Support Enforcement
P.O. Box 2006
Corner Brook, New Foundland
Canada A3H 6J8
Telephone: 1-709-637-2608
Fax: 1-709-634-9518

Northwest Territories
Commissioner
Government of the N.W.T.
P.O. Box 1320
Yellowknife, N.W.T.
Canada X1A 2L9
Telephone: 1-403-873-7400
Fax: 1-403-873-0223

Nova Scotia
Courts and Registries Division
Department of Justice
P.O. Box 7
Halifax, Nova Scotia
Canada B3J 2L6
Telephone: 1-902-424-4030
Fax: 1-902-424-4556

Prince Edward Island
Maintenance Enforcement Office
42 Water Street
P.O. Box 2290
Charlestown, P.E.I.
Canada C1A 8C1
Telephone: 1-902-368-6010
Fax: 1-902-368-0266

Ontario
Ministry of the Attorney General
Family Support Plan
London
55 Yonge Street, Third Floor
Toronto, Ontario M5E 1J4
Telephone: 1-416-326-2556
Fax: 1-416-326-2568

Quebec
Deputy Attorney General
Ministre de Justice
Government of Quebec
Direction de la loi sur
l'administration et privee
1200 Route De L'Englise 2 Etage
Sainte Foy, Quebec
Canada G1W 4M1

Saskatchewan
Saskatchewan Justice
Maintenance Enforcement Office
P.O. Box 2077
Regina, Saskatchewan
Canada S4P 4E8
Telephone: 1-306-787-8961
Fax: 1-306-787-1420

Yukon Territory
Maintenance Enforcement Program
P.O. Box 4066
Whitehorse, Yukon
Canada Y1A 3S9
Telephone: 1-403-667-5437
Fax: 1-403-667-4116

CZECH REPUBLIC
Central Office of International Legal
Protection of Juveniles
Benesova 22, 602 00 Brno
Czech Republic
(Ustredi Pro Mezinarodne Pravni,
Ochranu Miadeze)

FIJI
Attorney General
Attorney General's chambers
Government Bldg.
Suva, Fiji

FINLAND
Ministry of Foriegn Affairs
c/o Embassy of Finland
Groot Hertoginnelaan 16
2517 EG The Hague
The Netherlands
Mrs. Eila Kurki-Suonio, Legal Officer
Merikaaasarmi B 1
P.O.B. 176, Fin-00161
Helsinki, Finland

FRANCE
Ministere de la Justice
Service des Affaires Europeenes
et Internationales
Bureau L1
13 Place Vendome
75042 Paris
Cendex 01, France

GERMANY
Der Generalbundesanwait
beim Bundesgerichtshof
Zentrale Behorde
Neuenburger
Strasse 15
10969 Berlin, Germany

HUNGARY
Ministry of Justice
Igazsagugy Miniszterium
Ministry of Justice
Szalay U 16
Budapest, Hungary

IRELAND
Department of Equality and Law Reform
Mr. Michael Gleeson
43-49 Mespil Road
Dublin 4, Ireland

JAMAICA
Child Services Division
10A Chelsea Avenue
Kingston 10, Jamaica

MEXICO
Secretaria de Relaciones Exteriores
Consultoria Juridica Homero 213
Piso 17
Col. Chapultepec Morales
Mexico, D.F. C.P. 11570
Telephone: 011-525-254-73-18
Fax: 011-525-254-73-16

NEW ZEALAND
Secretary for Justice
Private Bag 180
Postal Center
Wellington, New Zealand

NORWAY
National Insurance Office for Social Insurance Abroad
Child Support Division
Post boks 8138 Dep N-0033
Oslo, Norway

POLAND
Ministry of Justice
(Ministerstwo Sprawiedlivosci)
Al, Ujazdowskie 11
00950 Warsaw, Poland

SLOVAK REPUBLIC
Center for International Legal Protection of Children and Youth
Centrum pre medzinzrodno-pravnu
Ochranu deti a miadeze
Pitalska 6
P.O. Box 57
814 99 Bratislava
Slovak Republic

SOUTH AFRICA
Director General
Departy of Justice
Attn: Diverse Legal Matters
Private Bag x81
Pretoria, South Africa 0001

SWEDEN
Stockholm County Social Insurance Office
Enforcement Division
(Forsakringskassan, Stockholms Lan, Utlandsavdelningen)
BDF, S-105 11 Stockholm, Sweden

UNITED KINGDOM

England and Wales
Reciprocal Enforcement of Maintenance
Lord Chancellor's Department
Selborne House 54/60 Victoria Street
London SW1E 6QW, U.K.

Scotland
The Scottish Courts
Administration
Hayweight House
23 Lauriston Street
Edinburgh EH3 9DQ, Scotland

Northern Ireland
The Lord Chancellor's Department
Windsor House
Bedford Street
Belfast, BT2 7EA, Northern Ireland

Voodoo Spice Number 25

CHILD ABUSE STATISTICS

CHILD ABUSE AND NEGLECT SUBSTANTIATED CASES

Number of Substantiated Victims in 1996 .... **1,000,502**

Type of Mistreatment	**Percent**
Neglect	52.3%
Physical Abuse	24.5
Sexual Abuse	12.6
Emotional Maltreatment	4.5
Medical Neglect	2.9
Other and Unknown	4.5

SOURCE: U.S. Department of Health and Human Services, National Center of child Abuse and Neglect, National Child Abuse and Neglect Data System, Working Paper 2, 1991 Summary Data Component, May 1993. Child Maltreatment–1992, May 1994; and Child Maltreatment–1993, April 1995, Child Maltreatment–1994, May 1995; and Child Maltreatment–1995; U.S. Census.

Voodoo Spice Number 26

DOMESTIC ABUSE AND VIOLENCE HOTLINES

National Domestic Violence Hotline
(National Coalition Against Domestic Violence)

1 (800) 333-SAFE (7233)

For Hearing Impaired: 1 (800) 873-3636

National Child Abuse Hotline

1 (800) 422-4453

National Rape Crisis Center Hotline

(202) 333-7273

DIRECTORY OF DOMESTIC VIOLENCE AND ABUSE SUPPORT GROUPS

Abusive Men Exploring New Directions
8000 East Prentice Avenue, Suite C-3
Englewood, CO 801111
(303) 220-1707

Action Ohio Coalition for Battered Women
P.O. Box 15673
Columbus, OH 43215
(614) 221-1255
Fax: (614) 221-6357

Alabama Coalition Against Violence
P.O. Box 4762
Montgomery, AL 36101
(334) 832-4842
Fax: (334) 832-4803

Alaska Network on Domestic Violence and Sexual Assault
130 Seward Street, Room 501
Juneau, AK 99801
(907) 586-3650
Fax: (907) 463-4493

American Association For Protecting Children
9725 East Hampden Avenue
Denver, CO 80231

American Bar Association's National Legal Resource Center for Child Advocacy and Protection
Second Floor
1800 M Street, NW
Washington, D.C.
(202) 331-2250

Anti-Violence Project
National Gay and Lesbian Task Force
2320 7th Street, N.W.
Washington, D.C 20009-2702
(202) 332-6483
Fax: (202) 332-0207

Arizona Coalition Against Domestic Violence
100 West Camelback Street, Suite 109
Phoenix, AZ 85013
(602) 279-2900
Fax: (602) 279-2980

Arkansas Coalition Against Domestic Violence
#1 Sheriff Lane, Suite C
Little Rock, AR 72114
(501) 812-0571
Fax: (501) 371-0450

AYUDA
1736 Columbia Road N.W.
Washington, D.C. 20008
(202) 387-0434

Battered Women's Justice Project
Minnesota Development, Inc.
4032 Chicago Avenue South
Minneapolis, MN 55407
(612) 824-8768
Fax: (612) 824-8965
(800) 903-0111

California Alliance Against Domestic Violence
619 13th Street, Suite I
Modesto, CA 95354
(209) 524-1888
Fax: (209) 524-0616

Center for Battered Women's Legal Services
105 Chambers Street, Suite 5A
New York, NY 10007
(212) 349-6009

Center for the Prevention of Sexual and Domestic Violence
936 North 34th Street, Suite 200
Seattle, WA 98103
(206) 634-1903
Fax: (206) 634-0115

Child Abuse Institute of Research
P.O. Box 1217
Cincinnati, OH 45201
(606) 441-7409

Child Abuse Listening & Mediation
1236 Chapala
P.O. Box 90754
Santa Barbara, CA 93190
(805) 965-2376
Fax: (805) 963-6707
calm4kids@aol.com

Child Welfare League of America
Suite 310
440 First Street, NW
Washington, DC 20001-2085
(202) 638-2952
Fax: (202) 638-4004
http://www.cwla.org

Clearinghouse on Child Abuse and Neglect Information
P.O. Box 1182
Washington, D.C. 20013
(703) 821-2086

Colorado Domestic Violence Coalition
P.O. Box 18902
Denver, CO 80218
(303) 831-9632
Fax: (303) 832-7067

Connecticut Coalition Against Domestic Violence
135 Broad Street
Hartford, CT 06105
(860) 524-5890
Fax: (860) 249-1408

Crossroads
3945 Rivers Avenue
North Charleston, SC 29405
(803) 747-6500

CUNY Battered Women's Clinic
1867 ACP Jr. Blvd.
New York, NY 10026
(212) 662-7509

D.C. Coalition Against Domestic Violence
P.O. Box 76069
Washington, D.C. 20013
(202) 783-5332
Fax: (202) 387-5684

Delaware Coalition Against Domestic Violence
P.O. Box 847
Wilmington, DE 19899
(302) 658-2958
Fax: (302) 658-5049

Delaware Domestic Violence Coordinating Council
900 King Street
Wilmington, DE 19801
(302) 577-2684
Fax: (302) 577-6022

EMERGE (Men's Counseling)
Second Floor
280 Green Street
Cambridge, MA 02139
(617) 547-9870

Family Violence Prevention Fund
383 Rhode Island Street, Suite 304
San Francisco, CA 94103-5133
(415) 252-8900
Fax: (415) 252-8991

Family Violence Project
1001 Portero Avenue
Building One, Suite 200
San Francisco, CA 94110
(415) 821-4553

Florida Coalition Against Domestic Violence
410 Office Plaza
Tallahassee, FL 32301-2757
(800) 500-1119
(904) 668-6862
Fax: (904) 668-0364

Georgia Advocates for Battered Women and Children
250 Georgia Avenue, S.E., Suite 308
Atlanta, GA 30312
(404) 524-3847
Fax: (404) 524-5959

Georgia Coalition on Family Violence, Inc.
1827 Powers Ferry Road
Building 3, Suite 325
Atlanta, GA 30339
(770) 984-0085
Fax: (770) 984-0068

Hawaii State Coalition Against Domestic Violence
98-939 Moanalua Road
Aiea, HI 96701-5012
(808) 486-5072
Fax: (808) 486-5169

Health Resource Center on Domestic Violence
Family Violence Prevention Fund
383 Rhode Island Street, Suite 304
San Francisco, CA 94103-5133
(800) 313-1310
Fax: (415) 252-8991

Iowa Coalition Against Domestic Violence
2603 Bell Avenue, Suite 100
Des Moines, IA 50321
(800) 942-0333
(515) 244-8028
Fax: (515) 244-7417

Idaho Coalition Against Sexual and Domestic Violence
815 Park Blvd., Suite 140
Boise, ID 83712-7738
(208) 384-0419
Fax: (208) 331-0687

Illinois Coalition Against Domestic Violence
730 East Vine Street, Suite 109
Springfield, IL 62703
(217) 789-2830
Fax: (217) 789-1939

Indiana Coalition Against Domestic Violence
2511 E. 46th Street, Suite N-3
Indianapolis, IN 46205
(800) 332-7385
(317) 543-3908
Fax: (317) 568-4045

Institute for the Community as Extended Family
P.O. Box 952
San Jose, CA 95108
(408) 280-5055

Interagency Council
Domestic Violence Program
2180 McCulloch Boulevard
Lake Havasu City, AZ 86403
(520) 453-5800
Fax: (520) 453-2787

International Society for Prevention of Child Abuse and Neglect
1825 Marion, Suite 320
Denver, CO 80218
(303) 864-5316
Fax: (303) 864-5326
kim_svevo@sba.com
http://child.cornell.edu/ispcan/ispcan.html

Kansas Coalition Against Sexual and Domestic Violence
820 S.E. Quincy, Suite 416
Topeka, KS 66612
(913) 232-9784
Fax: (913) 232-9937

Kentucky Domestic Violence Association
P.O. Box 356
Frankfort, KY 40602
(502) 875-4132
Fax: (502) 875-4268
kdvasac@aol.com

Louisiana Coalition Against Domestic Violence
P.O. Box 3053
Hammond, LA 70404-3053
(504) 542-4446
Fax: (504) 542-6561

Maine Coalition for Family Crisis Violence
128 Main Street
Bangor, ME 04401
(207) 941-1194
Fax: (207) 941-2327

Maryland Network Against Domestic Violence
6911 Laurel Bowie Road, Suite 309
Bowie, MD 20715
(800) MD-HELPS
(301) 352-4574
Fax: (301) 809-0422
mnadv@aol.com

Massachusetts Coalition of Battered Women's Service Groups
14 Beacon street, Suite 507
Boston, MA 02108
(617) 248-0922
Fax: (617) 248-0902

Michigan Coalition Against Domestic Violence
913 W. Holmes Road, Suite 211
Lansing, MI 48910-0411
(517) 484-2924
Fax: (517) 372-0024

Minnesota Coalition for Battered Women
450 North Syndicate Street, Suite 122
St. Paul, MN 55104
(800) 646-0994
(573)646-6177
Fax: (573) 646-1527

Missouri Coalition Against Domestic Violence
415 East McCarty
Jefferson City, MO 65101
(573) 634-4161
Fax: (573) 636-3728
mcadv@sockets.net

Missouri Shores Domestic Violence Center
P.O. Box 398
Pierre, SD 57501-0398
Crisis (605) 224-7187
(605) 224-0256
(800) 696-7187
Fax: (605) 244-6274

Mississippi State Coalition Against Domestic Violence
P.O. Box 4703
Jackson, MS 39296-3234
(800) 898-3234
(601) 981-9196
Fax: (601) 982-7372

Montana Coalition Against Domestic Violence
P.O. Box 633
Helena, MT 59624
(406) 443-7794
Fax: (406) 449-8193

National Assault Prevention Center
P.O. Box 0205
Columbus, OH 43202
(614) 291-2540

National Center for the Prosecution of Child Abuse
Suite 200
1033 North Fairfax Street
Alexandria, VA 22314
(707) 739-0321

National Clearinghouse on Child Abuse and Neglect Information
P.O. Box 1182
Washington, D.C. 20013-1182
(800) FYI-3366
(703) 385-7565
Fax: (703) 385-3206
http://www.calib.com/nccancl

National Clearinghouse on Marital and Date Rape
2325 Oak Street
Berkeley, CA 94708
(510) 524-1582

National Coalition Against Domestic Violence
P.O. Box 18749
Denver, CO 80218-0749

National Coalition Against Sexual Assault
P.O. Box 21378
Washington, D.C. 20009
(202) 483-7165

**National Committee for
Prevention of Child Abuse**
Suite 950
332 South Michigan Avenue
Chicago, IL 60604
(312) 663-3520

**National Council on
Child Abuse and Family Violence**
Suite 400
1155 Connecticut Avenue, N.W., Suite 400
Washington, D.C. 20036
(202) 429-6695

**National Court Appointed
Special Advocate Association**
Suite 202
909 N.E. 43rd Street
Seattle, WA 98105
(206) 547-1059

**National Exchange Club
Foundation for the
Prevention of Child Abuse**
3050 Central Avenue
Toledo, OH 43606
(419) 535-3232
Fax: (419) 535-1989
www.preventchildabuse.com

National Network to End Domestic Violence
701 Pennsylvania Avenue, N.W., Suite 900
Washington, D.C. 20004
(800) 903-0111 Ext 3
(202) 434-7405
Fax: (202) 434-7400

National Network to End Domestic Violence
c/o Texas Council on Family Violence
8701 North Mopac Expressway, Suite 450
Austin, TX 78759
(512) 794-1133
Fax: (512) 794-1199

National Organization for Victim Assistance
1757 Park Road N.W.
Washington, D.C. 20010
(800) 879-6682
(202) 232-6682
Fax: (202) 462-2255
nova@try-nova.org
http://www/access/digex.net/-nova

**National Resource Center
on Domestic Violence**
Pennsylvania Coalition
Against Domestic Violence
6400 Flank Drive, Suite 1300
Harrisburg, PA 17112
(800) 537-2238
Fax: (717) 545-9546

National Victim Center
2111 Wilson Blvd.
Suite 300
Arlington, VA 22201
(703) 276-2880

National Woman Abuse Prevention Project
Suite 508
2000 P Street, N.W.
Washington, D.C. 20036
(202) 857-0216

**Nebraska Domestic Violence and Sexual
Assault Coalition**
315 South 9th, #18
Lincoln, NE 68508-2200
NE Only (800) 876-6238
(402) 476-6256

**Nebraska Network Against
Domestic Violence**
2100 Capturro Way, Suite E
Sparks, NV 89431
(800) 500-1556
(702) 358-1171
Fax: (702) 358-0546

**New Hampshire Coalition
Against Domestic and Sexual Violence**
P.O. Box 353
Concord, NH 03302-0353
(800) 852-3388
(603) 225-9000
(603) 224-8893
Fax: (603) 228-6096

New Jersey Coalition for Battered Women
2620 Whitehorse/Hamilton Square Road
Trenton, NJ 08690
(800) 224-0211
(609) 584-8107
Fax: (603) 228-6096

**New Mexico State Coalition
Against Domestic Violence**
P.O. Box 25363
Albuquerque, NM 87125
(800) 773-3645
(505) 246-9240
Fax: (505) 246-9434

New York Asian Women's Center
39 Bowery Street, Box 375
New York, NY 10002
(212) 732-5230
(888) 888-7702

**New York State Coalition
Against Domestic Violence**
79 Central Avenue
Albany, NY 12206
(800) 942-69906
(518) 432-4864
Fax: (518) 432-4864

**North Carolina Coalition
Against Domestic Violence**
P.O. Box 25189
Durham, NC 27702-5189
(919) 956-9124
Fax: (919) 682-1449

North Carolina Victim Assistance Network
505 Oberlin Road, Suite 151
Raleigh, NC 27605
(919) 831-2857
Fax: (919) 221-6357

**North Dakota Council on
Abused Women's Services**
State Networking Office
418 East Rosser Avenue, Suite 320
Bismark, ND 58501
(800) 472-2911
(701) 255-6240
Fax: (701) 255-1904

**NOW Legal Defense and
Education Fund**
99 Hudson Street
New York, NY 10013
Ohio Domestic Violence Network
4041 North High Street, Suite 400
Columbus, OH 43214
(800) 934-9840
(614) 784-0023
Fax: (614) 784-0033

**Oklahoma Coalition Against Domestic
Violence and Sexual Assault**
2200 North Classen Boulevard, Suite 610
Oklahoma City, OK 73106
(800) 626-HOPE (4673)
(405) 557-1210
Fax: (405) 557-1296
ocdvsa@swbell.net

**Oregon Coalition Against
Domestic and Sexual Violence**
520 N.W. Davis, Suite 310
Portland, OR 97204
(503) 223-7411
Fax: (503) 223-7490

Otter Tail County Intervention Project
Box 815
Fergus Falls, MN 56538
(218) 739-0983

**Pennsylvania Coalition
Against Domestic Violence/National Resource
Center on Domestic Violence**
6440 Flank Drive, Suite 1300
Harrisburg, PA 17112-2778
(800) 932-4632
(717) 545-6400
Fax: (717) 545-9456

Red Cliff Band of Lake Superior Chippewaw
Family Violence Programs
P.O. Box 529
Bayfield, WI 54814
(715) 779-3707
Fax: (715) 7779-3711

**Resource Center on Domestic Violence:
Child Custody and Child Protection**
National Council of Juvenile and Family
Court Judges
University of Nevada
P.O. Box 8970
Reno, NV 89507
(800) 527-3223
(702) 784-6012
Fax: (702) 784-6628
http://ncjfcj.unr.edu
admin@ncjfcj.unr.edu

**Rhode Island Coalition
Against Domestic Violence**
422 Post Road, Suite 202
Warwick, RI 02888
(800) 494-8100
(401) 467-9940
Fax: (401) 467-9943

Sanctuary for Families
P.O. Box 413
Times Square Station
New York, NY 10108
(212) 582-2091

**South Carolina Coalition Against Domestic
Violence and Sexual Assault**
P.O. Box 7776
Columbia, Sc 29202-7776
(800) 260-9293
(803) 750-1222
Fax: (803) 750-1246

**South Dakota Coalition Against Domestic
Violence and Sexual Assault**
P.O. Box 141
Pierre, SD 57401
(800) 572-9196
(605) 945-0869
Fax: (605) 945-0870

**Statewide California Coalition
on Battered Women**
6308 Woodman Avenue, Suite 117
Van Nuys, CA 91401-2347
(818) 789-0072
Fax: (818) 787-0073

Task Force on Families in Crisis
Suite 223-B
4004 Hillsboro Road
Nashville, TN 37215
(615) 383-4575

**Tennessee Task Force
Against Domestic Violence**
P.O. Box 120972
Nashville, TN 37212
(800) 356-6767
(615) 386-2967
Fax: (615) 383-2967

Texas Council on Family Violence
8701 north Mopac Expressway, Suite 450
Austin, TX 78759
(512) 794-1133
Fax: (512) 794-1199

Utah Domestic Violence Advisory Council
120 North 200 West, Suite 319
Salt Lake City, UT 84103
(800) 987-LINK
(801) 538-9886
Fax: (801) 538-4016

**Vermont Network Against Domestic
Violence and Sexual Assault**
P.O. Box 405
Montpelier, VT 05601
(802) 223-1302
Fax: (802) 223-6943

Victim's Services Domestic Violence Program
P.O. Box 157
Macomb, IL 61455
Crisis (309) 837-5555
(309) 837-6622
Fax: (309) 836-3640

Violence Intervention Project
515 W. 135th Street Suite 1C
New York, NY 10031
(212) 368-4596

Virginians Against Domestic Violence
2850 Sandy Bay Road, Suite 101
Williamsburg, VA 231185
(800) 838-VADV
(804) 221-0990
Fax: (804) 229-1553

**Washington State Coalition
Against Domestic Violence**
2101 4th Avenue E, Suite 103
Olympia, WA 98506
(800) 562-6025
(360) 352-4029
Fax: (360) 352-4078

**West Virginia Coalition
Against Domestic Violence**
P.O. Box 85
181B Main Street
Sutton, WV 26601-0085
(304) 765-2250
Fax: (304) 765-5071

White Buffalo Calf Women's Shelter
P.O. Box 227
Mission, SD 57555
(605) 856-2317
Fax: (605) 856-2994

**Wisconsin Coalition
Against Domestic Violence**
1400 East Washington Avenue, Suite 232
Madison, WI 53703
(608) 255-0539
Fax: (608) 255-3560

Women's Coalition of St. Croix
P. O. Box 2734
7 East Street
Christiansted St. Croix, VI 00822-2734
(809) 773-9272
Crisis (340) 773-9272
Fax: (809) 773-9062
wcscstx@worldnet.att.net

**Wyoming Coalition Against Violence and
Sexual Assault**
341 East E. Street, Suite 135A
Pinedale, WY 82601
(800) 990-3877
(307) 367-4296
Fax: (307) 235-4796

Voodoo Spice Number 27

MISSING CHILDREN HOTLINES

For Assistance to Runaway or Abducted Children:

CALL 1 (800) I AM LOST
(Child Find, Inc.)

COVENANT HOUSE
CALL 1 (800) 999-9999

For Assistance for Parental Abductors:

CALL 1 (800) A WAY OUT

NATIONAL CENTER FOR MISSING AND EXPLOITED CHILDREN
CALL 1 (800) 843-5678
CALL 1 (800) THE LOST

NATIONAL RUNAWAY SWITCHBOARD HOTLINE
CALL 1 (800) 231-6946

MISSING CHILDREN ORGANIZATIONS

Adam Walsh Children's Fund
Suite 200
Alternate A1A
Lake Park, FL 33403
(561) 863-7900
(800) 892-7430

Boys Town
(800) 448-3000

Children's Defense Fund
122 C Street N.W.
Washington, D.C. 20001
(202) 628-8787

Child Find of America
P.O. Box 277
New Paltz, NY 12561-0277
(800) IAM-LOST
(914) 255-1848
Fax: (914) 255-5706

Find the Children
11811 West Olympic Boulevard
Los Angeles, CA 90064
(213) 477-6721

National Child Safety Council
P.O. Box 1368
Jackson, Michigan 49204
(517) 764-6070

National Clearinghouse on Runaway and Homeless Youth
P.O. Box 13505
Silver Spring, MD 20911
(301) 608-8098

National Center for Missing and Exploited Children
Suite 600
1835 K Street, N.W.
Washington, D.C. 20006
(202) 634-9821

Voodoo Spice Number 28

ALCOHOL AND SUBSTANCE ABUSE SUPPORT GROUPS

Al-Anon Headquarters
1372 Broadway
New York, NY 10018
(212) 302-7240

Alcoholics Anonymous Headquarters
Grand Central Station
P.O. Box 459
New York, NY 10164

Narcotics Anonymous
P.O. Box 9999
Van Nuys, CA 91409
(818) 780-3951

**National Council on Alcoholism
and Drug Dependence, Inc.**
12 West 21st Street
New York, NY 10010
(212) 206-6770
1 (800) NCA-CALL
Fax: (212) 645-1690
http://www.ncadd.org

**National Council on Alcoholism
and Drug Dependence, Inc.**
1511 K Street NW
Washington, D.C. 20005
(202) 737-8122
1 (800) NCA-CALL
http://www.ncadd.org

**National Parents' Resource Institute
for Drug Education**
Suite 1002
100 Edgewood Avenue
Atlanta, GA 30303
(404) 651-2548

302 Voodoo Divorce

Voodoo Spice Number 29

Form **8332**
(Rev. June 1996)
Department of the Treasury
Internal Revenue Service

Release of Claim to Exemption for Child of Divorced or Separated Parents

▶ ATTACH to noncustodial parent's return **EACH YEAR** exemption claimed.

OMB No. 1545-0915

Attachment Sequence No. **51**

Name(s) of parent claiming exemption

Social security number

Part I Release of Claim to Exemption for Current Year

I agree not to claim an exemption for _____
                                        Name(s) of child (or children)

for the tax year 19_____ .

_____   _____   _____
Signature of parent releasing claim to exemption   Social security number   Date

If you choose not to claim an exemption for this child (or children) for future tax years, complete Part II.

Part II Release of Claim to Exemption for Future Years (If completed, see **Noncustodial Parent** below.)

I agree not to claim an exemption for _____
                                        Name(s) of child (or children)

for the tax year(s)_____ .
                   (Specify. See instructions.)

_____   _____   _____
Signature of parent releasing claim to exemption   Social security number   Date

General Instructions

Paperwork Reduction Act Notice.—We ask for the information on this form to carry out the Internal Revenue laws of the United States. You are required to give us the information. We need it to ensure that you are complying with these laws and to allow us to figure and collect the right amount of tax.

You are not required to provide the information requested on a form that is subject to the Paperwork Reduction Act unless the form displays a valid OMB control number. Books or records relating to a form or its instructions must be retained as long as their contents may become material in the administration of any Internal Revenue law. Generally, tax returns and return information are confidential, as required by Internal Revenue Code section 6103.

The time needed to complete and file this form will vary depending on individual circumstances. The estimated average time is: **Recordkeeping,** 7 min.; **Learning about the law or the form,** 5 min.; **Preparing the form,** 7 min.; and **Copying, assembling, and sending the form to the IRS,** 14 min.

If you have comments concerning the accuracy of these time estimates or suggestions for making this form simpler, we would be happy to hear from you. See the instructions for the tax return with which this form is filed.

Purpose of Form.—If you are a **custodial parent,** you may use this form to release your claim to your child's exemption. To do so, complete this form and give it to the **noncustodial parent** who will claim the child's exemption. Then, the noncustodial parent must attach this form or a similar statement to his or her tax return EACH YEAR the exemption is claimed.

You are the **custodial parent** if you had custody of the child for most of the year. You are the **noncustodial parent** if you had custody for a shorter period of time or did not have custody at all.

Instead of using this form, you (the custodial parent) may use a similar statement as long as it contains the same information required by this form.

Children of Divorced or Separated Parents.—Special rules apply to determine if the support test is met for children of parents who are divorced or legally separated under a decree of divorce or separate maintenance or separated under a written separation agreement. The rules also apply to children of parents who did not live together at any time during the last 6 months of the year, even if they do not have a separation agreement.

The general rule is that the custodial parent is treated as having provided over half of the child's support if:

1. The child received over half of his or her total support for the year from both of the parents, **AND**

2. The child was in the custody of one or both of his or her parents for more than half of the year.

Note: *Public assistance payments, such as Aid to Families with Dependent Children, are not support provided by the parents.*

If both **1** and **2** above apply, and the other four dependency tests in your tax return instruction booklet are also met, the custodial parent can claim the child's exemption.

Exception. The general rule does not apply if **any** of the following apply:

● The custodial parent agrees not to claim the child's exemption by signing this form or similar statement. The noncustodial parent **must** attach this form or similar statement to his or her tax return for the tax year. See **Custodial Parent** later.

● The child is treated as having received over half of his or her total support from a person under a multiple support agreement (**Form 2120,** Multiple Support Declaration).

● A pre-1985 divorce decree or written separation agreement states that the noncustodial parent can claim the child as a dependent. But the noncustodial parent must provide at least $600 for the child's support during the year. This rule does not apply if the decree or agreement was changed after 1984 to say that the noncustodial parent cannot claim the child as a dependent.

Additional Information.—For more details, get **Pub. 504,** Divorced or Separated Individuals.

Specific Instructions

Custodial Parent.—You may agree to release your claim to the child's exemption for the current tax year or for future years, or both.

● Complete **Part I** if you agree to release your claim to the child's exemption for the current tax year.

● Complete **Part II** if you agree to release your claim to the child's exemption for any or all future years. If you do, write the specific future year(s) or "all future years" in the space provided in Part II.

Noncustodial Parent.—Attach Form 8332 or similar statement to your tax return for the tax year in which you claim the child's exemption. You may claim the exemption **only** if the other four dependency tests in your tax return instruction booklet are met.

Note: *If the custodial parent completed Part II, you* **must** *attach a copy of this form to your tax return for each future year in which you claim the exemption.*

*U.S. Government Printing Office: 1996 - 405-493/40143   Cat. No. 13910F   Form **8332** (Rev. 6-96)

Voodoo Spice Number 30

BANKRUPTCY STATISTICS

SUMMARY OF BANKRUPTCY FILINGS

Year	Personal Non-Business Filings	Business Filings	Total Filings	Percentage of Personal Filings/Total
1980	287,570	43,694	331,264	86.81%
1981	315,818	48,125	363,943	86.78
1982	310,951	69,300	380,251	81.78
1983	286,444	62,436	348,880	82.10
1984	284,517	64,004	348,521	81.64
1985	341,233	71,277	412,510	82.72
1986	449,203	81,235	530,438	84.69
1987	495,553	82,446	577,999	85.74
1988	549,612	63,853	613,465	89.59
1989	616,226	63,235	679,461	90.69
1990	718,107	64,853	782,960	91.72
1991	872,438	71,549	943,987	92.42
1992	900,874	70,6439	71,517	92.73
1993	812,898	62,304	875,202	92.88
1994	780,455	52,374	832,829	93.71
1995	874,642	51,959	926,601	94.39
1996	1,125,006	53,549	1,178,555	95.46

Voodoo Spice Number 31

SAMPLE DISCOVERY PLEADINGS: INTERROGATORIES

EMPLOYMENT/INCOME:
Please state the name, address, and telephone numbers of any and all of your employers. In so doing, state the date that you commenced your employment with present employer(s); your present rate of gross monthly pay; the date on which that rate was established; the frequency that you receive your pay; and for each of your last twelve pay periods, state your gross pay, net pay, and the amount and purpose of each deduction from your gross pay.

Please state your total gross income for the last three (3) years and state, with particularity, the components, with dollar values undersigned, of each year's gross income.

Does your employer pay for or reimburse you for meals, entertainment, travel, automobile, and/or other expenses? If so, state: How you are reimbursed, what expenses are reimbursed, and whether you or your employer keeps records of these expenses and reimbursements.

Have you had your employment terminated within the last twelve (12) months? If so, state whether you quit or were fired.

RETIREMENT:
Please list and describe each pension, retirement, profit sharing plans, stock options, 401 k plans, or similar type of fund in which you have a present or future interest of any kind, stating for each fund, the name of the fund, the legal entity which maintains the fund, the amount of your vested and non-vested interest in that fund as of the date that you received these interrogatories, and the name, address, and telephone number of the administrator of the fund.

SCHOLASTIC AND VOCATIONAL DOCUMENTS:
Please identify any and all scholastic and/or vocational diplomas, awards, and/or degrees that you have received.

EXPENSES:
Please itemize, with numerical particularity, any and all of your expenses on a monthly basis. Include, with specificity, the amount of money expended each month for each of the following categories: housing, property insurance and taxes, household repairs, furniture payments, household supplies, utilities, telephone, cable, food, automobile expense/travel, clothing purchases, laundry, personal grooming, education, pet supplies, union dues, recreation, gifts/donations, medical insurance, medical expenses not covered by insurance, and miscellaneous expenses.

LIABILITIES/DEBTS:
Please list each liability/debt owed by you or your spouse, as of the date that you received these interrogatories, stating for each: the name, address and telephone

number of each creditor, the amount owed, the monthly payment required, the date on which the obligation was incurred, and the purpose for which the obligation/debt was incurred.

BANK ACCOUNTS:
Please list each checking, commercial banking, savings, credit union, and/or other depository account(s) of every nature in which you have an interest, showing as to each such account: the name and address of the institution; account number; the name(s) listed on each account; the amount in the account as of the date that you were served or otherwise received these interrogatories; for each withdrawal, indicate the date, amount, and purpose; and for each deposit, state the date, amount, and source of funds deposited.

BUSINESSES:
Do you have an ownership or equitable interest in any business entity of any kind? If so, please state the name, address, and telephone number of each business, and your percentage interest therein; the form of that business operation, i.e., a sole proprietorship, joint venture, partnership, corporation, etc.; and whether any other person has an ownership or equitable interest in that business.

FINANCIAL STATEMENTS:
Please state whether you have prepared or has had prepared for you, any financial statements during the last three (3) years. If so, please state whether you have furnished any financial statements to any banks or other lending institution(s) within the past three (3) years. In so doing, state the date on which the statement was furnished, and the name of the bank or institution to whom the statement was furnished.

SECURITIES:
Please list any and all stocks, bonds, certificates, options, or other securities of whatever nature, owned by you, or by someone on your behalf, for the last three (3) years. State the location of each security.

REAL ESTATE:
Please list any and all real property in which you have, or had, a legal or equitable ownership interest for the last three (3) years; stating for each such property: the acquisition date, purchase price, initial down payment; whether each property has been sold or donated, and if so, for how much, to whom and when. If not sold or donated, what mortgages are outstanding on each property, and for each such mortgage, state the mortgagor's name and address.

PROPERTY:
Please describe in detail any property which you allege to be your separate (non-marital) property. State for each property, the description, location, date of acquisition, the method of acquisition, including source of funds used to acquire the property; and the facts relied on to support your allegation that the property is your separate (non-marital) property.

Please describe in detail any property which you allege to be your community property. State for each property, the description, location, date of acquisition, the method of acquisition, including source of funds used to acquire the property; and the facts relied on to support your allegation that the property is allegedly community property.

VEHICLES:
Please list all motor vehicles, boats, motor cycles, motor homes, trailers and/or airplanes owned by you or by someone on your behalf, stating for each: the make, model, and identification number, purchase price, and (if any) down payment, the chattel or mortgage holder and amount of any note and amount remaining unpaid, and the amount of monthly payments of each note and/or chattel mortgage(s), and the identity of the registered owner(s).

JEWELRY AND OTHER VALUABLES:
Please list each piece of jewelry and other items of personal property owned by you having a value in excess of $100.

CONTENTS IN SAFETY DEPOSIT BOXES/SAFES:
Do you maintain a safety deposit box and/or safe? If so, state as to each such safety deposit box and/or safe: the institution in which the safety deposit box is maintained, the address of that institution, the number or other identification for the safety deposit box, the description of the contents of the safety deposit box and/or safe, and the signatories for the safety deposit box.

TRUSTS:
Are you the beneficiary of any trust? If so, for each please state the date that the trust was established, the name, address, and telephone number of the trustee(s) and/or administrator(s), the amount of money and/or description of property held in trust, and the income or funds received by you, or someone on your behalf, during the past three (3) years, specifying the dates and amounts of each transaction.

PRIOR SPOUSES/CHILDREN:
Have you been married to someone other than your present spouse? If so, state the name, address, and telephone number of each prior spouse, the names of all children, the birth dates of all children whether you are under a court order or agreement to pay alimony and/or child support to any other person. If so, state the amount of alimony/child support owed.

CHILD SUPPORT:
Please provide any and all basis for which you aver should be made for a deviation from the state child support guidelines.

DAY-CARE/TUITION:
Please state the cost of any day-care, child care, tuition, camp, and/or educational expenses for the children of the parties. In so doing, provide the name, address, and telephone number of each school and/or provider of child care.

INSURANCE:
Please list every type of insurance policy, whether life, health, disability, liability, automobile, or other, owned or purchased by you or your spouse, stating for each policy, the name of the insurer(s), the policy number, the date of issuance, the type of insurance policy, the face value (if any), the current cash surrender value (if any), the name, address, and telephone number of each beneficiary, whether there is a loan on the policy, and if so, what is the amount of the loan, who obtained the loan(s), and for what purpose.

FAULT:
If you are alleging that any "fault" should be placed on any party that lead to the break up of the marriage, please state with specificity any and all allegations regarding the alleged fault of any party.

WITNESSES:
Please identify the name, address, and telephone number of each witness you may or shall call at the trial of this matter or any incidental proceeding.

EXHIBITS:
Please list any and all documents and things that you may or shall introduce into evidence, or use as demonstrative evidence, at the trial of this matter or any incidental hearing.

Voodoo Spice Number 32

SAMPLE DISCOVERY PLEADINGS

REQUESTS FOR PRODUCTION OF DOCUMENTS AND THINGS

EMPLOYMENT/INCOME:
Any and all pay checks, pay stubs, federal tax returns, state tax returns, cash register receipts, contracts for work, accounts receivable records, appointment calendars, cash register tapes, purchase receipts, tax refunds, and/or daily log of cash receipts.

Any and all documents regarding reimbursements and/or payments for the past three (3) years, including but not limited to: travel, automobile, meal, health club, country club, and entertainment expenses.

Any and all employment records for the past three (3) years.

RETIREMENT:
Any and all documents and things regarding pensions, retirement, profit sharing plans, stock options, 401 k plans, and/or deferred compensation.

SCHOLASTIC AND VOCATIONAL DOCUMENTS:
Any and all of your scholastic and/or vocational diplomas, awards, and/or degrees.

EXPENSES:
Any and all documents and things referencing the expenses of either you or your spouse within the past three (3) years, including but not limited to invoices, canceled checks, check book registries, and the like for the following categories: housing, property insurance and taxes, household repairs, furniture payments, household supplies, utilities, telephone, cable, food, automobile expense/travel, clothing purchases, laundry, personal grooming, education, pet supplies, union dues, recreation, gifts/donations, medical insurance, medical expenses not covered by insurance, and miscellaneous expenses.

LIABILITIES/DEBTS:
Any and all documents and things referencing each liability/debt owed by you or your spouse within the past three (3) years.

BANK ACCOUNTS:
Any and all documents and things regarding each checking, commercial banking, savings, credit union, and/or other depository account(s) of every nature in which you have an interest within the past three (3) years.

FINANCIAL STATEMENTS:
Any and all financial statements rendered by you, or on your behalf, for any purpose, within the past three (3) years.

SECURITIES:
Any and all stock certificates, bonds, options, and other evidence of securities that you had or have a legal or equitable interest within the past three (3) years.

Any and all documentation concerning the valuation of any and all securities, including but not limited to, stocks, bonds, and/or mutual funds, within the past three (3) years.

BUSINESSES:
Any and all documents and things regarding your business interests, including but not limited to, articles of incorporation, initial reports, annual reports, minute books, stockholder subscriptions, partnership agreements, counter letters, and/or other documents concerning any entity that either party to this litigation.

Any and all state and federal tax returns filed by you, or on your behalf, for the past three (3) years.

Any and all financial statements, balance sheets, profit and loss statements, and income statements of any and all proprietorships, joint ventures, partnerships, realty trusts, corporations, or other business interests that you had or have a legal or equitable interest within the past three (3) years.

TRUSTS:
Any and all evidence of trusts and/or custodial accounts in which you are a trustee, administrator, and/or beneficiary.

PRIOR SPOUSES/CHILDREN:
Any and all birth certificates, adoption decrees, affidavits of acknowledgment, divorce decrees, paternity/DNA test results, and/or decrees of emancipation regarding your children and/or any child made subject to this litigation.

INSURANCE:
Any and all insurance policies that you have or had within the past three (3) years.

MEDICAL EXPENSES:
Any and all medical bills regarding any party to this litigation and/or the minor children thereof.

CHILD SUPPORT:
Any and all documents and things indicating that you have paid and/or received child support payments within the past three (3) years.

DAY-CARE/TUITION:
Any and all documents and things evidencing that day-care, child care, tuition, camp, and/or educational expenses were paid and/or incurred associated with the children of the petitioner and defendant.

REAL ESTATE:
Any and all documents and things concerning any appraisal of any and all real estate owned by either party to this litigation.

Any and all mortgages, notes, titles, deeds, acts of sale, acts of donation, time share contract, associated with any property that you had or have a legal or equitable interest within the past three (3) years.

FURNITURE/OTHER PROPERTY:
Any and all documents and things concerning any evaluation of the worth of the furniture and/or furnishings owned by either party to this litigation

Any and all documents and things concerning the sale and/or acquisition, within the past three (3) years, of any property by either party to this litigation.

VEHICLES:
Any and all titles, acts of sale, acts of donation, and/or registrations to any vehicle, boat, motorcycle, motor home, and/or airplane owned by either party to this litigation within the past three (3) years.

Any and all documentation concerning the appraisal of any vehicle boat, motorcycle, airplane, owned by either party to this litigation within the past three (3) years.

GIFTS:
Any and all records of any gifts given to and/or received by you within the past three (3) years.

CONTENTS OF SAFETY DEPOSIT BOXES/SAFES:
Any and all documents and things in your safety deposit box(es) and/or safes.

ATTORNEY FEES:
Any and all invoices of your attorney of record paid with marital property.

PRENUPTUAL/POSTNUPTUAL AGREEMENTS:
Any and all prenuptial or postnuptual agreements between the parties to this litigation.

SURVEILLANCE:
Any and all surveillance reports in your possession, custody and/or control pertaining to any party to this litigation.

COUNSELING:
Any and all documents and things concerning counseling and/or psychological evaluations of any party to this litigation and/or of the minor children thereof.

FAULT:
Any and all documents and things, including photographs and recordings, relating to any allegation of "fault" that should be placed on any party that lead to the break up of the marriage.

WITNESSES:
Any and all resumes and/or ciriculim vitaes of any witness that you may or shall call as a witness at the trial of this matter or any incidental hearing.

EXHIBITS:
Any and all documents and things that you may or shall introduce into evidence, or use as demonstrative evidence, at the trial of this matter or any incidental hearing.

Voodoo Spice Number 33

DIRECTORY OF MEDIATION RESOURCES

Academy of Family Mediators
P.O. Box 10501
Eugene OR 97440
(503) 345-1205

Academy of Family Mediators
1500 South Highway Ste. 100
Golden Valley, NM 55416
(612) 525-8670

American Association of Marriage and Family Therapy
1133 15th Street N.W., Suite 300
Washington, D.C. 20005-2710
(202) 452-0109

American Bar Association Dispute Resolution Center
1800 M Street N.W.
Washington, D.C. 20036
(202) 331-2258

Association of Family and Conciliation Courts
329 West Wilson Street
Madison, WI 53703-3612
(608) 251-4001
Fax: (608) 251-2231
afcc@igc.apc.org

Certified Mediators, Inc.
3309 Williams Blvd.
Kenner, LA 70065

Conflict Resolution Center, Inc.
204 Thirty-Seventh Street
Suite 203
Pittsburgh, PA 15201-1859
(412) 687-6210
Fax: (412) 687-6232
crcii@conflictnet.org
http://www/igc.apc.org/crcii

Family & Divorce Mediation Council of Greater New York
114 West 47th Street, Ste. 2200
New York, NY 10036
(212) 978-8590

Family Mediation Association
9308 Bulls Run Parkway
Bethesda, MD 20817
(301) 654-7708

Family Service Associations of America
11700 W. Lake Park Drive
Milwaukee, WI 53224
(414) 359-2111

Louisiana Mediation Institute, Inc.
4004 Magazine Street
New Orleans, LA 70115
(504) 897-1003

Society of Professionals In Dispute Resolution
815 15th Street N.W., Suite 530
Washington D.C. 20005
(202) 783-7277

Voodoo Spice Number 34

ACTUAL VOODOO INGREDIENTS

VOODOO CANDLES

White Candles: Use white candles for happiness, peace, protection, purification, stopping gossip, spirituality, and strength. White candles can be used anytime.

Black Candles: Use black candles for "hexing" or destroying your enemy. Black connotes death. Black candles should be used on Mondays or with a New Moon.

Red Candles: Use to create love, lust, physical strength, courage, sensuality, and success. Red candles also are used as a shield and a sword. Red candles should be used on Tuesdays or Thursdays.

Green Candles: Use green candles to promote financial gain, employment, healing, fertility, and luck. Green candles should be used on Mondays or Fridays.

Purple Candles: Use purple candles to create business success and power. Purple candles should be used on Mondays, Wednesdays, and/or Saturdays.

Blue Candles: Use blue candles to promote health, protection, peacefulness, and happiness. Use blue candles on Mondays, Fridays, and/or Saturdays.

Brown Candles: Use brown candles to win your court battles and protect your home. Brown candles should be used on Mondays.

Orange Candles: Use orange candles to improve your memory and create success in legal matters. Orange candles should be used on Tuesdays, Wednesdays, Thursdays, and/or Sundays.

Yellow Candles: Use yellow candles to persuade, for psychic powers, and for good luck. Yellow candles should be used on Thursdays and Sundays.

Pink Candles: Use pink candles to repel evil and promote love, fidelity, and relationships. Pink candles should be used on Fridays.

VOODOO HERBS, INCENSES, OILS, AND ROOTS

Acacia: Enhances psychic abilities

Adam and Eve Root: Promotes compatibility

Ague Root: Destroys your spouse's ability to harm you

Alfalfa: Protects against poverty and hunger

Allspice: Promotes wealth and healing

Almond: Promotes wealth and healing

Aloe: Protects your home

Althea: Burnt will evoke the spirits and enhance psychic abilities

Angelica: Prevents evil from entering your home

Asafoetida: Protects you from colds

Ash Tree Leaves: Protects you from illness and promotes prosperity
Aspen: Protects against theft
Basil: Promotes prosperity, harmony, and success
Bayberry: Promotes wealth
Betony: Promotes physical strength
Black Mustard Seed: Causes your spouse stress when placed before his door
Bladder Wrack: Protects your travels over water
Blood Root: Promotes respect and kindness; also protects your home
Boldo Leaves: Protects your home from evil
Broom Tops: Repels evil
Buckwheat: Attracts money
Cactus: Promotes chastity
Calendula: Receive justice in court
Caraway Seed: Protects your children from illness; also protects from theft
Carnation: Promotes healing and power
Cascara Sagrada: Enhances your chances of winning your court case
Catnip: Creates luck
Cedar: Promotes courage and wealth
Celery: Increase your psychic powers and lust
Chamomile: Assists you in gambling
Cinnamon: Promotes purification
Cinquefoil: Protects your home from evil
Clover: Repels evil and promotes purification
Cloves: Promote friendship and love
Comfrey Root: Protects you traveling
Corn Flower: Promotes harmony
Couch Grass: Attracts a lover
Cowslip: Repels visitors from your home
Cypress: Protects and comforts
Damiana: Promotes a stray lover to return to you
Dill: Used for counterspells
Dog Grass: Protects you from depression
Dragon's Blood Reed: Promotes good luck
Elder Bark: Assists you in controlling your spouse
Elm Bark: Repels ugly rumors
Eucalyptus: Repels colds and promotes healing
Frankincense: Protects and repels evil
Galangal Root: Promotes luck with a jury

Gardenia: Promotes peace, harmony, and love
Garlic: Protects and repels evil and theft
Gilead Buds: Protects you against curses
Ginger: Put under your pillow to protect you from evil
Ginseng: Heals and promotes lust
Goat's Leaves: Provides you with more control
Gravel Root: Enhances employment opportunities
Heartsease: Makes you more attractive to your mate
Honeysuckle: Promotes wealth
Horseradish: Protects from evil
Huckleberry: Break hexes
Irish Moss: Promotes wealth and health
Jasmine: Promotes love
Job's Tears: Promotes healing
Lavender: Purifies and promotes chastity
Lemongrass: Promotes psychic abilities
Licorice: Promotes passion
Lilac: Promotes harmony and psychic abilities
Lucky Hand Root: Promotes wealth and employment
Magnolia: Promotes peace and fidelity
Marigold: Promotes success in legal matters
Mint: Promotes wealth
Mistletoe: Promotes fertility
Musk: Promotes courage and fertility
Mustard Seed: Protects against colds and increases mental abilities
Myrrh: Promotes healing and hex breaking
Nutmeg: Promotes psychic abilities
Olive: Promotes peace, fertility, and lust
Orris Root: Protects your home
Peony: Protects against evil spirits
Peppermint: Purifies and promotes psychic abilities
Pine: Promotes wealth
Pistachio: Breaks love spells
Poke Root: Breaks hexes
Primrose: Promotes respect of children
Rose Buds: Promotes peace and harmony
Rosemary: Promotes healing and power
Rose Petals: Promotes love, relationships, and enhances psychic abilities

Rue: Protects and promotes healing
Rye: Promotes fidelity
Sandalwood: Promotes healing and psychic abilities
Skullcap: Promotes fidelity
Slippery Elm: Stops gossip
Spearmint: Promotes healing and enhances psychic abilities
St. John's Wort: Protects and creates harmony
Sumbul Root: Promotes good luck
Sweetpea: Promotes happiness and friendship
Thyme: Promotes health, purification, and courage
Trillium: Promotes wealth and love
Vanilla: Promotes power and psychic abilities
Venus Flytrap: Promotes passion
Violet: Promotes healing and protection
Walnut: Promotes infertility
Yarrow: Provides courage

******

VOODOO DIVORCE DOLLS® and GRIS-GRIS BAGS:

To purchase, contact
www.voodoodivorce.com
or call 1-8707-4VOODOO

Voodoo Spice Number 35

SUBSCRIBE TO THE "VOODOO DIVORCE NEWSLETTER"

YES, I want to subscribe to the VOODOO DIVORCE NEWSLETTER. (Quarterly Newsletter)

Please send my new subscription to the following address:

Your name: _____

Address: _____

_____

City: _____

State: _____

Zip Code: _____

Home Telephone Number: _____

Work Telephone Number: _____

( ) I have enclosed my check for a year's subscription at $100.00

( ) Please charge the subscription on the following credit card:

Circle One: VISA   MASTERCARD   AMERICAN EXPRESS   DISCOVER

Account Number: _____

Expiration Date: _____

Your Signature: _____

Please mail or fax to the following address:

VOODOO DIVORCE NEWSLETTER
4004 Magazine Street
New Orleans, LA 70115
Fascimile: (504) 443-5533

Voodoo Spice Number 36

DISCLAIMER

Use of the foregoing spells, recipes, candles, voodoo dolls, gris-gris bags, and/or other ingredients are for entertainment purposes only, and are not offered as advice for legal, medical or physiological problems/ailments. Please consult a licensed attorney, health care provider, counselor, and/or religious advisor for real legal, medical, psychological, and/or spiritual needs. This book does not provide legal advice. The "Voodoo Tips" are merely concepts to be discussed with your attorney.

Every effort was made to present accurate information. The publisher and the author assume no liability associated for any errors and/or omissions. Consult your attorney as to the applicability and accuracy of the contents presented in this book.

The publisher and author offer this book for interest and entertainment only and specifically do not make any claims of supernatural or other effects and/or powers associated with any spells provided herein.

"Real Life Experiences" are excerpts from actual testimonials and/or are created from common experiences shared by many individuals under the same or similar circumstances. Many names and details have been changed to protect the true identities of the individuals involved. Except for any endorsing comments, all individuals referenced in this book are not intended to refer to any living persons or to disparage any company's products or services.

Voodoo Spice Number 37

ABOUT THE AUTHOR; TO CONSULT WITH THE AUTHOR

The author, **Stephen Rue**, is an aggressive attorney and businessman. Stephen is a graduate of Southern Methodist University in Dallas, Texas where he received a Bachelor in Business Administration degree. He also has received two post-graduate degrees from Loyola University—a law degree and an MBA. He also completed fellowships at The National Institute of Trial Advocacy and The Institute of Politics.

Since university, Stephen has become one of the most high profile divorce attorneys in New Orleans. He is a regular lecturer at seminars and classes for attorneys and law students throughout the country.

Stephen Rue has litigated well over 1,000 divorces. Stephen's notable cases include filing the first petition in Louisiana history seeking a sexually abused child's "divorce" of his father. He also litigated one of Louisiana's first "Baby Jessica" styled paternity/custody cases. Additionally, Stephen represented the mother in a custody battle after her children attempted to poison her. Stephen is aggressive in his pursuit for the rights of parents and their children.

Stephen is a familiar personality frequently interviewed on major New Orleans television and radio stations. He is routinely consulted as a legal advisor to these stations. Recently he has started a column on divorce issues currently shown in New Orleans' *Times Picayune* newspaper. Stephen Rue's legal profile also has been displayed in *New Orleans Magazine*. He was previously selected as one of the top ten "most eligible bachelors" in the city of New Orleans. This year he was chosen as one of the top ten "best dressed" men in the city.

With the completion of *Voodoo Divorce*, Stephen Rue has changed his professional focus to that of assisting people with their divorce problems throughout the country. He is well on his way to being the country's divorce lawyer. Stephen's goal is to become licensed to practice law in every state in the nation.

Stephen Rue is extremely involved in the civic and philanthropic projects. He is a recipient of New Orleans' "Great Gentleman Award," which recognizes outstanding volunteer work in the community. His activities have included the following: March of Dimes, Board of Directors; National Multiple Sclerosis Society, Member of Louisiana Chapter Board of Directors; President of Professional Support Group; American Cancer Society, Member, Board of Directors, Louisiana Chapter; and President of the Kenner Business Association.

For further information about author/attorney Stephen Rue call toll free

(877) 4VOODOO
(504) 887-4443

Additionally you may find information about Stephen Rue
on his web site:

WWW.STEPHENRUE.COM

or call The Voodoo Divorce® Helpline
1-877-4VOODOO

Index

A

abandonment	56
abuse	171, 172, 176, 177, 178, 182, 292
physical	172
sexual	172
accountant	221
adultery	56, 57, 59
age of majority	124
Air Force	147, 148
Alabama	54, 60, 140, 161, 254, 258, 274
Alaska	54, 60, 123, 140, 161, 254, 258, 274
Alcoholics Anonymous	95
alimony	65–69, 72, 114, 122, 201, 208–11
pendente lite	65
permanent	66
temporary	65
annulments	61, 260
antenuptial	38
apartment	35
appraisals	38, 156
appraisers	28
arbitration	223, 226
Argentina	190
Arizona	54, 60, 123, 140, 162, 254, 258, 274
Arkansas	54, 60, 123, 140, 161, 254, 258, 274
Army	147, 148
arrest warrants	131, 134
articles of incorporation	38
assets, hidden	154
ATMs	22
attendance record	94
attorney	9, 11, 12, 14, 15, 17, 29
Australia	146, 190
Austria	146, 190
automobile	39

B

baby-sitting	102
Bahamas	190
bank accounts	37
bankruptcy	128, 207–11, 213, 216
battered women's shelter	174
Belize	190
Bermuda	146
"best interest"	80, 82, 91
bigamy	57
bill, legal	30
bill, of sale	30
birth certificate	75, 142
bonds	37
bonuses	37
Bosnia	190
Burkina Faso	190

C

cable	39
California	54, 60, 140, 162, 254, 258, 274
camp	95
Canada	146, 190
caretaker, primary	87
central registry	144
check book registers	38

checks, canceled 38
child support 101–02, 109, 112–14, 122–24, 128–29, 142, 144, 146, 211, 208
child support enforcement agencies 274
Child Support Enforcement Office 131, 139, 273
child support guidelines 111
child support models 110
Child Support Recovery Act of 1992 134
child support, collection 128
child support, deviations for guidelines 116
child support, enforcing 130
child support, modification 125
child support, termination 125
children 6, 34, 81–82, 90, 179
Chile 190
circumstantial evidence 57
classes, co-parenting 90
clinic, legal 16
clothing 40
Coast Guard 148
COBRA 68
Colombia 190
Colorado 54, 60, 140, 161, 254, 258
common law 161–62
community property 161
computers 41
conflict of interest 17
Connecticut 54, 60, 123, 140, 161, 254, 259
Consolidated Omnibus Budget Reconciliation Act of 1985 (COBRA) 68
consumer credit counseling service 213
contempt of court 130, 132
corporeal punishment 180
court 228
court cost 19, 28–29
covenant house 300
covenant marriages 52
CPA 221
credit 207, 216
  bureaus 131
  cards 20, 21, 22, 23, 24
  report 24, 211
creditors suit 131
Croatia 190
cruel treatment 57
custody 79, 80–84, 89, 95–98, 104, 187, 199
  grandparent 103

joint 80
permanent 80
provisional 80
sole 80
split 80
temporary 80–81
worksheet 263
Cyprus 190
Czech Republic 146

D

day-care 40, 119, 120, 181
  expenses 117, 121
debt 157
Delaware 54, 60, 123, 140, 161, 254, 258
Denmark 190
dental expenses 117
dental insurance 117
dependent 198
depositions 28, 219–20
desertion 57
diplomas 37
disavow 76
discovery pleadings 219
District of Columbia 254
divorce 1, 51–53
divorce rate 51, 260

DNA 77
DNA test 28, 76
documents 37
domestic violence 292
domiciled 53
drugs 95
drunkenness 57

E

earnings capacity 71
Ecuador 190
education 40, 71
emergency 97
emotions 1
Equifax 212
equitable distribution 161
evaluations 38
  custody/visitation 92
  physical 219, 221

psychological	219, 221	**H**	
evaluator	28, 93	Hague Convention	190
Ex Parte	48	harassment	172, 177, 182
motions	42	Hawaii	54, 60, 123, 140, 161, 254, 258
orders	177	head of household	197
relief	45	hidden assets	71
exemptions	197	holidays	100
expenses	245, 250	Honduras	190
Experian	212	Hong Kong	190
experts	28, 70, 92, 93	house	35, 177
		Hungary	146, 190

F

I

Fair Credit Reporting Act	213	Iceland	190
Fair Debt Collection Practices Act	214	Idaho	54, 60, 123, 140, 162, 254, 258
Family support	122	identification record, child's	188, 264
Family Support Act of 1988	132	Illinois	54, 60, 140, 161, 254, 258
fault	52, 56	impotency	57
fees		*In Forma Pauperis* application	27, 115
attorney	29, 130, 209	income	250
legal	19	income tax refunds	130, 133
service	29	income withholding	130, 131
felony	57	Indiana	54, 60, 140, 161, 254, 258
Fiji	146	Individual Retirement Arrangements	203
filing status	194	injunctions	45
financial affidavit	115	insanity	57
financial information	243	inspections	219, 221
financial statements	37	insurance	38, 68, 118, 159
Finland	146, 190	International Social Service	147
Florida	54, 60, 123, 140, 161, 254, 258	interrogatories	219, 304
food	39	inventory	36
Form 8332	199, 302	Iowa	54, 60, 123, 140, 161, 254, 258
Form 8822	193	Ireland	146, 190
France	146, 190	IRS	193, 194
furnishings	35	Israel	190
		Italy	190

G

J

garnishment	130, 131, 147	Jamaica	146
genetic testing	77, 270	Jewelry	40
Georgia	54, 60, 123, 140, 161, 254, 258	joint tax return	195
Germany	146, 190		
gift certificates	25	**K**	
grades	94	Kansas	54, 60, 123, 140, 161, 254, 258
Greece	190	Kentucky	54, 60, 123, 140, 161, 254, 258
grooming	40	keys	38
grounds	56	kidnapping, parental	185–86, 189, 192
Guam	140		

L

lawyer	6, 9, 11–14, 16, 53, 98
Lawyer Referral Hotline	10
licenses, marriage	38
lien	210
linkage order	131
Lis Pendens	47
locks	35, 177
Louisiana	45, 54, 60, 83, 123, 140, 162, 255, 258
Luxembourg	190

M

Macedonia	190
maid	40
Maine	54, 60, 123, 140, 161, 255, 258
maintenance	65
Marine Corps	148
marriage	51
Maryland	54, 60, 123, 140, 161, 255, 259
Massachusetts	54, 60, 123, 140, 161, 255, 259
Maternity	75
Mauritius	190
mediation	92, 223–24, 312
mediators	28
medical	
deduction	200
expenses	117
insurance	117
records	39
memberships	37
Mexico	146, 190
Michigan	54, 60, 123, 140, 161, 255, 258
military	131, 138, 148
Minnesota	55, 60, 123, 140, 161, 255, 259
Minnesota Multiphase Personality Inventory Test	94
missing children organizations	300
Mississippi	55, 60, 123, 140, 162, 163, 255, 258
Missouri	55, 60, 123, 140, 161, 255, 258
Monaco	190
money	34
Montana	55, 60, 141, 161, 255, 258
"most wanted" lists	131, 135
murder, attempted	56
mutual funds	37

N

name change	61
narcotic drugs, habitual use of	57
Narcotics Anonymous	95
National Center for Missing and Exploited Children	188–89, 192, 300
National Child Abuse Hotline	175, 292
National Coalition Against Domestic Violence	175
National Domestic Violence Hotline	49, 175, 184, 292
National Rape Crisis Center Hotline	292
National Runaway Switchboard Hotline	300
Navy	147, 148
Nebraska	55, 60, 141, 161, 255, 258
Netherlands	190
Nevada	55, 60, 123, 141, 162, 255, 258
New Hampshire	55, 60, 141, 161, 255, 258
new hire reporting	131, 135
New Jersey	55, 60, 141, 161, 255, 259
New Mexico	55, 60, 123, 141, 162, 255, 258
New York	55, 60, 123, 141, 161, 255, 259
New Zealand	146, 190
no-fault	56, 60
North Carolina	55, 60, 123, 141, 161, 255, 258
North Dakota	55, 60, 123, 141, 161, 255, 259
Norway	146, 190

O

Ohio	55, 60, 123, 141, 161, 255, 258
Oklahoma	55, 60, 123, 141, 161, 255, 258
Omnibus Crime Control and Safe Street Act of 1968	59
Oregon	55, 60, 123, 141, 161, 256, 258
Orr v. Orr	91
ownership interest	252

P

Panama	190
papers	
adoption	38
divorce	38
Parent Locator Service	142
Parental Kidnapping Prevention Act	188
Parents Without Partners	146, 272
passport	97, 191
Passport Policy, Office of	191, 192

Index

paternity 75–77, 268
Pay checks 37
pay
   severance 37
   sick 37
   vacation 37
payment, methods of 126
payroll deduction 130, 131
payroll stubs 37
peace bond 177
Pennsylvania 55, 60, 123, 141, 161, 256, 259
Personal Responsibility
and Work Opportunity Act of 1996 135
pets 34, 40
photograph 36, 42
Poland 146, 190
police 178, 189
Portugal 190
postnuptial agreements 165, 169
preference
   child's 84, 85
   maternal 91
prenuptial agreement 38, 165–68
prescriptions 39
presumption 75
primary custodial parent 199
private eye 58
property 33, 153–587, 160, 162, 204
   division 153, 208
   seizure 130, 134
   settlements 203
   community 162
Puerto Rico 123, 141, 162, 256

Q

Qualified Domestic Relations Order 202
"Quick Facts" 51, 54, 57, 79, 81, 85, 109, 110, 113, 116, 118, 129, 131, 132, 133, 136, 139, 171, 173, 185, 207

R

rape crisis center 174
rape, spousal 176
real estate 253
"recapture" rules 202
receipts 37, 88
reconciliation 72

registrations 38
request for admissions of facts 219, 221
request for production of
documents and things 219, 220, 308
residency 56
   requirements 54
retirement 158
revocation of state licenses 131, 134
Rhode Island 55, 60, 123, 141, 161, 256, 259
Romania 190
Rue, Stephen 319, 320

S

safety deposit box 26, 38
savings accounts 38
school records 95
schools 181
separation 60
settlement 229, 230
shelters, battered womens' 98
Slovak Republic 146
Slovenia 190
Social Services, Department of 92
South Africa 146, 190
South Carolina 55, 60, 123, 141, 161, 256, 258
South Dakota 55, 60, 123, 141, 161, 256, 258
Spain 190
spousal support 65
St. Kitts 190
stalking 180
standard of living 110
state bar associations 254
state department 190
statistics 257, 258, 260, 261
   bankruptcy 303
statute of limitations 145
sterility 57
stocks 37
stress 4
support groups 271, 292, 301
Support Enforcement Office 133
surveillance 58
Sweden 146, 190
Switzerland 190

T

tax 37, 41, 72, 159, 194–97, 200–03

returns	37	Washington	55, 60, 123, 141, 162, 256, 258
telephone	14, 39, 46–47, 59, 103, 180, 266	Washington D.C.	55, 60, 123, 141, 161, 258
log	265	West Virginia	55, 60, 123, 141, 161, 256, 258
"tender years doctrine"	91	will	63
Tennessee	55, 60, 123, 141, 161, 256, 258	Wisconsin	55, 60, 123, 141, 162, 256, 259
Tests	94, 219, 221	witnesses	89
Texas	55, 60, 123, 141, 162, 256, 258	expert	231
titles	38	lay	231
training	71	Wyoming	55, 60, 123, 141, 161, 256, 258
Trans Union	212		
travel	101		
trial	227, 230		
tuition	117, 121, 130		

Z

Zimbabwe   190

U

U.S. Family Educational Rights
and Privacy Act   95
unemployment benefits, intercept of   131, 136
Uniform Child Custody
Jurisdiction Act   97, 188
Uniform Interstate Family Support Act   143
Uniform Reciprocal
Enforcement of Support Act   143
United Kingdom   146, 190
Utah   55, 60, 123, 141, 161, 256, 258
utilities   39

V

venereal disease   57
Venezuela   190
Vermont   55, 60, 123, 141, 161, 256, 258
videotape   36, 42

Virgin Islands   123, 141, 161, 256
Virginia   55, 123, 141, 161, 256, 258
visitation   79, 83, 98–99, 101–02, 104, 129
order   187
supervised   96, 179
terminated   179
worksheet   263
vocational rehabilitation   70
Voodoo Divorce® Checklist   238
"Voodoo Divorce® Newsletter"   317
Voodoo Dolls®   316

W

wage assignment   130, 131